ZOLTÁN
KODÁLY

ZOLTÁN KODÁLY

A HUNGARIAN MUSICIAN

PERCY M. YOUNG

GREENWOOD PRESS, PUBLISHERS
WESTPORT, CONNECTICUT

Library of Congress Cataloging in Publication Data
Young, Percy Marshall, 1912-
    Zoltán Kodály : a Hungarian musician.

    Reprint of the ed. published by E. Benn, London.
    Bibliography: p.
    Includes indexes.
    1. Kodály, Zoltán, 1882-1967.
[ML410.K732Y7 1976]   780'.92'4   75-45268
ISBN 0-8371-8650-1

YOUNG

Originally published in 1964 by Ernest Benn Ltd., London

Reprinted in 1976 by Greenwood Press
A division of Congressional Information Service
88 Post Road West, Westport, Connecticut 06881

Library of Congress Catalog Card Number 75-45268

ISBN 0-8371-8650-1

Printed in the United States of America

10 9 8 7 6 5 4 3 2

'The voice of Kodály in music is the
voice of Hungary'

SIR ARTHUR BLISS
3 June 1960

Foreword

A letter to the author from

ZOLTÁN KODÁLY

DEAR DR. YOUNG,

You want a foreword to your book. But what could I say, that you have not already written in it?

Perhaps this: I was fifteen, when a German booklet strayed into my hands; author and title are both forgotten, but the idea is still living in me. It depicts the career of an average German composer who, having reached the three-fold figure of Beethoven's opus-numbers, had to realise that he worked in vain; he should rather have used his time to do some work useful to his fellow-citizens. 'Less music!'—there is too much useless music written.

Since then I always pondered, when some musical idea occurred to me: is it worth while to be written down? This is why I published so few works.

As to nationalism:

Robert Schumann wrote some 100 years ago in his article about Gade: 'In der That scheint es, als ob die Deutschland angrenzenden Nationen sich von der Herrschaft deutscher Musik emanzipieren wollten; einen Deutschtümler könnte das vielleicht grämen, dem tiefer blickenden Denker und Kenner der Menschheit wird es nur natürlich und erfreulich vorkommen. . . . Und wie sie auch alle die deutsche Nation als ihre erste und geliebteste Lehrerin in der Musik betrachten, so soll sich niemand verwundern, wenn sie auch für ihre Nationen ihre eigene Sprache der Musik zu sprechen versuchen wollen. . . .'[1]

Schumann mentioned only four countries: Poland, Denmark, Holland and Hungary. Today he could say, that nearly all peoples in Europe begin to speak their own language. Even America is still seeking for the musical expression of her spirit.

---

[1] English version in Robert Schumann: *On Music and Musicians*, translated by Paul Rosenfeld, p. 244 (London, Denis Dobson, 1947).

vii

All of them had to start with the surface, the most accessible layer. As the miner penetrates gradually deeper, so the musician can reach deeper and deeper into the strata of the inscrutable national soul. We have attained more than our forerunners, our followers can detect new traits of Hungarian character, which is never to be exhausted; even if we go as far, as Vaughan Williams said: 'as to our abominable food'.

All my activity, musical or other, was devoted entirely to my country. It is for me an unexpected pleasure and satisfaction, that my work found so many friends abroad, especially in English-speaking countries.

Does this mean perhaps some mental affinity? We discussed that several times with the late Professor Edward Dent; both peoples are fond of singing, assert justice and exercise humanity.

I remember Professor Dent always with deep gratitude: his magistral translation opened the path for the "Psalmus Hungaricus", the first English performance of which was initiated in Cambridge by the late Professor Cyril Rootham.

The high level of English choral-singing was for us a stimulating example, and in spite of all unfavourable events of the last decades, we can be proud of some positive progress.

A German critic reproached me for not having any longer work than twenty to thirty minutes. Is it not pure loyalty to the listeners instead of boring them for hours?

Another one wrote: 'ganz problemlos'. Well, I think we have to resolve our problems at home, not before the public.

Furthermore, my device has always been: "Persicos odi, puer, apparatus!"

Salve egregie Doctor—atque vale.

BUDAPEST
3. 3. 1964

Contents

List of Illustrations

Preface

ZOLTÁN KODÁLY is one of the few men (a moment's reflection will show how few they are) who has effectively broken through the barriers that bedevil our age. That being the case, it is clear that he deserves some kind of memorial. Since he is a musician, the necessity for such is the greater, because the art of music, and the profession of music, are, or should be, enhanced thereby. In brief, what follows is a summary of the past, but also a testament to the future.

The last day I was with Kodály, in his flat in Budapest, we had a party. The guests were a Hungarian teacher, a group of children from her school, a little five-year-old British girl (competent in the Hungarian language and adept at singing the kindergarten songs of Hungary), and myself. The purpose was to demonstrate the fundamentals of musical education: in effect, the occasion turned out to be a multilingual exercise in social understanding—and the source of much amity and mutual respect. There are some things that are unforgettable. Unimportant, or relatively so, in themselves, they serve as tokens. On this July morning one became aware—in the intimate atmosphere of the composer's home and workshop—of the significance of this musician, of the basic virtues of music, of the purpose of education, of the experience of age comprehending the fervours of youth, of the points at which different traditions, and attitudes, meet. These furnish the main themes of the succeeding book.

Kodály is a great national figure. As such, his career has been described in Dr. László Eősze's admirable study. But he is equally a great international figure and it is, perhaps, not unfitting that the detachment which another nationality confers should be brought to bear. And it is noteworthy that Kodály has assumed a particular place in the musical life of Britain and of the United States. That this is so is due to his starting-point, which (as ours, in a national sense) is choral music. From here he has moved to a special branch of corporate music-making, that of the schools; Kodály's influence on musical education is profound, and likely to become more profound. In this field, wherein too often otiose, amateur, standards have prevailed, he has shown the merits of acute professionalism.

It was in this connection that I was drawn into more or less intimate connection with Kodály's music, being required to prepare certain works for an edition to be used in the English-speaking world. Thus studying some 200 pieces one begins to feel that one has acquired a certain amount of inner knowledge—of incentive, of style, of method, and of meaning.

When one looks at Kodály's works it becomes apparent that their character can only be understood in relation to the whole life of the Hungarian people and to the progress, hitherto sadly chequered, of their musical tradition. I have—aware of the general lack of material available in England on these issues—therefore tried to give some adequate background to the main biographical and critical narrative.

Regarding the central figure, I have been immensely helped by Professor Kodály himself. Since he has read everything that relates to his own life, and has corrected some errors that have otherwise been given currency and enlarged on episodes that would seem hitherto to have been given sparse treatment, I can, perhaps, lay claim to some degree of authenticity. Moreover, where I have exposed his points of view or otherwise interpreted his attitudes, he has not dissented from my presentation. I should, in private duty bound, set on record my gratitude for the frequent hospitality I have enjoyed from Professor and Mrs. Kodály, which has given many opportunities for far-ranging discussion. In fact, we have talked about most things under the sun.

A separate list of acknowledgements indicates that I have enjoyed the assistance of various institutions and people. At the risk of appearing invidious, I would pay special tribute to the Association of Hungarian Musicians, to the Music Department of the National Széchényi Library, and to the Staffs of the Hungarian Embassy in London and the British Embassy in Budapest, all of whom have been generous in transmuting what started as duty into friendship. But there are some whose claims to official recognition are slighter than those to more personal regard.

There was, for example, the old waiter in the café near the Library who, while acknowledging the stature of Professor Kodály, opined that for himself the music of Lehár and of the gipsy bands was preferable to what he—rather oddly—defined as the 'abstract music' of Kodály and Bartók. Thus he confirmed what Kodály, being a realist, understands: that the task of educating a new public still runs over the track of old prejudices. But, said the waiter, the children will understand it: they, he added, were being brought up to it. This conclusion was supported by the charming young woman (alas! I never learned her name) who daily superintended my breakfast during my last visit to Budapest. Her two children were following Kodályan principles, if from afar. And there was the hotel clerk whose assiduity in attention to his English visitors was in large measure a vicarious tribute to 'the Professor'. Artists, writers, university lecturers, doctors, conductors, orchestral virtuosi . . . : having met a fair cross-section of the people of Hungary, and in a private, non-official way, one may lay claim to some sort of feeling for the atmosphere. It is sufficient here to state that through such encounters one is able to appreciate the service that Kodály has done for his nation, and his unique position as a musician. This is a fit subject for the historian, the sociologist, the philosopher. That is why I am particularly conscious of the contribution made to this book by the Hungarian man- and woman-in-the-street. That is where Kodály expects one to begin.

This Preface, I notice, is running away from the conventions of musicological prologue. It is not necessarily any the worse for that, for it leads to this conclusion: that as between peoples who comprise separate nations there are certain principles and beliefs that are commonly held. Throughout a long and often troubled history, the greatest Hungarians have enunciated philosophical truths that, in other form, have found expression in our own tradition. On this foundation the work of Zoltán Kodály is reared: *Sic rerum summa novatur semper, et inter se mortales mutua vivunt.*

P. M. Y.

Acknowledgements

THE AUTHOR IS INDEBTED to the following, who have given valuable assistance in the preparation of this book: Professor and Mrs. Zoltán Kodály; the Association of Hungarian Musicians; the Széchényi National Library; the Hungarian Academy of Sciences (Folk Music Group); the Hungarian Institute for Folk-Art; the Hungarian Embassy to Great Britain and Northern Ireland (especially Mr. Lajos Nagy); the British Embassy to Hungary; Professor György Antal; Mr. Gábor Friss (Music Director of one of the General Schools for Music); Mr. Károly Gink; Mr. István Harmath; Mr. Gyula Kertész; Mr. Lajos Lesznai; Professor Ervin Major; Dr. Éva Palócz, and *Hungarofilm*; Mr. Miklós Róna; Mrs. Helga Szabó, and children from the Mogyoródi úti skola, Budapest; Professor Bence Szabolcsi; and to Editio Musica, Budapest, Messrs. Boosey and Hawkes Ltd., and Universal Edition, by whose permission also the music examples appear.

Particular thanks are due to Dr. István Kecskeméti for reading the proofs.

Illustrations appear by kind permission of Professor Kodály, Professor Antal, the Széchényi National Library, the Academy of Sciences, the Institute for Folk-Art, the Hungarian Embassy in London, the Hungarian News and Information Service, and Magyar Foto. For photographic work undertaken specially for this book the author acknowledges the ready cooperation of Mr. István Harmath, Mr. Károly Gink, and Mr. Gyula Kertész.

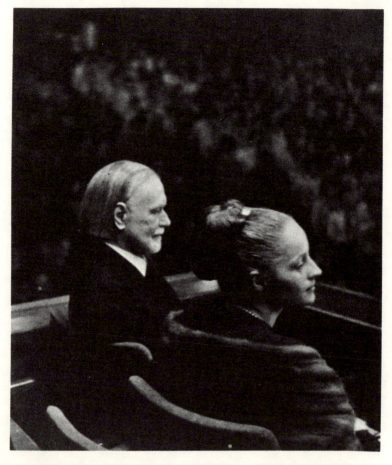

Professor and Mrs. Kodály at eightieth birthday celebrations
at the Erkel Theatre, Budapest, 1962

The Historical Background

FROM ROMAN TIMES TO THE WAR OF INDEPENDENCE

The history of Hungary is both long and tragic; a sequence of invasions, subjugations, and uprisings, amid which national leaders have from time to time arisen to fight for national freedom and independence, and the arts have struggled fiercely for existence and survival. In countries where such conditions have obtained the sense of history is keen, so that yesterday and the day before yesterday are never forgotten.

There was a time when Celtic people lived in what is now Hungary and these became the subjects of the Roman legions who settled themselves on the banks of the Danube to establish a firm boundary to the Empire. There are many remains of the Roman occupation, both in the countryside and in the settlement of Aquincum (in the museum of which is what is said to be the oldest organ—a 'water-organ' or *hydraulus*—in the world), north of Budapest. Of the legionaries of the Transdanubian province of Pannonia some came to Britain—the first link with this country— to occupy the Lancashire fortress of Ribchester, where recent discoveries of ornaments established the Danubian origin of these visitors. When the power of Rome passed and the Empire contracted the plains of Hungary were open to invading tribes; of Huns, whose great leader was Attila, of Avars, and of Magyars. The Magyars whose origins were in the same Finno-Ugrian group as the Finns, ultimately gave their name to the Hungarian nation as a whole. (The basic connection between Hungarians and Finns, marked in some aspects of vocabulary and speech structure, is acknowledged by Zoltán Kodály in the selection of certain cantos from the Finnish *Kalevala* which are incorporated into the collection entitled *Bicinia Hungarica*, and in *Vejnemöjnën muzsikál*.) Under the influence of the Carolingian Empire Hungary became

Christian (not, however, before the missionary Bishop Gellért had been thrown into the Danube from the hill that now bears his name), and the organisation of a centralised State was accomplished in the tenth and eleventh centuries by Prince Géza and his son István (Stephen) I.

Despite internal dissensions, and continual threats from without, ordered ecclesiastical life provided the Hungarians with such splendid Romanesque buildings as those at Esztergom and Pécs; while a vigorous assault on royal privilege and the reigning monarch, András II, led to the Golden Bull of 1222 (a Charter similar in intention to the English Magna Carta of the same period).

A nation is at the mercy of geographical circumstance. Hungary, Christian and feudal, lay on the overland route to Constantinople and inevitably it found itself important to western Europe as a bastion against the pagan East; conversely, as a barricade against the West. The strategic value of Hungary led to it being continually coveted by those powers with imperial aspirations, whether in Germany, Byzantium, or Mongolia; and in the fourteenth century after the tribe of Árpád had died out, the crown passed to the Neapolitan House of Anjou. Although aggressive in foreign affairs, the two principal members of this dynasty, Róbert Károly (Robert Charles) and Lajos (Louis) I, not only kept their recalcitrant nobility in order, but also built up the trade and culture of the cities. The most striking relics of this era are the sculptures about the great portico of the church at Ják, and in the Church of St. Elizabeth at Kassa[1]; the miniatures in the *Illustrated Chronicle* done by order of Lajos I; and the art of the goldsmiths—a traditional craft in Hungary from Magyar times.

A decline in royal power, indifference to national interests on the part of a squabbling nobility, and popular discontent largely focused on the Hussite activities which spread to Hungary from Bohemia, left Hungary ill-equipped to ward off the advancing armies of the Turks. In the middle of the fifteenth century, however, János Hunyadi, a minor nobleman of Wallachian descent, emerged to take command of the situation, to keep the Turks at

1 Now Košice, in Czechoslovakia.

bay, and to establish himself as a greatly loved national hero—the subject of many folk legends. At the end of the fifteenth century Hunyadi's son, Mátyás, became king, and he, a cultivated, scholarly, and humane ruler, introduced to Hungary the rising impulses of Renaissance culture. Mátyás set up a printing press, founded the Corvina library, and encouraged such scholars as Janus Pannonius, who, although his means of expression was Latin, is regarded as the first of the Hungarian lyric poets.

It may be said that from Renaissance until relatively modern times the Latin language has occupied a special place in Hungarian culture. In later time of oppression, when the Magyar tongue was proscribed, Hungarians insisted on the official use of Latin, by which means they were able to register some kind of protest. It is noteworthy that Kodály (as the dedications of certain works show) has often recalled this tradition.

After the reign of Mátyás, weaker government followed, and the depredations of the Turks intensified until in 1526 the independence of Hungary was extinguished at the Battle of Mohács. For practical purposes, the greater part of the country was now a Turkish province, and so it remained until 1699, when, as a result of the Peace of Carlowitz, Hungary and Transylvania were ceded to Austria, which set a new yoke on the necks of the unfortunate Hungarians.

Hating both Turks and Habsburgs (who also considered Hungary as within their zone of interest) the Hungarians, inspired both by their own traditions and the general ferment of the Reformation, threw their pride, courage, resentment, and passion into literature, and three great names stand out in the sixteenth and seventeenth centuries: those of Péter Bornemissza[1], Bálint Balassi,[2] and Miklós Zrinyi. These are honoured as patriots, as the founders of a literature in the vernacular, and are all to be met within the choral settings of Zoltán Kodály.

The cultural tradition of Hungary up to the seventeenth century was one of continual absorption and reconstitution. So it was with music, which, in so far as art-music was concerned,

---

[1] Musical settings of whose poems were published in *Cantio optima* (1553 ?).

[2] See *Deutsche dreistimmige Lieder,* 1576, by the Dresden composer, Jacques Regnart.

was based on plainsong[1] and minstrelsy, and any new tendencies
were generally appreciated only in the polyphonic works of
visitors or immigrants. During the reigns of Mátyás and of Lajos
II there was a brief climax under the direction of Thomas Stoltzer,
the Court Kapellmeister, whose Latin psalms and motets were
widely known in the first half of the sixteenth century. Of his
Geistliche Gesänge, one[2] reflected his Hungarian employment in
somewhat Gothic manner, being based on an acrostical arrangement of words which revealed the inscription 'König Ludwig'.
A similar motet celebrated Queen Maria. Stoltzer was a German,
and after the Battle of Mohács the majority of Hungarian-born
composers took their talents abroad; among them were Bálint
Bakfark, the lutenist commemorated in the verses of the Polish
poet, Jan Kochanowski, and pictured in the frontispiece of his
Intabulatura of 1552,[3] Johann Kusser, who eventually occupied
important posts in Dublin, Georg Strattner, and the Neusiedlers.
In Hungary the musical genius of the people found its expression
in liturgical music—especially the often reissued *Cantus Catholici*
of 1651 and János Kájoni's *Organo Missale,* of 1667, and in folk-
song. The songs that were sung in the seventeenth century are
still, having been unconsciously absorbed into the common
practice of peasant music-making, a living part of the Hungarian
tradition. Now, as then (and this point will be expanded later),
the folk tradition reflects almost every influence that has played
a part in Hungarian musical life, whether sacred or secular.

In the middle of the sixteenth century there was, however, an
interesting revival of bardic music by Sebestyén Tinódi, to which
Sir Philip Sidney, who visited Hungary as diplomat in 1573,
made reference in *An Apologie for Poetrie.* 'In Hungary', he wrote,
'I have seen it the manner at all Feasts, and other such meetings,
to have songs of their Ancestors' valour; which that right soldier-
like Nation thinks the chiefest kindlers of brave courage.'
In his *Cronica* (1554) Tinódi set historical records to melodies
contrived in a style that combined ecclesiastical, native folk-

---

[1] See, for examples, the *Psalterium Blasii* (Pozsony), 1419.

[2] *König, ein Herr ob alle Reich.*

[3] Bakfark has lately become more public property through the three fantasias
arranged and orchestrated by Gábor Darvas (1962).

music and Turkish influences. Outside of Hungary the vitalising possibilities of Hungarian dance music was recognised by a number of lutenist composers in search of novelty. In a collection of pieces issued in 1562 Wolfgang Heckel, of Strasbourg, included a sharp-edged *Magyar Dance*

etc.

initially set above a tonic-dominant pedal. Eleven years later Bernhard Jobin, also of Strasbourg, arranged a *Passamezzo ongaro* in a lute book. While in 1620 Giovanni Picchi, one of the leading Italian harpsichord composers, displayed a *Ballo ongaro* in his *Intavolatura di balli d'arpicordo*. Such works, however, had no more national significance than the pieces in the English collections that acknowledged occasional Celtic stimulus. The intention was to provoke audience interest by reference to romantically distant, but second-class peoples. The practice continued until well on into the nineteenth century.

Social organisation in seventeenth-century Hungary showed the greater noblemen, opportunistically collaborating with the alien oppressors and consolidating their own estates; the lesser noblemen, mostly impecunious, from whose often thoughtful and patriotic ranks sprang such great heroes as Zrinyi and Ferenc Rákóczi—the latter immortalised in the march that bears his name[1] and in other popular music; and the peasantry, whose role, as until modern times, was necessarily almost entirely passive.

Rákóczi attempted to unite all patriotic Hungarians, but also to relieve the peasants of some at least of their disabilities. A skilled politician and diplomat, he joined with the French in the War of the Spanish Succession and, having defeated the Austrians, won for his country a brief spell of independence. He himself was elected Prince of Transylvania, a dignity which he enjoyed between 1705

[1] See Introduction by Ervin Major to *Old Hungarian Piano Duets, III* ('The Original Rákóczi Song', 'Rákóczi March'), Editio Musica, Budapest, 1959.

and 1711. In this year Rákóczi's struggle for national independence was ended when some of his commanders treated with the Austrians behind his back, and the French deserted him. Then the Austrians reimposed their suzerainty. Hungary, under Maria Theresa and Joseph II, became a province, with her trading interests subordinated to those of Austria, with German language and method made compulsory, and with the claims of the Roman Catholic Church held as supreme—except where, as in Debrecen, stubborn pockets of Calvinism persisted.

This particular form of resistance to the established order in Debrecen—a proud city with its Charter granted by Lajos I in 1361—had important consequences for Hungarian popular music, and one aspect of the work of Zoltán Kodály derived from the eighteenth-century pioneer work of a Debrecen musician. This was György Maróthy, Professor in the College of that city, who promoted polyphonic singing among the students, reorganising the choir so to do, founded a Collegium Musicum, and, in 1743, published an *Abridged Method of Harmonic Singing* (*A' Hármoniás éneklésről valo rövid tanítás*).

During the period of the 'Enlightenment' the great noblemen of Hungary firmly fixed their sights on Austrian culture, and were rewarded for their political fidelity with vast accessions to their personal fortunes. Possessed of great wealth, their influence was enormous. Hungarian literature, also kept under ecclesiastical observation, was trimmed to the prevailing standards of neo-classicism, and it suffered a temporary decline. Towards the end of the century, however, a reconsideration of the structure and vocabulary of the language—with a view to ensuring its viability in the modern world—coupled with an enthusiasm derived from French revolutionary thought, gave encouragement to those who, like József Katona, wished to make literature a driving force in the aspiring nationalism that was growing anew. As for music the aristocracy plumped for opera, and for the symphonic style. Private theatres were erected at Pozsony (Pressburg, now Bratislava), Nagyvárad (now Oradea Mare), Pécel, and Eszterháza (now Fertőd), and music and musicians, as well as actors, were brought in from Germany and Austria in large numbers. Of the princely establishments the most famous was that at Eszterháza, where Miklós Esterházy, whose annual income was almost two million gold forints, installed József Haydn as musician-in-chief.[1] As a court servant, Haydn did all that was required of him, and the quality of his work at Eszterháza was appreciated by Maria Theresa herself, and described in glowing terms by the French Ambassador in Vienna, the Duke of Rohan. But Haydn did more: through his compositions he made Hungary music-conscious in the wider sense. His symphonies were acclaimed not only in Eszterháza, but also in Kismarton (now Ersenstadt), Pozsony and Budapest, while towards the end of the century his oratorios were especially appreciated in Győr and Sopron. More than this, 'in small Hungarian country towns, wherever there were schoolboys, civil servants or others who could play the fiddle, they sat down and played the string quartets of Haydn. For these people, more often than not, this was the only road leading towards the higher spheres of classical music. But whoever as a young boy caught a glimpse of the wonderful realm of music, never rested until gaining access to it. It is in this way that Haydn's œuvre became one of the cornerstones of Hungarian musical culture.'[2]

Kodály added to this that Haydn 'was the first to announce to the world at large, in his music inscribed *all' ongarese*, that a musical mode of expression, specially Hungarian and differing from any other had come into being. . . . But even compositions not marked *all' ongarese* also indicate sufficient Hungarian elements.'

The Hungarian elements, as in the *Menuetto—Allegretto alla Zingarese* of the String Quartet in D major (Op. 20 No. 4), or in the Rondo of the Trio in G major of 1795, were sometimes specified by Haydn; but often they were not, and a comprehensive list of works in which Hungarian influences are to be found is given by Szabolcsi.[3] Sometimes it was a matter of rhythm, or melodic outline, sometimes a matter of colouring, and it is not difficult to see how the so-called *Zigeuner* style of free, improvisatory, fiddling lies behind the *affettuoso* of the second movement of

---

[1] For a detailed account of music, and especially opera, at Eszterháza, see *Das Esterhazysche Feenreich*, Mátyás Horányi, Budapest, 1959.

[2] Zoltán Kodály on the 150th Anniversary of Haydn's death: quoted in *Haydn Compositions in the Music Collection of the National Széchényi Library*, Budapest, 1960, p. vii.

[3] *Op. cit.*, pp. ix-x.

Op. 20, No. 4, or the ornamental ejaculation in the first violin part of the *Finale* of Op. 33. In such ways did Haydn show his acquaintance and approval of the below-stairs music of eighteenth-century Hungary.

During Haydn's life-time this branch of music was revivified by a particular form, known as *verbunkos,* and it is this dance that was to become one of the principal supports for a genuinely Hungarian school of composition. For centuries the Hungarians had been notable for their dances,[1] and during the eighteenth century all were funnelled into that which initiated the young men into the soldiery. The *verbunkos* (derived from the German word *Werbung*—enlisting), showing elements of native folk-dance, but also of Balkan influences in general, of Turkish, Viennese, and gipsy music, was a simple two-sentence structure in $\frac{2}{4}$ time, accommodated by an elementary harmonic scheme (mostly tonic and dominant) that admitted the maximum or improvisation. Melodically, the *verbunkos* was distinguished by a wealth of syncopation, ornamentation, and wide leaps.

The *verbunkos* served a practical purpose, but, since its popularity raised it to an emblematic plane, it attracted attention for its own sake and examples, which hitherto had existed only rarely in manuscript form, were published. One of the earliest such publications was József Bengráf's[2] *XII Danses Hongroises pour le Clavecin ou Piano-Forte,* issued in Vienna in 1790. Other early collections— in which the dances were arranged in contrasted order in respect of tempo or tonality—included Ferdinand Kauer's 12 *Neue Ungarische Tänze für das Forte-Piano* (1798), and two volumes of dances from the gipsy musicians of Galánta—from which Kodály borrowed for his *Dances from Galánta* suite—which appeared in 1804.[3]

The early development of *verbunkos* was more or less fortuitous,

---

[1] Chronicles of the eleventh century noted how Hungarians raiding in the west celebrated their victories with dances; while a sixteenth-century preacher tried to persuade the 'dancing Hungarians', as he called them, to a more sober way of living.

[2] 1745 or 6 - 91, Kapellmeister and Composer in Pest.

[3] For examples and discussion of *verbunkos* music, see: (*a*) *Ungarische Tänze aus Haydn's Zeit,* ed. B. Szabolcsi and F. Bónis, Editio Musica, Budapest, 1959. (*b*) *100 Jahre Ungarische Klaviermusik,* ed. Ervin Major and I. Szelényi, Zeneműkiadó Vállalat, Budapest, 1954.

and in this respect, it may be seen to belong to the folk-music tradition (even though modern Hungarian musicologists are reluctant to admit it to the same company as the true songs of the peasants). But once its popularity was established, composers, as distinct from arrangers, of *verbunkos* came forward, of whom the chief were János Lavotta (1764-1820), János Bihari (1764-1827), and Antal György Csermák (1774?-1822). All were performers and made the famous 'virtuoso trio' of the *verbunkos* tradition. This melody by Bihari

2   Allegro

was later rearranged by Liszt in his *Ungarische National-Melodien* and also by Kodály in *Háry János*.[1]

A further composer of importance was Márk Rózsavölgyi (1789?-1848), who developed the *verbunkos* cyclically, and also saw the replacement of that dance by the derivative *csárdás*. The significance of this expressive type of music is emphasised by consideration of the history of Hungary during the same period, when much happened to stimulate a national consciousness and an intellectual and artistic renaissance.

The Napoleonic Wars, in which the military nobility of Hungary attached themselves to the Imperial forces of Austria—and suffered a crushing defeat at Győr for their pains—brought a particular incentive to the intellectuals and, in spite of Napoleon's ultimate defeat, they formed secret societies with the connivance and assistance of some lesser members of the aristocracy to overthrow the Habsburg rule. The plight of the latter (there was a great gulf between the higher and lower aristocracy) was bad, for they were in poor economic condition and were

[1] See vocal score of *Háry János*, p. 60.

victims of the violent censorship and generally tyrannic overseer-
ship imposed on the country by Metternich; but that of the
peasants was impossible. So H. A. L. Fisher wrote: 'While the
nobility of Austria and Hungary enjoyed every form of social
privilege, while they were exempt from military services, relieved of
taxation, and placed beyond the reach of the common law courts,
the peasantry were hard bound in the fetters of medieval subjection.'

A state of general misery, governmental incompetence, and
economic incapacity compelled protestations in the Hungarian
Parliament of 1825-7, and certain concessions from the Austrians.
The leader of reform was Count István Széchenyi, an aristocrat
concerned at the backwardness of his country and the social
inequalities that were increasingly apparent. To Széchenyi may
be attributed the improvement of transport, particularly on the
Danube, which was bridged by the Englishman William Clark
and on which steamers began to appear, and Lake Balaton, and
the foundation of the Hungarian Academy of Sciences. Cultural
developments followed; the Theatre, for the erection of which
voluntary labour was forthcoming, and the Kisfaludy Literary
Society were founded. The Kisfaludy brothers, Károly and
Sándor, were prime movers in romanticism of thought in
Hungarian literature, which, by referring the present to the past
and by expanding a literary consciousness of the free play of
individual and collective emotion, now took on characteristics
of other national-romantic schools. Another prominent literary
figure in the Reform Era was Ferenc Kölcsey, a great lyric poet,
a critic who laid the foundations of scientific literary criticism in
Hungary, an active participant in political life, and the author of
the words of the present national anthem. Sándor Kisfaludy and
Kölcsey were also among the first literary figures to appreciate the
cultural place of music in society—their criterion was the works of
Haydn,[1] and they also appear among the poets whose works have
been set by Kodály.

The next stage of Hungarian emancipation is dominated by the
personality of Lajos Kossuth, whose patriotism was founded on
an acute perception of economic possibilities—given social reform

---

[1] Some of Haydn's songs were published in Vienna to Hungarian texts by
Verseghy in *Hat magyar énekek* (1791).

and industrial development—and a burning zeal for justice. In 1848 the Hungarians rose again. But a year later another war of independence was crushed—because of the numerical superiority of foreign arms, including some allowed to the Austrians by the Russian Government. 'The emotions of Western Europe', wrote H. A. L. Fisher, 'were deeply stirred by the tragedy of the Hungarians who, if they had acted oppressively[1] towards their own subject peoples [i.e. national minorities, Slovak, Serb, Transylvanian, Rumanian, etc, living within the borders of the country as it then was], were yet in their passionate and tenacious struggle for personal liberty and responsible government, members of the fellowship of progress and freedom.'

HUNGARY IN THE LATTER PART OF THE NINETEENTH CENTURY

After the collapse of the War of Independence, Hungary was submitted to a ruthless campaign of subjection, put into effect by the notorious Alexander Bach, Austrian Minister of Home Affairs; and Transylvania and Croatia were put under the direct administration of Vienna. During the next troubled decade the development of industry in Hungary was hindered by the abolition of the Customs frontier, which flooded the country with Austrian products. Dislike of the Austrians and contempt for their autocracy was reflected in the non-cooperation of many of the citizens and in the novels of Mór Jókai and the poems of János Arany. In 1861 the Austrians, having suffered defeat from the French and the loss of territories in Italy, reorganised the Empire and offered the already restive Hungarians improved provincial status, with a Parliament responsible only in a colonial sense. This being rejected, the *status quo* was maintained until 1867, after Ferenc Deák had proffered a scheme for compromise and the restoration of fuller powers, and after the Austro-Prussian War. In this year Transylvania and Croatia were restored to Hungary, a separate government (though with defence and foreign affairs controlled by joint Austro-Hungarian Commissions) was acknowledged in Budapest, with Count Gyula Andrássy as Prime Minister

---

[1] The word is not well chosen. In a highly complex situation it should be pointed out that representatives of the 'minorities', especially the Slovaks, were often welcomed as full partners in the national development.

and Franz Joseph was separately crowned as King of Hungary.

In Hungary the Austrian influence was strong and German was the official language until 1861, but there were benefits. Compulsory education, for instance, was introduced by the Minister for Education, József Eötvös, the novelist, and economic development was encouraged, particularly by the implementation of a Customs union that opened the Austrian market to Hungarian agriculture. In so far as social organisation was concerned, the biggest advance was represented by the results of the abolition of serfdom, as from 1848, and the technical acknowledgment of the equality of the peasantry before the law. The generally feudal relationship between the classes, however, was fully maintained by the ruling classes—the large landowners, whose interests, as always, lay in Vienna. The peasants accepted that the Almighty, whose ministers were many and persuasive, had His own good reasons for making them peasants (until the agrarian disasters of the 1890's), and were, within their limits, happy. That is to say, they cultivated their land, and sang folk-songs. In the cities, however, there was an increasing industrial population which, beginning to organise itself, began to give a new turn to the theme of nationalism as preached by the intelligentsia. None approved the support given by the Prime Minister, now Kálmán Tisza, to the Monarchy, which occupied Bosnia and Hercegovina and allied itself with the Prussian Government in Berlin.

LISZT, MOSONYI, ERKEL, AND OTHER CONTEMPORARY MUSICIANS

Despite political and military disasters, however, Hungarian culture had moved forward, and in the works of Sándor Petőfi— who died during the War of Independence—and János Arany— like Petőfi, of peasant stock—a new, more direct, literary manner emerged, in which habits of colloquial expression and simplicities borrowed from folk-poetry displaced the artificial diction of earlier romanticism. While folk-poetry affected the literary development, so also did folk-music come directly into the province of the Hungarian composer. Three composers particularly claim attention at this juncture: Liszt, Mosonyi, and Erkel. These were the virtual founders of modern Hungarian music.

Ferenc Liszt, a native of Doborján in the former western Hungary, is of first importance in that he played a large part on the stage of European music, whereon he succeeded in establishing some kind of musical image of his country. He was brought up on one of the Esterházy estates, on which his father was steward. When the Esterházy family—patrons of Haydn and of Hummel (who ended his tenure of the office of Kapellmeister at Eisenstadt in 1811, in which year Liszt was born), and occasional hosts of Cherubini —discovered that the young Liszt had the gifts of a prodigy they were delighted. A committee of the nobility was formed and Ferenc was provided with a generous six-year subsidy to further his musical education in Vienna. It was nearly twenty years before he revisited his native country, and when he did so it was—so far as the rest of Europe was concerned—as the most distinguished, and most successful, of living Hungarians. Although he largely forgot the Hungarian language (which had in any case been subordinate to German) Liszt never forgot that he was Hungarian, and as the years passed, and as Hungarian affairs obtruded in the political sphere, he became increasingly conscious both of his inheritance and his responsibility. In 1838 he gave a concert in aid of the victims of the floods in Buda and Pest—which were not united into one city until 1873. In 1840, after a triumphal reception at Pozsony, where he had given his first recital as a boy, he was welcomed into the capital by serenading choirs and military bands, and at a concert in the new, State-owned, theatre in Pest[1] was presented with a 'sword of honour'—the gift of the aristocracy. National fervour was stimulated by Liszt's playing of his arrangement of the *Rákóczi March*, which he himself described as a *Marseillaise aristocratique hongroise*.[2]

[1] Founded in 1837. The present Opera House was built by Miklós Ybl in 1884.

[2] The earliest version of the *Rákóczi March* was published in 1820 by Miklós Scholl, Bandmaster of the 'Prince Miklós Esterházy No. 32 Infantry Regiment' in Pest. The March was popularised by the playing of János Bihari, and by Berlioz's arrangement. In 1859 the March, together with the *Rákóczi Song* and a piece entitled *The Battle*, was issued by F. Glüggl of Vienna in a volume edited by Count István Fáy (*Pearls of Old Hungarian Music*, Vol. IV). Fáy surmised that the *Rákóczi Song* had been composed by Mihály Barna, a gipsy musician in the service of Rákóczi. Further legends concerning the music associated with Rákóczi are summarised by Ervin Major in the Foreword to *Eredeti Rákóczi Nóta*; *Rákóczi Induló* (Editio Musica, Budapest, 1959).

In nostalgic mood, Liszt, having paid a visit to his birthplace, inquired whether the gipsies he used to hear in childhood were still about. Learning that they were he went to their encampment and renewed acquaintance with their music, as he described in his *Die Zigeuner und ihre Musik in Ungarn* (1859)—a book which in due course misled many people as to the proper origins of Hungarian folk-music.

From such experience, and fired with the proved patriotism that distinguished every Hungarian after the tragic War of Independence, Liszt composed much 'Hungarian' music—rhapsodies,[1] in which the *verbunkos* style was ever prominent and the sounds of the gipsy orchestras, particularly of the cimbalum, were simulated, and csárdás for pianoforte; the symphonic poem *Hungaria* for orchestra; the *Esztergom Mass*, written for the Prince-Primate, the *Coronation March* and *Mass*—with vivid colours and striking rhythms—for the inauguration of Franz Joseph I as King of Hungary in the dual monarchy of Austria and Hungary. At the end of his life Liszt memorialised Petőfi, first in the setting of Petőfi's ballad, 'The God of the Magyars', and then in the elegiac pianoforte piece, *Dem Andenken Petőfis*. This music was arranged by Liszt from that composed for the melodrama, based on a poem by Mór Jókai—*Des todten Dichters Liebe*. In respect of Liszt's synthesis of Hungarian elements in his last music, Ervin Major comments that 'it already opened a new perspective in the combination of basic Hungarian music and art music and led to the early works of Béla Bartók'.

Liszt and the violinist Reményi, who had been involved in the insurrection of 1848 and compelled to flee the country, succeeded in romanticising Hungary. (Reményi claimed to have been a gipsy musician, but, of Jewish stock, his credentials did not carry real authenticity.) This was partly through personal magnetism, partly through the idiomatic inflexions they brought to bear on the common musical style of the age.

In Hungary national events were commemorated in Lisztian

---

[1] Notice the use of material from the 'Wedding Dances from Tolna' in *Hungarian Rhapsody*, Vol. IX, No. 5. The dances in this collection were also used by Brahms in his *Hungarian Dances*, and one was rediscovered as living folk-music by Béla Bartók in 1912. (See Ervin Major's notes in *100 Jahre Ungarische Klaviermusik*.)

language by such composers as Ferenc Doppler, who was director of the Band of the National Guard in Buda in 1848, József Müller, Kapellmeister of the Honvéd Regiment, and Béni Egressy, all of whom seized the spirit of *verbunkos*, and of the *csárdás* that had prevailed from the early 1840's, and, because their works were popular in a revolutionary period, helped to formalise concepts of Hungarian music for the Hungarians themselves. But the field of opportunity was widening. As the national ideal was politically and militarily frustrated, so it looked for its symbols in terms of art, and musical expansion was encouraged by the foundation of such institutions as the pioneer music school at Kolozsvár,[1] in Transylvania, in the operas of the National Theatre in Pest, and, later, in the Philharmonic Society (1853), the Academy of Music (1875), and the Opera House of Budapest (1884). Of the Academy Liszt, by now ennobled by the Hungarian Government, became first President.

Outwardly it would seem that Liszt dominated the scene; but within Hungary the two musicians who most effectively built the foundations, and on the foundations, were Mihály Mosonyi and Ferenc Erkel.

Mosonyi, born in 1815, was of German descent and bore the family name of Brand until he adopted one that was Hungarian (Mosonyi means 'from Moson') in 1859. Of modest family, he was intended to become a schoolmaster, but a natural gift for music persuaded him to relinquish this objective and to go to Pozsony. Here, in the intervals of working as a type-setter, he had some lessons in piano and in the rudiments of harmony. In the main, however, he acquired the craft of composition from text-books, and in due course appeared as a promising composer nicely obedient to German conventions. Mosonyi was music-master in various aristocratic families until he arrived in Pest with various large-scale works, of which a symphony was favourably received in 1844. At the same time the potent, German, quality in his writing was noticeable and soon to become the target of nationalist critics, and the cause of a psychological disturbance in Mosonyi's pattern of life. Thus between 1845 and 1848 he gave up composition, and when he recommenced it was with the

---

[1] Clausenburg, now Cluj (Rumania).

intention of evolving a more purely national idiom, initially based
on the *verbunkos*.

In 1856 Mosonyi's second symphony was heard, and in the last
movement was evidence of his new style. In pianoforte works he
let Hungarian "programmes" into romantically-styled miniatures
—as in *Puszta-Life, Hungarian Children's World* (dedicated 'To the
Youth of Hungary'), *Homage to the Memory of Kazinczy,* and
Funeral Music for István Széchenyi, all composed in 1859-60. From
this last work (which was later orchestrated) two excerpts show
the melodic, rhythmic, and harmonic characteristics of Mosonyi's
'Hungarian' idiom:

The bass in the second excerpt is used throughout as a ground-
bass. The augmented interval, also plangently featured in
Mosonyi's *Orphan Girl,* belongs to the so-called 'Hungarian scale'.
Liszt borrowed this theme for one of his historical portaits.

Mosonyi forsook the poets—Lenau, Geibel, and Burns—who
had inspired his earlier songs, and turned to Arany, Tóth, and
Petőfi. A strongly pedagogic strain caused him to anticipate
Bartók and Kodály by writing didactic pieces for the young—
Studies for Developing the Performance of Hungarian Music—which
were esteemed by Wagner, for whom, in turn, Mosonyi had the

Woodcut from 'Dózsa' series, by Gyula Derkovits, symbolising
the Peasant Uprising of 1514

MS. score of Erkel's *Bank Ban*, showing the use of cimbalum

highest regard. The general Wagnerian apparatus, indeed, served Mosonyi as a useful background when he turned to opera, even when as in *Szép Ilon* (*Pretty Helen*), produced in the National Theatre in 1861, he endeavoured to compose 'entirely in the Hungarian idiom to the exclusion of all foreign elements'.

Mosonyi was an indefatigable composer, but even more important was his function as educationist. As the founder of *Zenészeti Lapok*, the first musical journal in the Hungarian language, he exercised a considerable influence on the musical thinking of his fellow-countrymen. What he was trying to do in this respect was what Schumann had done for German musical culture in the *Neue Zeitschrift*. Mosonyi, who was a vigorous contributor to his own magazine, discussed many aspects of national music, but in looking forward to a compromise between European and Hungarian styles, and in championing the music-dramas of Wagner, he alienated the sympathy of those who, like Ferenc Erkel, were not inclined to accept any compromise solution. This attitude, of course, mirrored political tensions and the facts of life as they then were. Mosonyi also wished to see musical education expanded and the institution of a national academy in the capital. This was achieved, but five years after his death. To Mosonyi honour is due in that he attempted to democratise music, to push it past the barriers set up by wealthy patrons of cosmopolitan tastes and into the ambit of the people as a whole: he was at least partly rewarded by the popularity of his choral pieces among the male voice choirs that had developed during the nineteenth century after the model of the German *Liedertafel*.

A historic date in the record of Hungarian music was 21 September 1868, for on that day the National Federation of Choral Societies was founded. This was four years after the inauguration of a large-scale competition for male voice choirs. The National Federation was instituted at Debrecen, a traditional centre of choral music, and fifty-four choirs, comprising 845 singers, participated. The direction of the Federation was entrusted to Ferenc Erkel, who was elected conductor-in-chief for life.

Erkel was five years older than Mosonyi and one year older than Liszt—with whom he was closely associated—and his place in Hungarian music has been likened to that occupied by Glinka in Russia and Verdi in Italy. He became a great opera composer, and through this medium something of a national hero; and so he remains, with an opera house[1] as his memorial, and two of his operas in the regular repertoire. The focal point of Erkel's life was *Hunyadi László*, which was first produced in 1844 when the urge to national independence was about to burst into flame. Hunyadi László was the elder son of János, and his execution by László V in the middle of the fifteenth century induced his near beatification. An opera based on such a theme of martyrdom (the libretto was prepared from Lőrinc Tóth) was certain to appear as symbolic in the mid-nineteenth century, and when the chorus 'Dead is the intriguer' was sung the effect was electrifying. The melody which Erkel used for this chorus was one later to be discovered anew by Bartók in the course of his folk-song expeditions.

Erkel was a native of Gyula and educated in Pozsony, a city with its own musical traditions, where the Neusiedlers and Hummel were born, where Sigismund Kusser began his career, where Mozart visited in 1762, and where the symphonies of Haydn, Mozart, Beethoven, and Schubert were first esteemed outside of Austria.[2] There was also a tradition of music in Erkel's family, and his father, steward to an estate, was an excellent amateur violinist. His early lessons were from Károly Turányi— also Mosonyi's master—and his apprenticeship to the profession was served in Kolozsvár, where gipsy music attracted him, and then, according to precedent, in aristocratic service. At the age of twenty-five, however, he benefited from the cultural first-fruits of the Reform Era and was appointed musical director to the Hungarian theatre company in Buda; a year later he crossed the river to become deputy conductor of the German theatre in Pest.

Here, by a rare combination of musical and administrative talents, he promoted first-class opera productions and by so doing built up a general fund of enthusiasm for opera. Erkel founded the Philharmonic Orchestra, whose concerts he conducted, and undertook the direction of the Academy of Music. As has already been stated, he also superintended the national work of the Choral Federation.

[1] The Erkel Opera House, erected on the centenary of the composer's birth, shares its artistes with the National Opera.
[2] See *Béla Bartók*, Lajos Lesznai, p. 14.

Directly in touch with the practical side of music, and passionately devoted to the causes of national regeneration and general musical emancipation, Erkel was a notable example of a 'committed' artist; it was his ambition as a composer also to show how a style rooted in some part of the national heritage of music could be honourably connected with the main stream of European music and then brought into communion with the appreciative inclinations of the people of his country as a whole. It was fortunate that in the history of Hungary many subjects existed that were ideal for opera libretti, and also for the temper of the age.

An incentive came from the one Hungarian opera that had so far been composed—József Ruzitska's *Béla Futása* (*The Flight of Béla*), which was produced in Kolozsvár in 1822 and in Budapest in 1827, where it remained in the repertoire for two decades.

Erkel's first opera (1840), which had been preceded by a mere handful of minor works, was *Bátori Mária*. This two-act piece—to a libretto by Béni Egressy, based on a story by András Dugonics —owed much to the styles of Bellini and Donizetti, whose operas Erkel was accustomed to conduct; but a vivid sense of the dramatic and an evident intention to modify the language of music in favour of native inflections ensured its popularity. The success of *Bátori Mária,* however, was far exceeded by that of *Hunyadi László*, and thus inspired Erkel (after collaborating with the Doppler brothers in *Erzsébet*) turned to a famous play by József Katona (1791-1830), *Bánk Bán*, out of which strenuous epic of thirteenth-century history came his next opera. Although completed in 1852, *Bánk Bán* had to wait on political developments for its first performance, which did not take place until 1861.

The evocative quality of Erkel's score (of which the fair copy was made by various members of the Erkel family) is shown in the opening bars of the Prelude to Act I:

5 Moderato andantino

which later reaches this intense climax:

6

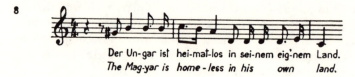

Here the dramatic quality is enhanced by a characteristically Hungarian change from major to minor tonality. The addiction to the augmented 'Hungarian' interval is frequent, as for example:

7

while the incorporation of a *Csárdás* in Act I is another obvious and deliberate gesture. In such a setting Erkel places powerful statements in language that is the more effective because it is commonplace. Thus:

8

Der Un-gar ist hei-mat-los in sei-nem eig-nem Land.
The Mag-yar is home-less in his own land.

or, from the Finale:

9

All-mächt-ger gieb der ar-men See-le Frie-den.
Al-migh-ty give to the poor soul peace,

9

E - wi-ge Ruh sei dem Lei-be be-schie - den!
Rest e-ver-last-ing al - low to the bo - dy.

It is not difficult to appreciate the overwhelming effect of such sentiments, so plainly exposed, on the audiences for whom Erkel wrote, even though the critics and high society scoffed at the 'barrel-organ' music. *Bánk Bán* still remains an essential part of the Hungarian repertoire of opera.

Other historical subjects that engaged Erkel were György Dózsa, leader of the peasant revolt of 1514, Prince Brankovics (with quotations from Turkish and Serbian folk-music and based on a prose drama by Mór Jókai), and St. Stephen (István I) of Hungary. He also composed two comic operas, *Sarolta* and *Névtelen Hősök*.

Erkel, whose *Hymnus* of 1845 to words by Kölcsey became and has remained the national anthem of Hungary, consistently made use of native musical characteristics, from *verbunkos* and *csárdás*, from folk-song, and from the popular songs that belonged to the local *Singspiel* tradition. In a more general way, he never departed from the lyrical quality inherent in the Hungarian style of singing (*bel canto* remains the ideal in opera performance), and absorbed the sense of instrumental colour that distinguishes all Hungarian scores. Erkel seized on the cimbalum[1] and put it into *Bánk Bán*, where it was played at the first performance by his son Sándor.

Erkel had four sons, each of whom became a musician. Gyula, the eldest was an educationist, conductor, and composer, among whose works is an overture on themes from Ruzitska's *Béla Futása*; Elek became a composer of operetta; László returned to Pozsony where, in 1894, he had the young Béla Bartók as piano

[1] The cimbalum was first employed in major works by Xavér Ferenc Szabó (1846-1911), and by Albert Siklós (1878-1942). In his *Magyar rapszodina* Siklós includes two cimbalums in his score.

pupil; and Sándor succeeded his father as conductor of the Opera in 1875.

Of the nineteenth-century Hungarian composers, Mosonyi, Liszt, and Ferenc Erkel were the most prominent and possessed of the most far-reaching influence. But there were others who also enjoyed some esteem as supporters of the national movement. András Bartay composed the first Hungarian comic opera— *Csel* (*The Trick*)—for the opening of the National Theatre in 1837. In the revolutionary year of 1848 György Császár wrote his patriotic opera, *A Kúnok* (*The Cumans*), which had more than a hundred performances. Kornél Ábrányi, once a pupil of Chopin, first Secretary and Professor of Composition at the Academy, infected the principles of his masters with Hungarian rhythms in slender piano pieces, and August von Adelburg, after the successful production of *Zrinyi*[1] at the National Theatre in Pest, in 1868, was already marked as an important figure in the new music of Hungary. Von Adelburg was born in Turkey and educated in Vienna, and he excelled as violinist and string quartet leader. But he also had musicological intuitions, which led him to publish a pamphlet[2] in 1859, where he joined issue with Liszt on the subject of gipsy music. Liszt claimed that the music played by the gipsies of Hungary was the basis of Hungarian folk-music. Von Adelburg disputed this, stating that gipsy music was in fact international, whereas true folk-music was the essential concomitant of folk-poetry. He ended his pamphlet passionately asking for a worthy exponent of the cause of the national music of the 'noble Hungarian people', one who was in true sympathy with its ideals and could, therefore, show it in its Eastern (*orientalisch*) quality, and in the fullness of its 'glowing life'. Then, he said Hungarian music would, without doubt, burst out 'from the womb of the nation and from the unjustly suppressed national consciousness'.

One more name remains: that of Ferenc Korbay. He, a godson of Liszt and a pupil of Mosonyi, gained a considerable reputation

---

[1] 'A dramatical, musical picture', in five acts, based on a text by Theodor Körner. Among von Adelburg's other works were an oratorio, *War and Peace,* and a *Thème originel et Variations dans le stile Hongroise* (Op.4), for violin and piano.

[2] *Entgegnung auf die von Dr. Franz Liszt in seinem werke auf gestellte Behauptung dass es keine ungarische Nationalmusik, sondern bloss eine Musik der Zingeuner gibt*, Pest, Verlag von Robert Lampel, 1859.

at the end of the nineteenth and the beginning of the twentieth centuries as singer, pianist, lecturer, and teacher. In the latter capacity he was on the staff of the Royal Academy of Music, London, for the last nine years of his life. It was, however, through his arrangements of Hungarian folk-songs that he was best known, and these, immensely popular in Britain, were the principal introduction for many to Hungarian music. Unfortunately, Korbay, although not unaware of the true situation, contented himself with making capital out of the bastardised songs (many composed by indifferent eighteenth- and nineteenth-century composers) of the gipsy repertoire.

Thus far, then, the story is chequered. Hungarian music was particularly vulnerable to the pressure of historical circumstances, and until von Adelburg's ideal of a champion should be realised the best that could be achieved was a compromise. Those who attempted compromise—and the Hungarians and English musical situations in the nineteenth century were comparable—were defeated. Cultural standards were set in Vienna—the true metropolis to the more substantial classes of Hungarian society—and in so far as native impulses were accepted it was rather on account of their curiosity. In the context of musical technique of the period composers (with the exception of Liszt in his last works) were bound fast by the *verbunkos* tradition on the one hand and by accepted, academic, harmonic method on the other.

The situation of a small country dominated both politically and culturally by a larger neighbour, or neighbours, was not at all uncommon in the nineteenth century (or the twentieth, if it comes to that); some found their political emancipation, some attained cultural independence. Hungary, like Ireland, had long to wait for both. That Hungarian music now exists in its own right is almost entirely due to the work of two men, Béla Bartók and Zoltán Kodály. The latter, having remained in his country through the course of a long life, having touched music at every point and ever relating it to the people he would claim as its true creators, and having at the same time established an international reputation, stands out as one of the most remarkable figures in modern times.

2

Kodály's Social and Musical Origins

GALÁNTA

In the railway age the need for improved communications led to the rapid extension of railroad facilities in Hungary. Those who worked in the administrative branch of this industry, in a country where all officials automatically enjoyed respect, were regarded highly, and a stationmaster was presumed to belong to the intelligentsia. To reach this grade, however, took time and a degree of patience. Frigyes Kodály was seventeen years of age when he entered the service of the railways in 1870. Diligent in his duties, he sought relaxation in playing the violin. In 1879 he married Paulina Jaloveczky, who was an accomplished pianist and singer, and of this marriage there were three children—Emilia, Zoltán, and Pál. Zoltán was born in 1882—in which year the association between Austro-Hungary and Germany was extended by the contractual accession of Italy, and a potentially disastrous power bloc was created. At that time Kodály senior, who had previously been in Budapest, was booking-office clerk at Kecskemét, a small town fifty miles south-east of the capital in the Great Hungarian Plain, where Katona, the dramatist, had been born. Kecskemét was famous for its fruit, and especially as distilled into apricot brandy, and a far more attractive place than Szob, now the frontier station, to which the family was compelled to move in 1883, when Frigyes took over the administration of the station. Two years later there was another move, Frigyes being appointed stationmaster at Galánta. Galánta, a rather dreary place on the main line from Budapest to Bratislava, Vienna, and Prague, was ceded to Czechoslovakia by the Treaty of Trianon in 1920, but briefly returned to the dominion of Hungary after the dismemberment of Czechoslovakia by Hitler. A village with a mixed population of Hungarians (the majority), Slovaks, and Germans,

Galánta found it difficult to forget its Hungarian associations across the years and the transference of 1938 was not entirely unwelcome, if for no other reason, because it was then possible to honour Zoltán Kodály by making him a honorary citizen, or Freeman.

To be a boy in Galánta in the 1880's was bliss. There was the companionship of one's equals, freedom to roam the countryside, lively games into which the traditional songs of the country were artlessly set, the excitement caused by the inherited skills of those schoolchildren whose parents comprised the local Mihók's gipsy band. Galánta, where the Kodálys lived for seven years, is memorialised in the *Dances of Galánta*, in which the *verbunkos* pattern is evident, and in the *Bicinia Hungarica,* while in the bass-less *Serenade* (Op. 12) of 1920 Szabolcsi finds echoes of the high-pitched instrumentation of the gipsy musicians. It is also to be remembered in this connection that the chamber-music ensemble of the Kodálys was without a 'cello until Zoltán, having learned violin and piano, turned to this instrument—being his own teacher. The Kodálys stuck firmly to the classics, but a new world was apparent in the arrangements from Erkel that came Zoltán's way.

'I see you still', writes Kodály of his school-friends in his Preface to *Bicinia Hungarica*, 'as you were when we were children: barefooted rascals, fighting among yourselves, throwing stones into the air, exploring the countryside for birds' eggs, but ever sturdy and fearless; and the girls—demure and always busy at home. I remember your singing and your dancing: but where have you all gone? . . .'

In 1952 one of Kodály's early companions read these words—and wrote to him. It gave great pleasure to Galánta's greatest son, whose view of the world has always been conditioned by his boyhood view of the world that was his village. In the village school there was a sense of equality and of common purpose. What experience taught him in those days Kodály has never forgotten. His philosophy is still that of a countryman; his attitude that of one who in growing old has not ceased to remain young.

'If', he concluded his Preface to *Bicinia Hungarica,* 'we had been taught what I try to teach in this book (as well as other important

things) life would have been very different in our little country.'
But what Kodály teaches is, in fact, what he learned: being an
artist, however, he was able to see purpose in and to give shape
to what he had learned.

NAGYSZOMBAT

When he was ten years old Zoltán's father was again moved,
this time to the neighbouring town of Nagyszombat—now
named Trnava and in Czechoslovakia—where Miklós Zrinyi
had once lived: a town to which officials of the Church had
evacuated themselves from Esztergom after the Turkish conquest
of the sixteenth century, and where they had built churches and
founded a University,[1] Nagyszombat had a mixed population,
mostly Slovak. By the late nineteenth century its importance had
declined (though now it is a thriving centre of engineering) and
the population about 14,000. There were, however, two institutions which maintained something of the prouder traditions
of former times: the grammar school and the Cathedral. In the
former teaching standards were high, and the intellectual discipline
was strict. Zoltán, in accordance with the principle that a stationmaster's son belonged to the intelligentsia and must, therefore,
be given a higher education, was enrolled as a pupil, and remained
in the school for eight years. A solid classical training gave him
particular skill in understanding the structure of language, and an
analytical capacity to discuss problems of translation from one
language to another, and particular aspects of semantics, is yet
evident as is reflected in his notes for an address in Israel in 1963.[2]
At school Zoltán immersed himself in German and Hungarian
studies (his guide to old Hungarian literature being a book by
Cyril Horváth), also developing a deep interest in history. He
never regretted that he went to a provincial grammar school,
for the German atmosphere of musical education in Budapest he
would have found uncongenial.

Music, in which the domestic background of music-making was
a decisive influence, was extra-curricular—but none the worse for
that. As a member of the school orchestra, he distinguished
himself by composing an overture which was given a public

---

[1] Closed in 1777, and its faculties transferred to Budapest.   [2] See p. 199.

performance in 1898, under the direction of the friendly school-master, Béla Toldy. This was recorded in one of the newspapers in Pozsony,[1] the metropolis of that north-western part of Hungary. Out of school, Kodály found the music in the Cathedral, while not in any way perfect, rewarding. Apart from the stimulating effect the combination of music and ritual has on the sensitive young mind the sight of instruments lying about in disrepair caught the practical sense. If they were there they should be used. A broken bassoon became, said Kodály, 'a symbol of how, if musical culture was to be recreated in Hungary, one would have to build it with fragments of its past'. At this time the notion that he might become a composer began to form, and, aware that music was a craft to be learned, he analysed the music that he heard. Having understood from the music of the Church, especially from those works of Haydn and Mozart that formed the local repertoire, that musical ideas must be shaped and ordered, he set about studying scores. Among these were Beethoven's Mass in C Major, Liszt's '*Esztergom*' *Mass,* and Bach's 'Forty-eight'. Among Kodály's original essays of this time were also an *Ave Maria* for voices, organ, and strings, and an incomplete Mass. The words of the Mass, he said one day, were for him of particular poetic significance, and all-embracing. It is not difficult to see how, in due course, Kòdály's art should produce such works as the *Psalmus Hungaricus,* the *Te Deum,* and the *Missa Brevis.*

BUDAPEST

In 1900 Kodály went to Budapest (where he heard the music of Brahms for the first time), and proceeded to read Hungarian and German at the Pázmány University, and to enrol as a student in the Academy of Music. The director of this institution, in succession to Erkel, was Ödön Mihalovich (1842-1929), who remained in office for thirty years, and whose principal work was to persuade the authorities to provide a new building worthy of the function it was expected to perform. The standards of music in Budapest had lately been raised by the Opera House, which had had the benefit of Mahler's direction some years before—this, it

---

[1] The *Westungarischer Grenzbote*, which commented that the work was 'pleasing to the ear, logically constructed, talented'.

was said, because of Mihalovich's insistence. Mihalovich, formerly a pupil of Mosonyi, and a keen Wagnerian and founder of the Budapest Wagner Society, was an able administrator, and he made for his Academy an international reputation; he was generous in recognising talent; and he was a competent composer. There is something to be said for the head of a musical academy not being a composer, for when he is it is more than likely that his attitudes to composition will be circumscribed by his own talents and predilections. Mihalovich considered that the only style to be cultivated was a German style.

The senior professor of composition in the Academy was Hans Koessler (1853-1926), a cousin of Max Reger, a composer who attracted Bartók in those days and repelled Kodály. Koessler, who followed Robert Volkmann (1815-83) as head of the composition department, was an ardent Brahmsian, and he too lived to inculcate his students with the idea that the German hegemony must not be questioned.[1] At the beginning of the century, none the less, he was sufficiently 'advanced' as a composer to attract the notice of Henry Wood, who included a set of Koessler's *Variations* in a Queen's Hall programme on 30 January 1902. Koessler was exacting in his standards and would not admit to his classes any other than those of proved competence in harmony and counterpoint. It is a measure of Kodály's achievement so far that Koessler was ready to allow him to go straight into a second-year class: This privilege Kodály refused, for he preferred to strengthen his foundations. It was, after all, a formidable task to be a pupil of Koessler.[2] He held four classes weekly, and when students were assembled each must play his latest exercise on the piano—an American Chickering that had once been the property of Franz Liszt—the others being expected to criticise. And then Koessler would weigh in. Deviationism he deplored and he held as sacred the '*Lied* form', into which all young composers were expected to pour their thoughts. He complained that what the young men of 1900 lacked was the ability to write slow movements, which should be primarily vehicles of 'love'. Adagios,

[1] Volkmann went to Leipzig in 1836, where he came under the strong influence of Schumann.

[2] See Lajos Lesznai, *op. cit.,* p. 22 *et seq.*

he said, should come from the experiences of life—should contain the emotions. Koessler's pupils, who included Bartók, Dohnányi, Leo Weiner, and Kodály, found this attitude reactionary, and Kodály was particularly put off when his professor refused to acknowledge that Hungarian themes could be the basis of a musical style. These, responded the Professor, were all right in their way, but they could never be more than ornamental. In so saying, however, Koessler was doing no more than defining what hitherto had taken place when Hungarian idiom came into contact with the main stream of European music. On the other hand, Koessler did, perhaps unwittingly, point to new horizons. He was, for instance, an ardent supporter of the musical primacy of song; and introduced into the curriculum *a cappella* singing. In later years Kodály, by-passing his early discontents, observed of Koessler that he was good at teaching the fundamentals of composition.

General insistence on his own dogmas, however, resulted in the young men more firmly embracing the vocation they set themselves: to found a genuinely native style of music. Kodály, nevertheless, was not unaware that there were many things of value that Koessler, despite his anti-modernism, could impart, for Kodály held, and still holds, that there are basic values in the techniques of traditional practice, relating to the organisation of sound, which should join the other values that arise from the conditions of the moment. So he laboured away to produce string quartets that, whatever their content, should be suitable for the medium. After four years he gained his Diploma, and in token of his promise he was given a subsidy which enabled him to visit Bayreuth. Academic success in the one field was matched by similar achievements in the other and Kodály satisfactorily graduated from the University.

Kodály may justly be described as a born teacher. Gifted with that insight that enables the good teacher quickly to assess the pupil's capacity (often unknown to the student himself), with the patience and persuasiveness that encourages the latent talent to blossom, with a fluent and direct manner of exposition, with a sense of authority, and with creative genius to underwrite the authority, he has made for himself a unique place in the pedagogic field. Yet he never took things for granted, and his specialist training for the profession of teacher was thorough.

In Budapest there was an excellent institution to which a limited number of students were sent for a rigorous course of pedagogic instruction. This was the Eötvös College, which was a memorial to the former Minister of Education, and novelist, József Eötvös (1813-71). At this institution Kodály supplemented the narrower professional training by taking courses in English, French, and German, and by following the researches of Professor Sievers[1] in the musical quality of language. At the same time he walked and swam (a lifelong routine of such exercise followed), attended concerts and the opera, and continued his practical music-making. Kodály conducted the students' orchestra, and when music was required for a dramatic performance, or other occasion, then he wrote it.

[1] Edward Sievers (1850-1932), an expert in linguistics, and a pioneer in the use of phonetics, who was successively professor at Jena, Tübingen, Halle, and Leipzig, and the author of an Anglo-Saxon grammar.

3

Looking for Folk-songs, and Collaboration with Bartok

IN 1905, one year after leaving the College, Kodály obtained his doctor's diploma. To become a doctor at that time it was deemed necessary intimately to know the examining Professor's published works. Kodály was well prepared; but a week before his final test the Professor was changed. By chance, Kodály—whose power of memory in such things is phenomenal—had lately and by chance read a long article by the newcomer, and was thus able to give convincing answers to the important questions. In the same year his first published composition appeared—an *Adagio* for violin and pianoforte—while others were taking shape. But if he would be a composer he would be a Hungarian composer. To be a Hungarian composer he must start on the ground floor. The necessary foundation was folk-song—the genuine, then uncharted, music of the peasantry, not the second-hand sentimental songs transmuted by the café ensemble into what the world took to be Hungarian.

An English layman's experience of music in Hungary at that time is given in a book recording the visit of a group of Liberal politicians: *Hungary: Its People, Places, and Politics: The Visit of the Eighty Club in 1906* (T. Fisher Unwin, 1907). So we read that at Pozsony 'the operetta *Die lustige Wittwe* [was given]. For eleven months in the year Hungarian pieces only are performed in this theatre, this arrangement being demanded by the terms of the subsidy granted by the Hungarian Government. But in September a short German season is given . . .' (p. 34). What was Hungarian, however, was primarily displayed by the czigány bands, which 'are distinctly a feature in Hungarian national life, and thought not of Magyar extraction [clearly the politicians had enlightened

31

guidance], nevertheless reflect in the passionate manner of their playing something of the Magyar temperament and character' (p. 37). In Budapest an absurd compromise—not unknown elsewhere—was practised in the Opera House when in *Lohengrin* 'the part of Lohengrin was sung by the famous German, Herr Anthes,[1] the singing of whose part in Italian, while the rest sang in Magyar, in no way impaired the enjoyment of a brilliant performance . . .' (p. 233).

It was to clear up this ambivalent situation that Kodály turned to folk-song. But in order to discover the content of folk-music one had to go out and look for it.

To-day one may visit the Academy of Sciences in Budapest and discover the whole history and corpus of Hungarian folk-music in the department (the 'Folk-music Group') devoted to this work. This, his creation and that of Bartók, is still the main centre of Kodály's activity, but it represents a memorial also to other poets and scholars, and musicians, who have laboured in this field—often in the face of opposition—for a century and a half. In 1803 Mihály Csokonai enjoined that attention should be paid, 'to the singing of the village girl and the simple peasant in the vineyard'. Twenty years later Ferenc Kölcsey observed that 'the seeds of truly national poetry must be looked for in the songs of the common people'. In 1832 the Hungarian Scholars' Society (as the Academy of Sciences was then called) considered a request from the counties of Esztergom and Komáron that folk-songs should be collected, and a year later a resolution was adopted that this should be done and publication undertaken. Nothing concrete, however, was achieved, and in 1844 the newly founded Kisfaludy Society—a literary group—urged that steps should be taken towards fulfilling the earlier intention. Between 1846 and 1848 three volumes of *Folk-songs and Tales* were issued by János Erdélyi, but without melodies. Beginning in 1847, two books of *Hungarian Folk-songs,* with pianoforte accompaniments arranged by János Fogarassy (1801-78) and János Travnyik (1816-64)—both of whom were lawyers—were published, but further progress

---

[1] Georg Anthes (1863-1922), notable as a Wagner singer in Dresden and New York before joining the Budapest Opera in 1903. He remained in this city until his death, and was also a professor of singing in the Academy.

Title page of Mosonyi's *Hungarian Children's World*

Hungarian folk-singers
from Csongrád County,
Nográd County and
Czechoslovakia

in this direction was stopped by the War of Independence. When it was possible to resume the project in 1852, the melodies that Erdélyi had collected from various sources,[1] amounting to 1,000, had all been lost. The Kisfaludy Society unfortunately were more concerned with folk-poetry than with folk-music (not realising that the two were inseparable) and subsequent publications— such as the seven-volume collection of István Bartalus, which appeared between 1873 and 1896—were inconsistent in respect of the melodies. Bartalus printed some 730 melodies, half of doubtful authenticity, and all with poor and inappropriate pianoforte accompaniments. So far as folk-music was concerned, the nine-teenth century saw no more than the publication of perhaps 200 specimens of melody, all in unscientific form and with irrelevant pianoforte accompaniments added. In all the collections (e.g. *101 Hungarian Songs*) which came from music publishers some authentic melodies were given, but side by side with popular, urban songs of recent date. The unscientific attitude was carried on into the twentieth century, expecially by Ferenc Korbay. Korbay's versions of Hungarian folk-songs, of doubtful provenance, were, as has been noted, taken at their face value in Britain and America, where they were extremely popular.[2]

In 1896, however, further incentive to proper research came from Béla Vikár, who used the phonograph (the first time this instrument had been tried anywhere in the world) to record folk-song, and in 1900 he exhibited his anthology to the International Folk-lore Conference in Paris. Vikár was no musician and unable, therefore, to transcribe his melodies, which fortunately came to Kodály's notice in the course of his philologic studies.

Such was the situation when Kodály, reminding himself of Liszt's never-fulfilled intention of 1838 'to get into the most

[1] The Kisfaludy Society had appealed to musicians and scholars to submit material in 1844.

[2] Korbay, however, was not unaware of the situation, and echoed von Adelburg when he wrote: 'it is . . . astonishing that the hypothesis that Hungarian music is of gypsy origin should ever have become the subject of any serious discussion. The gypsies play our songs and dances at dinners, balls, or weddings with a dash and fire, and with the instinctive rhythmical verve, which is so imperatively demanded by our music. As composers, they have no more claim to it than a German street band has to *Norma* or *Trovatore*, to *Home, Sweet Home* or *Robin Adair* (Preface to *Hungarian Melodies*, Vol. I., Rösler, Leipzig, 1891).

backward districts of Hungary . . . alone, on foot, with a knapsack on my back' in search of folk-music, went back to the district of Galánta in the summer of 1905, to return with a first catch of some 150 specimens. The next months were spent in intensive study, and in April 1906 a dissertation on 'The Stanza Structure of Hungarian Folk-song' was accepted as suitable for his doctoral thesis.

While Kodály was beginning his researches into folk-music, so also was Béla Bartók, who, through Mihalovich's recommendation, was able to obtain an allowance from the State in order to investigate the subject. Bartók's interest in folk-music was first aroused, so it is said, when he heard the singing of a Transylvanian maid in his home. But he, even more than Kodály, was a composer in search of a style.

Kodály and Bartók never met when they were students at the Academy, their lessons with Koessler being on different days, and they became intimates only by chance. One of the most hospitable drawing-rooms in Budapest was that of Mrs. Emma Gruber. She, of Jewish origin, and forever consumed with a characteristically Jewish passion for justice, was the sister of Pál Sándor, who was conspicuous in the business life of the city, and she had, when very young, married Henrik Gruber, a business man and amateur violinist. Intellectual, and highly musical, Emma, whose father was a friend of Koessler, was a brilliant pianist and a composer of no mean talent, as her Brahmsian *Variations and Fugue* (published by Editio Musica in 1957) show. At her flat she arranged lively evenings of chamber music, at which Koessler, Mihalovich, Viktor Herzfeld, and others of the senior musicians attended together with their protégés and those who commended themselves to Mrs. Gruber. Bartók, two years older than Kodály, but reserved and ill at ease in company, was grateful for Kodály's friendship and, as he himself wrote in later years, for 'his clear insight and sound critical sense'.

In one sense Bartók was more single-minded than Kodály. Unaffected by the demands of a broader education, his objectives were narrower. He would be a pianist—he was a distinguished pupil of István Thomán (1862-1941)—and a composer. In 1902 he published settings of four poems by Lajos Pósa; in the next year a sequence of four piano pieces, one being a study for the left hand; while on 13 January 1904 his *Kossuth Symphony* was given a first performance, under István Kerner (1867-1929)[1]. There were numerous other works of this period, many of which were first heard, and discussed at Mrs. Gruber's house.

The *Kossuth Symphony* was a great demonstrative piece of programme music, in which the influences of Strauss and Tchaikovsky, as well as of the Mosonyi-Erkel-Liszt Hungarian tradition, were patent. Scored for a large orchestra and under-rehearsed, this symphony encountered difficulties with the orchestral players, who took exception, not only to its idiom, but also to its content. Those who were German and Austrian found the parody theme which underlies the eighth section (describing 'the slow approach of the Austrian troops') objectionable and impertinent. But this kind of gesture

was in tune with the sentiments of the young intellectuals of Budapest—a rejection of alien influence. A month after its first performance, the *Kossuth Symphony* was played in Manchester, under the Hungarian-born Richter, and Bartók was present, also in the role of pianist. Among other works of this period, the *Rhapsody*, for pianoforte and orchestra (Op. 1), which was dedicated 'To Emma', also brought a qualifying degree of recognition; by this time the Budapest newspapers were devoting much attention to this young prodigy, who, if the *Rhapsody* was anything to go by, promised to be the natural successor to Liszt. It was after completing this work at Vésztő, where he was staying with his sister, however, that Bartók became more strongly aware of the immediacy of a living folk-music tradition. This would be the point of departure for the style he would fashion for himself. In this way Kodály and Bartók independently reached the same

[1] Kerner has some claim on British gratitude, in that he gave the first performances in Budapest of Elgar's works. Later in 1904 he conducted *In the South*, an event which Kodály recalled sixty years later.

conclusion. The partnership between the two was fruitful in every way.

In 1906, after further excursions into the border territories of Hungary where small Hungarian pockets preserved their ancient folk-traditions in the midst of Slovaks, Ruthenians, Rumanians, Croats, and Serbs, a modest book of twenty folk-songs, edited by Bartók and Kodály, was published by the firm of Rózsavölgyi.[1] The first ten songs were harmonised by Bartók, the remainder by Kodály, who also wrote the preface in characteristically pragmatic terms.

One should, said Kodály, choose from the best and popularise the selection through the right kind of accompaniment. In transplanting the folk-song from the country to the town the editor must, in his setting, retain the atmosphere of the countryside and of the village. Hungarian folk-songs should take their place beside the great works of music of the world and, of course, folk-music of other lands. But this could only be done when mass-produced and fabricated songs masquerading as Hungarian were driven out of circulation. In respect of performance, it was boldly stated that no one could make mistakes if they knew the peasant manner of singing, or if they spoke Hungarian properly. Speech-rhythm was the unfailing guide, and on no account should extraneous rhythmic habits be imposed on those which were indigenous.

The work entailed in thus beginning to realise intention was considerable. The peasants, so far removed in every way from the town-dwellers, were often suspicious of educated visitors from Budapest and required some coaxing before they would commit their view to the mysterious phonograph. As in England at the same period, the older people were most reliable in repertoire; but women who sang in public were held guilty of impropriety, and men preferred to sing when drunk. On the whole it was easier to catch the peasants at work, when they sang with fewest inhibitions.

During the immediate pre-war years there were several profitable folk-song excursions, especially in Transylvania (later to be

[1] Between 1906 and 1938 only 1,500 copies of this work were sold, an index to the lack of enthusiasm which the pioneers encountered.

transferred to Rumania), where valuable work was done on the tenuous instrumental tradition of the peasantry, and of the gipsy musicians.[1] In 1913, Kodály and Bartók, having by now collected some 3,000 folk-songs, proposed to the Kisfaludy Society that these should be published under the aegis of the Society, whose officers, however, were unresponsive. And soon the war was to prevent any possibility of action in this direction, even if indifference could be overcome. Nevertheless, Kodály continued his patient researches, even during the war years. In 1917 two folk-songs from Zobor (*Woe is me* and *Blooming on the Hill-top*[2]), in Kodály's arrangement, were coldly received. This, it was said, was not music, and if it was then it should not be. The blend of metrical oddity and melodic succinctness with Kodály's individual manner of harmonisation and vocal lay-out were too much for those whose principles were deep in the sanctity of S.A.T.B. disposition.

When the folk-song project could be initially accepted as in being, in 1906, Kodály, like Bartók, turned once more to the matter of his own ambitions as a composer. He went abroad, first to Berlin, and then to Paris. In the one city he was captivated by the playing of the Joachim Quartet; in the other he became acquainted with Romain Rolland, Jules Ecorcheville—a brilliant writer and musical historian—and the music of Debussy.

[1] See *Folk Music of Hungary*, p. 111 *et seq.*
[2] English titles as in U.E. edition (1923).

4

The Young Composer

THE AIMS OF A NEW GENERATION

At the beginning of the century all, superficially, was well in Budapest. There was an apparent prosperity, based on heavy financial investment from outside the country and on profitable ventures in industrial development in Bulgaria, Greece, and Serbia. New buildings were erected to symbolise the current importance of Budapest, particularly the Parliament building and the grandiose Basilica (echoing the Cathedral of Esztergom, as rebuilt in 1822), while the traditions of the nation were recollected in the monuments of Heroes' Place, which was designed to celebrate its millennium. But the appearance of well-being was a façade. There was discontent among the peasantry, who were oppressed by taxes and the victims of a sequence of bad harvests, and also among the industrial workers, many of whom were suffering periods of unemployment as the result of over-production. The intellectuals too were restive. In general they disliked the fact that Hungary's destiny was inevitably linked with those of Austria and Germany. But most of all they deplored the philistine conservatism, based on foreign models, that looked with disfavour on fresh and provoking ideas. Bartók and Kodály were trying to achieve a break-through in one way—and they were not to find their ideals long in attainment—but there were artists in other fields whose aims were similar.

The restoration of aims was in many cases attained under the liberating influence of Paris—the common factor in all progressive Hungarian art of the period. Of the painters, Mihály Munkácsy, having freed himself from academic training, established himself in Paris, and his graphic gifts there became greatly appreciated. László Paál and Pál Szinnyei-Merse were also strongly affected by French art, but it was József Rippl-Rónai and István Csók who principally reorientated Hungarian attitudes to painting by their distinctive use of Impressionism. János Tornyai and József Koszta turned to village life to depict it as it was and not, as in the nineteenth century, as it had been idealised, while Tivadar Csontváry's individual genius explored and expressed the fantastic. In literature the revolutionary figure was Endre Ady.

Ady, like other young writers, deplored the decline of Hungarian literature—especially in poetry, where a mock-romantic style, based on the tenets of 100 years earlier, was, once again, generally thought adequate—and it was in Paris that he found the key that unlocked his own genius. There Ady became deeply aware of the backwardness of Hungarian culture, and he went back home, inspired by Baudelaire, Verlaine, Rimbaud, Gaugin, Matisse, and Rodin, to revivify his native literature with a combination of passion and verbal beauty that was quite new.[1] 'My writings', he said, 'especially the poems, simply aroused indignation. I was mad, a comedian, meaningless, un-Hungarian, a traitor—in a word, I attained everything that a new poet in Hungary could achieve, but I did not die.' Ady wished to be regarded as the true heir to the great traditions of Hungary—'I am', he once wrote, 'the grandson of György Dózsa'[2]—but at the same time as an exponent of western European culture.

In 1908 the focal point of Hungarian literature was the journal *Nyugat* (*The West*) and writers subscribing to its progressive ideals became known as the 'Nyugat Group,' complementary to the painters who formed the School of Nagybánya (the district in which they worked), and to the two-man school of Bartók and Kodály. The identity of outlook between poet and musicians is signified by Kodály's settings of Ady's works in Op. 5 and Op. 9, and Bartók's in his Op. 16.

Before visiting Berlin and Paris, Kodály had presented his *Summer Evening* at the graduation concert of the Academy of Music. In this work (rewritten in 1929 for Toscanini) Kodály broke with one convention by using only a small orchestra.

---

[1] A natural affinity between Hungarian folk-poetry—'an allusive art, with intimate undertones'—and French Symbolist poetry is admirably demonstrated in Serge Moreaux's *Béla Bartók* (English edition, Harvill Press, 1953).

[2] See p. 21.

'*Summer Evening*', said Kodály, 'was conceived on summer evenings, amidst harvested cornfields, over the ripples of the Adriatic.'[1] After returning from Paris, he made a thorough study of the scores of Debussy he had acquired, and particularly that of *Pelléas et Mélisande*, and in a *Méditation sur un motif de Claude Debussy* he paid tribute to the French composer.

In 1907—one year after Bartók had joined its staff—Kodály became a professor at the Academy of Music. The official notice ran as follows:

'In view of the increasing number of students and the resignation of Professor Herzfeld, it became necessary to appoint a new Professor of Musical Theory to the Department of Composition. Dr. Zoltán Kodály was put in charge of this work. He has given proof of his ability as a talented composer and as a learned scholar and exponent of our national music. He also distinguished himself as a student of our institute.'

A year later Kodály took over the instruction of first-year students in composition, and from that time his influence on Hungarian composers has been stronger, perhaps, than any other teacher of this subject in any country during the same period.[2] As has already been stated, Kodály the instructor is clear, logical, and unambiguous. The same qualities distinguish his own music, and, for the same reason that students are enjoined to attend to Palestrina (with whom Kodály entertained certain conscious affinities), so they could, and can, discover much about the fundamentals of composition from the craftsmanship and logic of Kodály. The primary virtue of his music—and this is a reflection of the man—is that it stands indifferent to fashion.

In one sense one may look at his works of the first decade of the century and at the most recent to discover a homogeneity that is rare at any time, most of all in the twentieth century. That this is evidence of an unduly conservative attitude may make a superficially attractive, and easy, argument. But the validity of the argument depends on the validity of the premises on which it is based. It is hoped to show that in this particular case the premises leading to a charge of conservatism are invalid. Kodály would be

---

[1] *New Hungarian Quarterly*, 8, 1962, p. 20.   [2] See Chapter 16.

the first to support the absolute integrity of individuality, and his collected works are its symbol.

Yet Kodály's interpretation of the individual function of the artist is fundamentally different from that of the nineteenth-century romantic. In Kodály's view the individual can only freely operate as a member of a community, which will nourish him, but at the same time equally expect to be nourished by him.

The foundations of Kodály's attitude to musical composition are simple to define. Music is a means of communication, and as such has meaning on at least two planes. Music by a Hungarian conveys particular meanings to other Hungarians, but, because there is no form of isolationism, either possible or desirable, such music also bears significance in the wider, international field. Communication, on both planes is, to a great extent, determined by precedent, by tradition. Communication, however, must be put into such a form that the audience to whom it is addressed is more likely to be receptive than unreceptive. The prescription for this is persuasion, and not dogmatism. At the same time it is to be appreciated that tradition can, and often does, ossify into convention, cliché, mannerism; and when this happens communication fails because the individual factors out of which it is constituted have become meaningless. This, precisely, is what had happened to Hungarian music as it had been left by its German sponsors at the beginning of the century. The end of music, in the progressive view of Kodály, was not merely to be music, but to add dignity to life, and to inspire national self-confidence. At once there should be added Kodály's own sharp distinction between nationalism and chauvinism—the latter being a false nationalism and therefore not nationalism at all.

'It is our belief', wrote Kodály, 'that every nation will survive while it has some message to communicate to the rest of humanity. Hungary has yet to tell her message to the world. She has yet to tell that, particularly in the field of culture, for many centuries she was compelled to take up arms to defend her bare existence. And the mission of the nations cannot gain a lasting expression save in works of peace.'

The problem for Kodály and for Bartók was that they must, in one sense, inaugurate a tradition, and there was only one way in which that could be done. 'From an artistic point of view, folkmusic means more to us than to nations which created a musical style of their own already several centuries ago. In those countries folk-music was assimilated by art music and that is the reason why, for example, a German musician can find in Bach or Beethoven that which we can seek as yet only in our villages: the organic life of a national tradition.'[1]

Given that the half of music—or more—arises from words the thesis thus proclaimed is unassailable. And in so far as Kodály himself is concerned the procreative power of words is ubiquitous. Even in purely instrumental music this is so, its double guarantee being the idiom based on folk-song and the principle that melody should at all times be in the broad sense vocal. Thus John Weissmann could write: 'On examining Kodály's instrumental music, we become aware of the problems which confronted him. His idiom, and generally that of Hungarian music, is essentially vocal in character. In this respect it is significant that the number of his orchestral works—including here *Háry János Suite*, but otherwise excluding those for voice or voices and orchestra— is comparatively small.'[2]

EARLY SONGS AND MUSIC FOR PIANOFORTE

We may then turn to the works by which Kodály established himself as a new voice in music, in Budapest, between 1907 and 1910. Op. 1 consists of a set of sixteen 'songs on Hungarian popular words' (taken from several collections of Hungarian folk-poetry), published under the title of *Énekszó*[3] in 1921.

In the melodic contours folk influence is clear in every detail. There is the rhythmic starting-point, from a strong beat—there being no general iambic opening in the Hungarian language;

---

[1] 'The Tasks of Musicology in Hungary', Z. Kodály, in *Studia Musicologica*, Tomus I, p. 5, Budapest, 1961.

[2] 'Kodály's later orchestral music', in *Tempo*, No. 17, 1950, p. 19.

[3] This is published, with English words by Cecil Gray, by Zeneműkiado, Budapest, 1955. The only singer ever to give performances of the complete cycle was Keith Falkner, now Director of the Royal College of Music, London. From 1937 he gave ten to fifteen performances (including two broadcasts) in England and America.

the completeness of each phrase within itself—emphasised by the interjectory character of the accompaniment; the reliance on pentatonic structure; the frequency of falling cadences; the use of modality; and the rhythms are fluid. Germinal motivs from *Énekszó* may be set beside motivs from folk-song;[1] thus Kodály No. 1 opening may be compared with the folk-song opening on page 53 (*op. cit.*):

Three the ways I may go

"Which one shall I choose, then?

Kodály No. 4 opening with the folk-song opening on page 109:

I nei-ther toil nor spin

Kodály No. 1 end with the end of folk-song on page 45

I shall leave her ne-ver—

and Kodály No. 2 end with end of folk-song on page 150:

back re-turn-ing—

With regard to the organisation of his melodic material in these songs Kodály retains the primitive simplicity of folk-song:

[1] Taken from *Tiszán innen, Dunán túl: 150 Magyar népdal*, Zeneműkiadó Vállatat, Budapest, 1959.

indeed, in some cases and in certain respects he is even more economical. The first song, for instance, is in the form A B (the end of B being a transposition of the end of A), repeated stanzaically; the fourth song is hardly more than a single sentence (A), repeated three times. But these are art-songs and not folk-songs, and the melodic statements are related to the accompaniments which support them by a subtle double standard of tonal relationships. That is to say, in, for example, No. 4 the first melodic statement commences in E and ends on A, while the repetitions follow between D and G, E and A, and G and C—the latter, in fugal terminology, being an 'answer' to the subject: the whole song is unmistakably in the key of C major.

In this way it is seen how the first hurdle was cleared—to ensure that the idiom sounded convincing in its new environment. At this point the matter of pianoforte accompaniment should be considered. As a composer, Kodály takes it as axiomatic that an instrument must be allowed to live according to its own nature. Pianoforte music must inevitably convey the essence of pianism. In accompaniment, however, it must collaborate and not control. It is not always, in these songs, that the composer is successful. Youthful enthusiasm produced dramatic, or otherwise illustrative, figuration that overlaps the vocal gestures, and preludial and postludial passages (e.g. No. 9) are sometimes of Schumann dimensions, though without Schumann's emotional warrant. It is, however, interesting to see how the harmonic scheme is developed. Basically, Kodály's harmonic method is classical, with a definite relationship of one chord to another (this is even more clearly seen in pianoforte pieces of the same date as the songs of Op. 1) within the limits of accepted tonality. The range is from a simple diatonicism, exemplified in the greater part of Nos. 9 and 13, to the post-Wagnerian shifts shown in No. 16. The method, however, is flexible, and susceptible to the mood changes implicit in the verbal pattern (see the end of No. 10 and the climax of No. 12) It is also clear that the chordal clusters are compounded of internally moving contrapuntal lines or suggestions of lines, and that sometimes extremes are reached by the incorporation of unessential notes, as in

19

All my des — — pair and grief, all

—an excerpt from No. 11. This again shows the evaluation of verbal significance and of the possibilities of its musical extension. Interest is added to the harmonies by their relation to timbre—by the placing of chords on the keyboard or by their breaking-down into figuration, wherein may be felt the impressive influence of Liszt; by occasional abandonment of the vocal melody (see No. 3); and by ellipsis (see the final cadence of No. 13). So far we have the method of a well-schooled craftsman, which partly contains the exuberance of youth and partly exposes the maturity of judgment that Bartók noted. But there is also the mark of the explorer. Kodály saw the virtues of Debussy (from whom he learned the possibilities of synthesising two familiar, but apparently unrelated, chords). The principle of light emission is contained in Impressionist hints—in the flickering semiquaver alternations of No. 2 (and in the beautiful B—D major sequence of the conclusion of the accompaniment); in the crisp E major—E minor *plus* C major background of the first three lines of No. 5; in the dissolvent *tierce de picardie* chord *plus* major ninth at the end of No. 8, or in the heaped fifths and fourths that bring No. 11 to a nebulous conclusion. Finally, from Debussy came the rows of consecutive fifths that in 1907 added a new factor to the harmonic vocabulary (see No. 2, bar 7 *et seq.*, No. 3, bar 16 *et seq.*, No. 4, and No. 6) and the cultivation of the diminished triad. In detail it may be noted that where Kodály uses fifths (in the bass) they are used with varying effect, not being seen as phenomena in themselves, but only as adjuncts of dynamic and rhythmic stresses.

In Op. 1 we contemplate the problem that faced Kodály at the outset of his career: the union of apparent opposites. On the one hand there is the compulsive directness of the folk-song idiom—with its own rhythmic, tonal, and structural properties inherent; in the other the richly cultivated storehouse of European urban tradition. Vaughan Williams faced a not dissimilar problem. His solution was the protestant one of exclusion. Kodály's was a catholic (indeed, we might say Catholic) solution. He was reluctant to jettison anything that he had learned, but by no means reluctant to modify. Moreover, his technical capacity was great; thus in the early songs the conclusion is that they are good songs. The pianoforte pieces of the same period likewise show similar embracive qualities. At one point of the compass is the engaging *Valsette,* in which contrasts of rhythmic and harmonic behaviour and a nice insouciance prelude Prokofiev and also Kodály's own music for children. At another lie the *Music for Pianoforte* (Op. 3), of which the *Valsette* at first formed part. This cycle comprises nine pieces of varying mood, in which the evolution of a more unitary style based on folk-song research is evident, although the form of expression is controlled by Liszt (No. 3) and by Debussy (No. 8). The climax of Kodály's first period (a period only in the sense that his works, exclusively in the field of chamber music, were practically unknown except for the uncharacteristic *Adagio* for Violin and Piano) was the First String Quartet: by any standards a great achievement.

THE FIRST STRING QUARTET (Op. 2)

When he was a student Kodály was required to write string quartets, and, a perfectionist, he would sometimes write as many as nine or ten movements before submitting a final exercise.

Kodály belongs to the classical tradition in that he comprehends the finiteness of an abstract musical structure, which is designed so as to fill a particular space in time. In this sense each of his works is complete in itself. Thus the first quartet is laid out in this manner. After an introduction a sonata-form *allegro,* with two-subject exposition, development, and recapitulation follows. The second movement is a ternary *Lied* intermission, and succeeded by another ternary movement—*Presto.* The final movement is a set of variations.

This is the outline of the architecture.[1] But architecture—as in Budapest—is affected by situation. Kodály's structure in this instance is set within the Hungarian atmosphere as he felt it. If one looks for folk-song motivation one has not far to look. The cello at once announces

This indeed is a folk-song, but, Kodály says, was added later as a 'motto' to the material assembled by the composer and was not (unless unconsciously) part of the first design.

Repeated sequentially throughout the eighteen bars of intro-duction, this theme is then modified in contour so that—against an urgent, chordal, pulsation in the upper strings it merges with first thoughts thus to become the first subject of the *allegro*:

The second subject (in the region of E major) is another extension of the same idea:

The first form of the first movement of this work appeared in the volume issued in 1957, in honour of Kodály's seventy-fifth birthday. In the slow movement, in both main sections, the original interval lay-out of the original introductory motiv is

[1] For a full, analytical, survey see Pál Járdányi's introduction (with an English translation) in the miniature score (Zeneműkiadó Vállalat).

closely followed, in A major and in B minor. In the scherzo a more bucolic element is admitted in the shape of

23

which is simply placed against the primitive oscillation of tonic and dominant in the bass. In the finale the process of *éclaircissement* is carried a stage further in the presentation—after an introduction which indexes the melodic gestures of the previous movements— of a straightforward, Haydnesque, melody in C major, to serve as the theme of the subsequent variations. At one point these variations refer to a significant landmark in the composer's biography, for the lively $\frac{5}{8}$ section is acknowledged to 'Emma Kodály'. On 3 August 1910 Kodály married the by now divorced Emma Gruber—considerably his senior in years, 'but', says Kodály himself, 'much younger in soul.'

The quartet is marked by fine organisation. This is, indeed, music for stringed instruments—and for no other—and this particularity is summarised in the spacing of the parts and in their inter-relationship. The basis of the writing is counterpoint (out of which the harmonies spring), and the counterpoint in itself is of varied complexion. It is, for example, a matter of rhythmic thesis and antithesis when the 'cello commences the introduction against the chordal contrary movement of the upper voices, or when the same instrument launches the first subject against the evanescent throb of the superimposed chord of C minor (which pattern is repeated in the different context of the scherzo). And even when the simple theme of the last movement is first stated (at figure 4) there is throughout a nervous energy and an elasticity within each subordinate part that disallows the use of the generally constricting term 'harmonisation'. In the slow move- ment the contrapuntal invention is of the order of that of Beethoven, and this, indeed, is not only the most striking move- ment in the quartet, but one of the peaks in the whole field of chamber music. Herein Kodály achieves the synthesis at which he aimed, for this from one angle is seen to be classical music,

A new style in painting: 'Promenade à Cheval', 1908, by Tivadar Csontváry

Bartók and Kodály
(*above*) Photograph, *c.* 1912 (*below*) Drawing by Emma Kodály

from another Hungarian. The latter quality grows from within and is not consciously applied from without. There is, in fact, no necessity to labour at folk-music characteristics (although, as the following extracts show, these are patent), because the total atmosphere—the sum of the technical parts—is both evocative and definitive.

The first section of the movement is based on

24

which, given to each instrument in turn, fluctuates in tonality and rhythmic detail and generates a new melodic contour. This new figure forms the basis of a beguiling cadence, being given to the 'cello, *pizzicato*, and in revised metre to anticipate the time change at figure 3. Here the figure lately quoted makes a fugue subject (cf. Ex. 23):

25

The entry of the second violin here shown allows a glimpse of the counter-subject, and in this may be felt the sense of passion which infects the working-out of this notion. The narrative quality is by no means impaired by the ultimate entry of the cello in augmentation. After the one fugal paragraph (in A modal minor, moving freely towards a final chord of G sharp minor) there follows another on this theme, which is not only derived from Ex. 20, but, unexpectedly, refers to the same tonal centre, thus giving homogeneity in a double manner:

26

After this has been developed and has returned to the environs of a half-close in the key of A major, Ex. 25 appears again, and is eventually bound together with Ex. 26 in a highly wrought climax. The end of the whole movement is an impressionistic extension of the opening section, the melody being set against fingered *tremolos* (such as distinguish the later string writing of Kodály, and also of Bartók), and intercalated arpeggios in the 'cello. In the last cadence a *pizzicato* reflection of Ex. 25 sinks beneath the high chords in the upper strings: the music rides away on a chord of A major sounded in harmonics. This music is generous in expression—the lines rise and fall and cover large areas of skyscape so that one is in mind, perhaps, of the third page of D. H. Lawrence's 'Strange Blossoms and Strange New Budding',[1] particularly of its cadential 'At evening [the clouds] were all gone, and the empty sky, like a blue bubble over us, swam on its pale bright rims'.

Kodály is undervalued by critics who mistake his simplicity for *naïveté*, who cannot examine his work without reference to standards outside his range of interest, who are disabled from sharing in the comprehensive vision that inspired such works as this, under-rated, quartet. Under-rated because while it is a complete work it spurs the imagination of the listener, or the player, to adventure further.

'CELLO SONATA (Op. 4)

In the two-movement *Sonata for Violoncello and Pianoforte* (Op. 4) Kodály is nearer to folk-music than in the Quartet, both in tune shape, and in figuration, and, to a point, in form. The opening movement is a fantasia, improvisatory and episodic in character, the whole being dominated by the fundamental Vaughan Williams motiv of *s d r s*. Since this figure plays a prominent part in Brahms's Double Concerto, it is worth pointing out that when he wrote the *Sonata* Kodály was unacquainted with this work. This figure, so to speak, is the beginning of music. The emancipating quality of the fantasia lies in the multiplicity of rhythmic changes: $\frac{6}{8}$, $\frac{5}{8}$, $\frac{7}{8}$, $\frac{9}{8}$, $\frac{5}{8}$, $\frac{9}{8}$, $\frac{6}{8}$, $\frac{9}{8}$, $\frac{4}{8}$, $\frac{9}{8}$, $\frac{6}{8}$. But there is also an abruptness in transition from one mood to another that is both striking and compelling.

[1] *The White Peacock*, Penguin ed., p. 171.

Kodály, as in the quartets and the later unaccompanied Sonata, writes eloquently for 'cello, which he succeeds in humanising by the urgency of the dominating lyrical passages. The pianoforte writing is improvisatory and freely decorative as in all music composed within earshot of the popularised *csárdás* style. In gesture Kodály here recalls not only Liszt, but also Mosonyi and even Rózsavölgyi. The second movement, in nominal sonata form, has its affinities with the *presto* of the Quartet, especially in the exploitation of fifths in the bass, and also with the traditional Tolna Dances. Once or twice the 'Hungarian' interval of augmented second occurs, but the unifying factor is the basic fourth. This being so it is not surprising that the movement is concluded by an imposing reference-back to the *fantasia*. In the last ten bars Kodály moves from F major (or note groups which can best be stated with F as the nodal point) to G major by an unexpected substitution of F♮ by F♯. This is extended melismatically and, in so far as the melisma is a previous statement of musical fact, acts as leading note to the terminal pianoforte chord of G major. Kodály leaves the 'cello lingering on F♯ until the pianoforte chord has sounded.

FOUNDATION OF A CHORAL IDIOM

While the peak of Kodály's first achievement lies in his early chamber music, a handful of choral works anticipate the character of later, and famous, pieces. Kodály's first (published) choral work is *Evening*, a setting of a slender, and, period-wise, soulful, piece by Pál Gyulai. He, a conservative influence on, if not impediment to, Hungarian letters at the beginning of the century was the dominant literary figure in the Academy of Sciences when Kodály first became acquainted with this institution.

Evening is an over-painted canvas. Kodály floods the score with redolent harmonies, often sited above pedal-points and squeezed out by the pressure of consecutive, and chromatic, thirds and sixths in the middle voices. The texture varies between three and eight parts, and melodic interest—despite occasional points of imitation—is largely centred in the top voice. However, this is highly expert choral orchestration, moving away from the staid *Liedertafel* conventions towards a new appreciation of the choral

potential in terms of tone colour. It is, moreover, qualifyingly
challenging to a lively body of singers in an Elgarian manner and
would make a happy choice for a competitive festival. The *Two
Hungarian Folk Song* arrangements of 1908 are also singers'
pieces. In both cases the songs are scored for three soprano and
three alto soloists, accompanied by a female-voice choir. The
result is an original type of work lying somewhere between choral
fantasia and concerto grosso, with affinities with both. These
works are rhythmically mobile, sharing in chromatic harmony, and
enchantingly coloured. Here indeed the country tunes are properly
dressed for town use, without loss of original impetus or character. There may be instanced the moving coda to the first of the
songs, in which the pathos of the young lover's dirge is contained
in the tonal asperities created by the melodic line against the
sustained chords, in the contrast between the chords themselves,
and in the concluding, and dying, bare fifths:

From a practical point of view this—and the same goes for all
Kodály's choral writing—is not difficult to sing, each voice
being adequately provided with hints as to how to progress from

one note group to another.[1] That choral singers should know what they are doing and that their way should be eased is a guiding principle with Kodály. It is characteristic that his first, slightly anxious, remarks on looking over a piece of contemporary English choral music was: 'It's not very easy, is it?'

PUBLIC REACTION

The year 1910 was a critical year, both for Bartók and Kodály, for by then they were in a position to proclaim their creed as progressive composers. Their immediate sponsors (in addition to Mrs. Gruber) were the forward-looking members of the group of artists known as 'the Eight'. Led by Róbert Berény, to whom Bartók was accustomed to play the sonatas of Beethoven, this society, which was responsible for a number of provocative art exhibitions, offered its gallery for a recital of the works of Bartók and Kodály. Imre Waldbauer, a pupil of Hubay, was persuaded to participate with his string quartet, of which the other members were János Temesváry, Antal Molnár, and Jenő Kerpely.[2] This quartet was seized with enthusiasm, and is said to have rehearsed 100 times before the concerts were to take place on 17 and 19 March. *Pester Lloyd* and the *Pesti Hirlap* advised both composers, rather more particularly Bartók, to eschew wildness and to cultivate 'beauty', with which concept neither Hungarian folk-melody nor *avant-garde* harmonies had any connection. On the other hand, there were sympathetic noises from elsewhere, and Béla Reinitz foretold that Kodály, whose Op. 3 and 4 were also given their first public performance, would one day be numbered among the most distinguished of Hungarians.

In December 1910 Debussy visited Budapest from Vienna,[3] and the performance of his quartet by Waldbauer and his colleagues was a revelation to those whose previous awareness was almost exclusively in the German-Austrian tradition. Bartók wrote of Debussy (in a memorial notice of 1918) that 'he was the

[1] The second of these songs was newly arranged in 1962.

[2] The Waldbauer Quartet visited London in 1927, when the programme given on 8 February included a new work by Géza Frid, a pupil of Kodály.

[3] He did not, as Lockspeiser states in his biography, conduct. See Lesznai, *op. cit.*, p. 95.

greatest composer of our time . . . [he] forsook the familiar paths and showed us new possibilities. . . . It was of great interest to us Hungarians that we could see the influence of eastern European folk-song in Debussy's melodies; certain pentatonic progressions were noticeable such as are to be found in the ancient Hungarian melodies, especially those of the Székely region.' In the villages of the Székely region—an isolated Hungarian 'pocket' in Transylvania, where Bartók and Kodály explored in 1910—there was a rich vein of folk-custom and folk-music. In due course Kodály made great use of the Székely traditions.

But at this point interest centres on Paris, where, between 1910 and 1913, Kodály's qualities as composer were resolutely placed before a curious, and sometimes enthusiastic, public. The artists responsible for presenting his works were the Waldbauer quartet (who appeared—apparently privately—in Paris, in 1910)[1] and Theodor Szántó. The latter, a pianist and pupil of Busoni, was living in Paris at the time, and distinguished himself by his general interest in contemporary music: it was to Szántó that Delius's pianoforte concerto in C minor was dedicated. After Szántó's playing of Kodály's Op. 3 at a meeting of the Société Musicale Indépendante, Sándor Kovács epitomised the impressions variously made by the new Hungarian music in the Society's *Revue Musicale* (No. 11, pp. 47-59), where No. 8 of *Zongora Muzsika* and Bartók's *Medvetánc* were also published.

'Les jeunes Hongrois, derniers venus à la vie musicale, ont un sens particulier, et pour ainsi dire exclusif, de ces affinités harmoniques. Ils se sentent attirés par le besoin de reculer les limites de ce domaine des oreilles. Bartók et Kodály triturent et expérimentent toutes ces matières sonores, sans aucun souci de ce plaisir immédiat, d'ordre purement esthétique, auquel le compositeur s'est si longtemps asservi. Les *Bagatelles* pour piano du premier, son *Quatuor*, sa *Suite*, ou bien les 10 *Morceaux* pour piano du second et sa *Sonate* de violoncelle et piano, font usage des mixtures les moins admises, et ne reculent devant aucune tentative. On s'en indignera certainement; et plusieurs crieront au sabotage. Car en musique, comme ailleurs, et peut-être plus qu'ailleurs, les moments

[1] In this year the de Boer Quartet played the *Quartet* in Zürich (See *Allgemeine Musikzeitung*, Zürich, 1910, pp. 510-11).

de transformation apparaissent à l'oeil inattentif ou prévenu, comme des périodes de décadence. . . .

'Un critique français, lors du dernier concert de la jeune musique hongroise, a parlé d'expériences de laboratoire, menées par des chimistes audacieux en quête de réactions nouvelles. En effet; et rien n'est plus juste. On se saurait mieux définir la signification de notre jeune école, telle que ses musiciens les plus avancés la représentent aujourd'hui. Hors de la Hongrie, elle ne peut avoir d'autre sens, pour le moment; elle représente un effort de la musique en marche. Chez nous elle prend une autre valeur. Nous y voyons les germes d'un art national, attendu, espéré depuis longtemps. Nous trouvons, en sa hardiesse révolutionnaire, la révolte de nos héros, qui depuis mille ans se défendent contre les Barbares; l'audace orgueilleuse de notre peuple. Ses sonorités évoquent l'âpre monotonie du paysage hongrois, les plaines où rougeoie le soleil, où chantent les grillons, les mers de blé doré, les allées de noirs peupliers, asiles de brusque fantaisie. Et nous l'aimons, comme nous aimons notre sol natal, notre mère!'

In 1912 M. D.Calvocoressi gave four lectures at the Ecole des Hautes Études Sociales on 'Some Tendencies of Contemporary Music in Europe'. In the first he dealt with the Russians—Scriabin, Stravinsky, Liapounov, Moussorgsky; in the second with the music of the Bulgarian composer Janco Binenbaum; next came Schoenberg and Wellesz. On the occasion of the fourth lecture, on 10 December, the Waldbauer Quartet made what was described as their first public appearance in Paris, playing a work by Miklós Radnai (1892-1935), Debussy's quartet, and Beethoven's Op. 95. The quartet recital was enormously successful, and an effective means of focusing further attention on the 'laboratory' in Budapest.

A year later there was another evening of Hungarian music in Paris, which Calvocoressi reported to England in the *Monthly Musical Record*.[1] 'After a long interruption', he wrote, 'the *Société Musicale Indépendante* has resumed its concerts. The first evening, devoted to the works of different schools, proved remarkably interesting and instructive. It began with a 'cello sonata by M.

[1] 2 June, p. 150.

ZOLTÁN KODÁLY (performers: Mm. A. Casella and Alexanian[1]) who is, with M. BÉLA BARTÓK at the head of the modern Hungarian School. M. Kodály, until now, was known to the Paris public solely by a set of pianoforte pieces, 'ZONGORA MUSIKA', which has been played at the same Society, three years ago, by M. Teodor Szanto—daring bewildering little pieces, the purport of which seems at first most recondite, but which on closer acquaintance prove as delightful as they are original. They may be given as typical instances of what Hungarian music of to-day is. Other no less characteristic specimens are to be found among M. Bartók's pianoforte works. The 'cello sonata, though instinct with absolute originality, is less forbidding; and perhaps, the would-be students of modern Hungarian music will do well to begin with it and, let us say, M. Béla Bartók's string quartet. A remarkable feature from the more technical point of view is the easy, simple way in which both instruments associate. In that respect M. Kodály has achieved a high feat of workmanship.'

The same Society was also presenting at that time other new music, some of which was also inspired by a national impulse. On 22 May Delius's *Appalachia* and Vaughan Williams' *Norfolk Rhapsody* were played at an orchestral concert, while a week later Theodore Byard gave a recital of songs by Cyril Scott and Vaughan Williams. Modern English music, however, proved less attractive to the Parisians than that from Hungary. At the same time the music of Delius was not unnoticed by both Bartók and Kodály. The former, indeed, had already, in 1911, written an article on his music.[2]

---

[1] Diran Alexanian (b. 1881), an Armenian, who became professor of violoncello in Paris, and a colleague of Casals.

[2] Reprinted by Szabolcsi in *Bartók, Béla: Válogatott Zenei Írásai*, Budapest, 1948, p. 76.

5

Trial by the Establishment

DIFFICULTIES IN THE WAY OF THE NEW MUSIC

One of the striking features of progressive musical activity during the first quarter of the present century is the way in which Ralph Vaughan Williams on the one hand, and Kodály and Bartók on the other were working towards an identical ideal: the enrichment of national (and, in the long run, international) music by uncovering the subconscious roots of a native genius for musical expression, and the enrichment of national life by the stimulation of a general self-esteem through co-operative energy in performance, particularly by amateurs. The intention of Vaughan Williams and the obstacles in the way of fulfilment are defined in an essay written for the English Folk Dance and Song Society,[1] which could easily (the necessary topographical adjustments having been made) have been penned by Kodály. For instance: 'In art, as I suppose in every activity', wrote Vaughan Williams, 'the best results are obtained by developing one's natural faculties to the highest. If an Englishman tries to pose as a Frenchman or a German, he will not only make a bad Englishman, he will also make a bad foreigner. If the English spirit is capable of being expressed in music, let it be so expressed; if not, let us honestly give up the attempt.'

In Britain it was possible to express such views without incurring more opprobrium than naturally settles on those who are qualified by the conservative as eccentric. In Hungary it was not. The patriot was liable to condemnation as being unpatriotic. Because this was so the crucial years of Kodály's career, in which he became a composer of world-wide significance, were marked by the opposition of his own integrity as man and artist to the

---

[1] Quoted in *Vaughan Williams*, Percy M. Young (London, 1953), pp. 200 *et seq.*

powerful, if scattered, forces of official attitudes. The misfortune of central Europeans was, and is, to live in central Europe, where national frontiers were defined and re-defined by horse-dealing of the most cynical order, and where the ruling classes, still feudal in outlook, had only the principal aim of self-preservation and -perpetuation. In the years leading up to the First World War Hungary was unhappily circumstanced. Culturally tied to the Austro-German tradition, and politically made to adhere to the imperialist designs of the Monarchy, coalition governments attempted to pursue a patently Hungarian line by blackmailing the ministries in Vienna on the one hand while adopting a ruthless attitude to the subservient mass of the Hungarian people (on whom the Russian Revolution of 1905 had made some consider-able impact[1]), and an even more ruthless attitude to the minorities living within Hungary on the other. The result was a general hatred of Hungary among the so-called minorities, for she, within the limits imposed from without, now appeared as more imperialist than the imperialists. But the comfortable middle-classes of Budapest mostly opted out of political and social issues, remaining negligent towards all save those which affected their personal comfort. They proved a formidable Philistine community, the more dangerous because of a superficial appear-ance of being 'cultured'. English Philistines of the same period mostly avoided this latter dishonesty.

Kodály and his fellow-workers were under increasing suspicion on these counts. Their attack on the romantic, Lisztian, conception of folk-music looked socially provocative; their extension of folk-music research to the minority enclaves was politically treacherous; their propaganda for a new style of music was culturally heretical. Opponents of the new ideas worshipped the *status quo*; they did not appreciate that the *status quo* never is, except phantom-wise.

Although Kodály and Bartók were not unacknowledged abroad —as appreciative articles in France and England[2] and the perform-ance of Kodály's First String Quartet by Franz Kneisel's Quartet

[1] See Endre Ady's 'Fölindulás (*Earthquake*)', *New Hungarian Quarterly*, Vol. III, No. 5, p. 92.
[2] See p. 203.

in America[1] showed—their reputation at home, was, to say the least, uncertain. One difficulty (as the first performance of Bartók's *Kossuth Symphony* had demonstrated) was to find performers able to tackle the new style competently. Therefore early in 1911 an optimistic group, lead by Kodály and Bartók, launched out ambitiously with a New Hungarian Music Association, of which the aims were the formation of an independent and self-supporting orchestra, and the issue of a new musical journal. In general terms, this Association—with its interest by no means narrowly confined to domestic issues—set out to provide for the musical what the *Nyugat* circle were achieving for the literary culture of Hungary. Neither orchestra nor journal escaped from the confines of wishful thought, and it was not until November that a modest beginning was made with a recital by Bartók. The programme consisted of pieces by Couperin, Rameau, Domenico Scarlatti, and a relatively unknown work by Beethoven. These were interspersed by Hungarian folk-songs arranged by Bartók and Kodály. An audience of little more than 100 applauded Bartók's playing, but refused to move towards enthusiasm for folk-music. The promoters persevered, and after one or two trials of strength in the realm of the classically unfamiliar, proceeded, tentatively, in the direction of the contemporary. Debussy, Ravel, and Leó Weiner were the mainstays of the programme. In the opening months of 1912 the Association, its audiences growing less and less, gave two concerts and then expired. Two years later a National Music Society (at which Kodály's Zobor folk-song arrangements were performed) was organised along official lines—with the implicit objective of countering the heterodoxies of Kodály and Bartók.

ORTHODOXY IN DOHNÁNYI AND WEINER

The way of orthodoxy was that of Dohnányi, a boyhood friend of Bartók in Pozsony (Dohnányi's father was a teacher of mathematics and science and as such Bartók's tutor at the Gymnasium). Dohnányi was a virtuoso pianist who was successful throughout

---

[1] The Kneisel Quartet was founded in 1885 and played a major part in establishing a taste for chamber music in America. In addition to Kneisel, its members in the pre-war years were Hans Letz, Louis Svečenscki, and William Willeke.

Europe and the U.S.A., and a more than competent (though less than inspired) composer in the Brahmsian classical manner. So far as folk-music was concerned, he was content to use any material denoted as Hungarian in a general way in order to give his otherwise solid style a face-lift. While Bartók and Kodály were pursuing their hard and unrewarding aim in Hungary, Dohnányi was enjoying voluntary expatriation, latterly as a professor of pianoforte at the Berlin Hochschule für Musik.

Leó Weiner (1885-1960), whose music featured in the New Music Association programmes, was a composer also standing on the threshhold of orthodoxy; but the quality of his music makes him a more interesting figure. Weiner was a pupil of Koessler at the Academy, to which he returned as professor (until 1949), after a period of travel in Germany and France and a subsequent period as *répétiteur* at the Komische Oper in Budapest. As composer and teacher, Weiner saw his role as the guardian of tradition. He was 'faithful to the forms of the classical masters . . . but he filled these forms with the melodies of the Hungarian instrumental heritage'. In fact, Weiner wears his Hungarianism lightly, preferring to contain it within that national capacity for sophisticated observation that distinguishes the living intellectual life of Budapest and provokes easy comparison with the spirit of Paris. The compatibility between the French and the Hungarian artist has already been instanced, and Weiner emphasises it by the lightness and elegance of his instrumental texture. His string quartets, of 1907, 1922, and 1949, have their place in the modern Hungarian repertoire, but the stranger will best appreciate his deft, unpretentious works for small orchestra—such as the *Concertino for Pianoforte and Orchestra* (Op. 15) and the *Pastorelle, Fantasie and Fugue* (Op. 23) for strings. In his *Divertimenti* (Op. 20, 24, 25) Weiner coloured his scores with reminiscences of folk instrumentation, and in certain other pieces, such as the *Hungarian Peasant Songs* for pianoforte (Op. 22) he made use of native melodies. But the overall impression was of urbanity. As a guardian of the traditions—of European music, that is—Weiner published a *Handbook of Musical Forms* in 1911, and two treatises on harmony, the first in 1911, the second in 1917.

POLITICAL ISSUES

Kodály was upgraded to a professorship in the Academy, but his views on the educational function were always more catholic than those of the specialist pedagogues. Thus in 1917 he joined *Nyugat* ('The West'), the progressive journal of the intellectuals associated with Ady and edited by Ernő Osvát, as music critic. The aim of *Nyugat* was not to imitate the West, but to raise Hungarian culture in its own right to the level of that of the western nations. Among Kodály's fellow-contributors—most of whom, like Kodály, were sensitive to the art of the West and able exponents also of the art of translation—were Mihály Babits, Gyula Juhász, Zsigmond Móricz, Margit Kaffka, Frigyes Karinthy, and Lajos Nagy. In 1918 Kodály also joined the critical staff of the radical newspaper *Pesti Napló*. Of his contributions to *Nyugat*, those discussing Bartók's Second String Quartet (Op. 17), of 1917, and the opera *Bluebeard's Castle* were the most important, and prefaced other essays on behalf of Bartók.[1]

As the war proceeded the Hungarians became increasingly disillusioned, and in 1917 the Russian Revolution won many adherents among the incarcerated prisoners of war and the hardly less free working-classes at home. There were demonstrations at the end of 1917 and throughout 1918.

On 16 November 1918 a Hungarian Republic, sponsored by a National Council, was proclaimed and separation from Austria was effected. On 21 March 1919 the Republic, the Communist Party having achieved virtual power, became the Hungarian Soviet Republic. Faced with appalling difficulties and threatened by Rumanian and French armies, this government lasted only 133 days, after which Rear-Admiral Horthy, a former aide-de-camp of Franz Joseph came to power. In 1920, by the Treaty of Trianon, Hungary lost Transylvania to Rumania, large territories in the north to Czechoslovakia, and some of the southern, Serbian, region to Yugoslavia, but all containing numerous Hungarians.

During this distressful era all departments of Hungarian life were disrupted, under the shadow of political intrigue and individual place-seeking. The Hungarian Republic of 1918 had put

---

[1] See p. 221.

Béla Reinitz (1878-1943) in charge of music organisation. He, known as a composer by his settings of Ady's poems, was an ardent supporter of Bartók (and so remained until his death), and when considering the Academy—by now the National Academy—of Music proposed to the Council of Ministers the retirement of Mihalovich, now seventy years of age, and his replacement as Director by Dohnányi, with Kodály as Deputy Director, and Bartók as the third member of the Music Council. Among those who took umbrage at being over-looked for the higher offices was Jenő Hubay, one of Hungary's greatest virtuoso violinists, who refused a lesser appointment as violin teacher and retired to the side-lines, in Switzerland, to await opportunity.

Bartók and Kodály, with Dohnányi's approval (he was absent in Scandinavia), began to formulate ideas on a broad and rational scheme of musical education. There was much concern at the vast amount of talent that, through deficiencies in the system, remained hidden. A radical reform was necessary, with at least three years of systematic training in singing and sight-reading.[1] Before anything could be effected, however, Reinitz was out of office and compelled to leave the country. Dohnányi, Kodály, Waldbauer, and Kerpely (1885-1954), a member of the Waldbauer Quartet and professor of the 'cello, were suspended, while Bartók was compelled to take an extended leave. Hubay returned to direct the affairs of the Academy, and an inquiry was set up to consider the activities of Kodály and others of his colleagues under the now defunct revolutionary government. The commission of inquiry was assisted by two of Kodály's former subordinates on the staff of the Academy, Rezső Kemény (1879-c. 1950), violin professor, and Béla Szabados (1867-1936). The latter, a late romantic with views on folk-music antithetical to those expressed by Kodály (most recently in the Zenei Szemle, 1917), was a not inconsiderable composer of his kind and his opera, A Bolond (The Simpleton), had a nine-year run in Budapest until it passed out of the repertoire in 1920.

The case against Kodály was drawn up, not without skill. He had, it was said, been a member of the governmental Council of

---

[1] See Lesznai, p. 118.

Music; had permitted the *Internationale* to be orchestrated; had allowed recruitment for the Red Army among students; had not been prompt in raising the national flag after the collapse of the Republican Government. Whether true or untrue, the statement of these charges was sufficient to arouse antipathy in conservative hearts. Added to these was another set of charges. The first stated that he had taken part in strike action by teachers. Three subsequent complaints were petty and applicable probably against any good teacher in any institution where red tape is conspicuous. Kodály had issued permits to singing teachers without first reference to the committee of management; had endorsed documents with a rubber stamp instead of with his own hand; had tended to behave in a manner detrimental to the smooth running of the office.

The long-drawn-out quasi-legal process was, of course, largely a cover for vindictiveness. There were those—and the point was openly expressed in one of the newspapers—who would have Kodály out, *et omne hoc genus*, because they disapproved of 'modern music'. Nothing like symbolism or cubism was to be encouraged (the connection of either with the style or teachings of Kodály seems implausible at any point), and 'what we want is an Academy that will train musicians, not foster young Kodálys'.[1]

If Kodály's enemies worked against him his friends were energetic on his behalf. Dohnányi, for instance, pointed out with considerable force that the responsibility for what went on at the Academy was his, as Director; further, that in all that he had done Kodály had his complete support. When Szabados stated that collecting folk-songs as Kodály had done was unpatriotic (in that recognition of the native talent of the former minorities was contrary to the chauvinism of those now in office) Dohnányi demolished the argument by observing that one who had spent as long in field research in the sphere of folk-song as Kodály had was obviously more patriotic than those who had not.

Bartók described the Commission as a comedy, but soon he found himself obliged to take action. On 20 February the *Szózat* announced a new Music Council. Under Hubay's presidency, its

[1] Article by Izor Béldi in *Pesti Hirlap*, 7 January 1920, quoted by Lászlo Eősze, pp. 23-4.

members were: Arpád Szendy,[1] Bartók, Szabados, István Kerner;[2] Ákos Buttykay,[3] with Aurél Kern[4] as Secretary. Having seen the constitution of this body, Bartók announced to the Press his unwillingness to serve, in view of the omission of the two best musicians in the country (Dohnányi and Kodály). At this point Bartók, who had been protected by the now discredited Béla Kun régime, partly on account of his association with Béla Balázs, his librettist, met the same criticism that raged about Kodály. He was unpatriotic. The newspapers said so, and Hubay said so. Bartók, disheartened by the turn of events in Hungary, went elsewhere for the time being, fortified by his 1918 agreement with Universal Edition in Vienna, who, in common with many in different countries of Europe, recognised his genius.

In the meantime Kodály, conscious of the strength of his cause, armed with dialectical skill and an appreciation of the comedy within the situation, and fiercely urged forward by Emma, battled on, in debate giving at least as good as he got. He spoke quietly, firmly, and fearlessly, with anger controlled.

'Let him,' he said, 'who has done more for Hungary than I . . . come forward to lecture me. All the work I have accomplished has been done without any financial aid from the State, but with an expenditure of my own money that might almost be called prodigal. . . . And from where have I obtained the energy for all this? Doubtless from that "anti-patriotic disposition" of which people are so anxious to find me guilty. I have never meddled in everyday politics. But, figuratively speaking, every bar of music, every folk-tune I have recorded, has been a political act. In my opinion, that is true patriotic policy: a policy of actual deeds, not of mere phrase-mongering. And it is for this I am being persecuted.'

At once—and the principles are the same now as they were then—Kodály appears as the least political of artists, and the most

[1] 1863-1922; pupil of Liszt and piano teacher at the Academy; a conventional, romantic, 'Hungarian' composer; collaborated with Szabados in the opera, *Mária* (1905).
[2] 1867-1919; the best-known Hungarian conductor of his generation. See p. 35.
[3] 1871-1935; pianist, and composer of the school represented by Szendy.
[4] 1871-1928; composer of *Lieder*.

Kodály, *c.* 1920

With Toscanini in Milan, 1928

political: it depends on the semantic interpretation of 'political'.

In the end, the trial (for that is what it was) ran out of breath—but not before the accused had stated his faith in Reinitz, a communist and now in exile, and his support for Waldbauer. The Ministry of Education, none the less, felt obliged to save its own face, and Kodály was brought down from the rank of Deputy Director to that of Professor. His salary was reduced (Reinitz had previously raised salaries of teachers), and he was given 'leave of absence'. It was Hubay's hope that Kodály would never come back to the Academy, and his efforts to ensure this result were persistent, but in the end unsuccessful.

The second decade of the century could hardly have been more discouraging from Kodály's point of view. It ended with his ideals no nearer realisation than when it started, and his own music had made precious little headway. His energy, however, was prodigious. He balanced physical with intellectual exercise, so that both body and brain were equal to all the demands made on him—most of all by himself. He was sustained by a stern conviction that what he was about was of vital importance to the nation, and by faith. An imperishable optimist, Kodály had the capacity, which he still retains, to see farther ahead than mere decades. Moreover, he was supported by Emma, who was equally convinced of the significance of his mission. Emma, intellectual in a general sense and sufficiently musically endowed to pass as a minor composer (and the purveyor of themes to Dohnányi and Bartók as well as Kodály), was fiercely protective, and if Kodály himself was a formidable opponent she was even more formidable. Kodály's critics, however powerful, could be made very uncomfortable. Emma Kodály belonged to that class of composers' wives—other members being Clara Schumann and Alice Elgar—who saw to it in every way that the creative function kept going at maximum capacity.

MORE SONGS

During this period Kodály's compositions, understandably, were not numerous, but included the *Serenade*. The composition of this work was a gesture to Emma, who, roused to fury by any injustice, was fearful lest Zoltán's career as composer should be halted. Apart from this, no works of more or less large dimension appeared, and in so far as solo songs were concerned the end of a stage of development was reached. (Although Op. 14 was published first only in 1929, the songs, by nature, belong to the main group which was complete by 1920.) To those which have already been considered, seventeen songs (Opp. 5, 6, 9, 14) were added. In Op. 5 and Op. 6 Kodály went back 100 years to treat the new-found lyricism of Berzsenyi, Csokonai, and Kölcsey. In Op. 9 he moved to his most notable contemporaries, Ady and Balázs. For Op. 14 he stretched towards the heroic period of the sixteenth and seventeenth centuries, setting one poem by Bálint Balassi and two by anonymous writers.

The two songs of Op. 5 were written in the first place for low voice and orchestra, and interest first lies in the commentatory material of the accompaniment. In the introduction to the first song (*A közelítő tél—The approach of winter*) the landscape is indicated, impressionist-wise, in isolated observations by solo instruments which rhapsodise in a manner to become characteristic of the composer. Rhythmic flexibility is marked, and the harmonic background is of a Delian subtlety and complexity. The vocal line, in both songs, is shaped towards folk-song in respect of both rhythmic and melodic contours. Whether the songs add up to a unity in either case is open to question, Kodály's fluency of technique running uneasily into his stylistic ideals. The picturesque properties of the pianoforte are often a handicap to the composer of fertile imagination (in Hungary there is no need to look further than the songs of Liszt to discover this), and in Kodály's songs as a whole there is a tendency to too much figuration and too much annotation. This is not surprising, in view of his primary devotion to the word as the origin of inspiration.

In Op. 6 and Op. 9 there is a good deal of busyness, sometimes of a too conventional order (see Op. 6, Nos. 4 and 5, and Op. 9, Nos. 2 and 4), and the image is falsified. At this point one is reminded of the aspiration of the period—to bring Hungarian music into the Western ambit on equal terms. When, however, the songs are looked at for a second time other aspects become clearer. There is a fluidity of vocal line, wherein the impulse of national idiom is assimilated within a personal style. The melodies of Op. 6, Nos. 1, 2, and 3, particularly show that the self-imposed discipline was indeed a liberating influence, so that the three songs give in fact a wide range of experience to the singer, and cover a good deal of emotional territory. Since discipline has been mentioned the effect of a zeal for melodic understatement, derived from the non-melismatic quality of folk music in the first degree, on an inbred feeling for lyrical expression, helps to produce a new type of melody. It is when the thus refined quality of melody is matched by similar refinement, and simplification of accompaniment, that Kodály's songs are most impressive. The first and last songs of Op. 6 illustrate the point. The first, *Magányosság* (*Solitude*), the words from Berzsenyi, is Brahmsian in mood and movement, spacious and controlled, and with a deep sense of spiritual awareness. (With this should be compared Op. 9, No. 5, *The Forest.*) The last song of the group, to words by Csokonai, and entitled *A farsang búcsuszavai,* (*Carnival*), is a wry comedy piece, which switches to a sardonic contemplation of Lenten penances in a middle section of engaging parody. The songs of Op. 9 are briefer, more lightly drawn, and thus in line with the more economical, though no less intense, method of Ady and Balázs. In this set the limits of expression are defined by the reflective, though ominous, character of No. 3 (*Éjjel— At Night*), and the exuberant, summer, mood of No. 4 (*Kicsi Virágom—Lovely flower*). In each of these songs there is evident a brilliant sense of design, that leads to imaginative climaxes. Here are relevant quotations, the first showing the vocal entry of No. 3, the second the melodic planning of the end part of No. 4:

28

[cont'd overleaf

The process of intensification and, at the same time, compression is carried a stage further in the three songs of Op. 14, in which the relationship between voice and pianoforte is closer, especially in No. 1, where, in a middle *parlando* section the two interchange functions, and, as fitting the historical necessity of the case (for the words are from the sixteenth and seventeenth centuries), the essentials of folk-melody are more firmly displayed. Common to all Kodály's songs is a sense of passion, which communicates the composer's involvement in the particular situation. Not all the refinement of technique, nor a strict application to first principles of classical design, could eliminate this essential quality. The quality is individual, but at the same time communal; it is of Kodály, but also of the Magyar *in toto*. Thus we conclude that a national idiom is more than an arrangement of sounds according to a limited scheme. It is the purposeful deployment of the particular arrangement to an expressive end; and this comes from within, from personal experience and experiment.

The songs are important in this stage of the composer's development, as leading from folk-music towards the style that would, in contemporary terms, have a similar effect to folk-music: that is, to unify a national community within the emotional compulsions of a musical expression felt to be nationally (at least) comprehensible, comprehensive, and also attuned to personal effort. In the twentieth century one may no longer create folk-music, but one may cultivate activities that, to some extent, cover something of the same area.[1] It was, therefore, in choral music— so firmly rooted in the Hungarian musical and social tradition— that Kodály was to discover his most potent medium. The solo songs, by their general vocal simplicity and their examination of the harmonic underlay or contrapuntal extension of melodic generalities, looked in this direction. In themselves they are incomplete, being unconsciously resistant to the means employed.

SONATA FOR SOLO 'CELLO (OP. 8), SERENADE (OP. 12), AND MINOR WORKS

On the other hand, this does not in any way apply to the chamber music of the same period, which is described with affectionate enthusiasm by Waldbauer in his article in *Cobbett's Cyclopaedia of Chamber Music*. In the works composed during the period of the First World War there are at least two which by themselves must rank as among the masterpieces. These two are the Sonata for Solo Violoncello (Op. 8), and the Serenade for Two Violins and Viola (Op. 12). The first was written for Jenő Kerpely, a member of the Waldbauer Quartet, and is a tribute to his virtuosity. A considerable work for unaccompanied stringed instrument is, of course, obliged to contain virtuoso properties; but of these the composer must be the master and not the slave. It is one part of Kodály's genius that he can control virtuosity so that his scoring, for whatever medium, never lies outside the boundaries of probability. This stems from an appreciation of the apparent personality of his chosen medium. In the present case the 'cello carries the characteristics assigned to it by Beethoven, Schumann, and Dvořák: it is passionate; it is lyrical. Accordingly, the

[1] Imre Kálmán's biographer, Bistron, suggested that operetta melodies (or, as we now might say, those of 'musicals') fulfil this function (E.K., 1932, p. 185).

opening instruction of the first movement includes *appassionato*, while the second is marked *con grand' espressione*. If it is passionate and expressive, it is not abstractly so, but about and of. The subject, if it can be put that way, is the composer's urge towards the realisation of his national and cultural ideals. A strong parallel to the quality and intention of the unaccompanied 'Cello Sonata (as well as other of Kodály's music of that period) is to be found in the works of the Bohemian school of painters active at the same time. 'To them', wrote Professor Jiři Kotalic, 'this art meant more than pure formalism. They interpreted it as a vehicle for expressing contemporary views and feelings, ideas and sentiments. Yet they did not dissociate modernism from the nation's cultural heritage.' And of the leader of the school. Antonin Slaviček, Kotalik observes: '[Landscape painting], more than any other genre, was his medium for consciously trying to grasp and express external reality without relinquishing his purely personal reaction to that reality.'[1] In this 'Cello Sonata Kodály reflects on the gestures of folk music—shown in the seemingly improvisatory quality of the whole, and in the simple melodic and rhythmic patterns that are fundamental. The interdependence of the three movements on germinal motivs, and on more deliberate transference of phrases from one movement to another, coupled with a tonal scheme that departs from and returns to the generating force of B major, gives balance and, therefore, form, even though traditional formal conventions are disregarded.

This work is eloquent in one way, the *Serenade* in another. Here there is, indeed, a distillation of classical propriety, in clear thematic definition and in the development, combination, and recapitulation of the stated themes. This was not the first time Kodály had attempted this medium. As a schoolboy, under the engaging influences of Haydn (the staple diet of his domestic music-making) and Schubert, and aware of the necessity to effect a *rencontre* between the classical style and folk-music, he had written a Trio in E flat major. Op. 12 is the corollary to this *jeu de jeunesse*. The first movement founded on a pervasive rhythmic idea, and a persuasive vocalise, is a gay sketch in sonata outline, but economical of intellectual effort. The slow movement,

[1] *Czechoslovak Life*, September 1962, p. 18.

punctuated by a reference back to the first, is in ternary form; while the finale, a conversation-piece in brilliant idiom, is paragraphed into what is virtually a set of highly integrated variations. In the disguising of procedure in the outside movements, as in the civilised gaiety, there is a palpable debt to Mozart. The easy, indeed prodigal, variety of colour derived from the unusual palette of instrumental colour is also, in a sense, Mozartian. In the slow movement, however, there is an intensity akin to Bartók: in no other work, in fact, does Kodály so nearly approach the more astringent idiom that Bartók derived from his analysis of the basic properties of Hungarian music. The first violin and viola conduct a dialogue against the almost continual murmuration of the mainly muted, and double-stopped, second violin. The outer parts speak fragmentarily, and in pointed prose rhythms. Dr. Eősze admits a detailed narrative to the *Serenade*, of a lover and his beloved (a trying woman, so it would seem), and Kodály's instructions to the players (*espressivo, ridendo, imitando, indifferente,* and so on in the second movement) convey the story clearly enough. But, the detailed programme removed, the music can equally stand as landscape delineation. In this one is reminded obliquely of the influence of French music according to Kodály's own assessment of French music. This is that it is at its best when appealing to the eye through the ear. 'The French', he said, 'must *see* music.' Which is another way of acknowledging the virtues of the Impressionist tradition.

Beyond the Sonata and the *Serenade* lie, in one direction the Second String Quartet, in the other the *Seven Pieces for Pianoforte*. The Second Quartet, dedicated to the Waldbauer Quartet, is akin to the *Serenade* in formal originality, in a narrative-like similarity in the slow movement, and in a skilful building-up of excitement in the vivacious, peasant-dance, exertions of the finale. There is, however, a greater distance between the folk elements—the intervals of fourth and fifth are more categorically stated—and the complex, post-Romantic, harmonic shifts. On the whole, the Second Quartet is less memorable than the trio. The piano pieces are a useful index to the composer's style, and more interesting on this account than for their intrinsic qualities. The truth is that Kodály managed keyboard music less than convincingly, with a tendency (already noted in some of his accompaniments) to over-write.

During the period of his enforced leave of absence, Kodály managed to continue teaching at home, and the loyalty of friends and pupils to some extent made up for official and semi-official disparagement. But when the critic observed that harmonic effects were sometimes 'laborious', after hearing Dohnányi's direction of the Op. 5 songs at the beginning of 1921, he was, in this particular, not unjust. Kodály's harmonies were inclined to monotony when the astringency implicit in his melodies was not conveyed to his chordal textures. Unfortunately, when musical criticism was blatantly mixed with personal abuse, the minimal truth contained therein was obscured.

Despite many efforts to denigrate Kodály in Budapest, however, his growing corpus of works was capturing attention abroad. Critical essays in Western countries were complemented by the publishing contract that came from Universal Edition, in Vienna. The main works written during the previous ten years were issued by this house in 1921. At this point his efforts to take up his professional appointment in the Academy again were successful, and a new phase of activity began.

6

Psalmus Hungaricus

IMPOVERISHED BY WAR, reduced through the Treaty of Trianon from a population of twenty millions to about seven millions, split asunder by revolution and counter-revolution, Hungary was at the nadir of her ever variable fortunes in the early 1920's. Nominally a monarchy, for the Emperor Charles succeeded to Franz Joseph on the death of the latter in 1916, the State since 1919 had been (and was so to remain until 1944) under the Regency of Admiral Horthy. In 1921 Count István Bethlen became Prime Minister. Controlling the country by means of a quasi-dictatorial system—the prevailing 'Party of Unity' being a coalition of right-wing interests and, since elections were judiciously rigged, unassailable at the polls—Bethlen pursued policies that defied any form of idealism save that which represented the desire for frontier revision. Pressed on the one hand by those neighbouring countries that had lately done well at Hungary's expense at Trianon, and on the other by the Allies (on whose orders the Habsburg Dynasty was ended by an Act of the Hungarian Parliament in 1921[1], Bethlen was faced with problems of consuming difficulty. Not least of these was the depreciated currency. In 1922 Bethlen managed to negotiate Hungary's acceptance as a member of the League of Nations and thereupon further manœuvred a 'reconstruction' loan. By 1924 the details of this loan were settled and other foreign money was invested in Hungary, with the result that within a short time there was an appearance of rapidly increasing prosperity. That is to say, those who had contrived to hold on to their assets, whether in industry or land, improved their fortunes. Those who had no capital, the industrial and agricultural workers, stayed as they were—indifferent or hostile to yet another government that evaded the basic issues of

---

[1] The Emperor Charles died in 1922.

social reform. Under such conditions education, especially musical education, could hardly be expected to broaden its base. Music was of value to an *élite* as a social accomplishment, to the virtuoso as a passport to fame in some other country, to the governors as an occasional means of flattering self-esteem or as part of the romantic façade that was dropped across the sober realities.

By 1923 Kodály, like Bartók, had strengthened his position inside Hungary by having gained a considerable reputation abroad. On two occasions he had gone to some lengths to demonstrate to his compatriots the quality of his achievement. In 1923 the opportunity came to him to apply his ideals to a commission that was surely his by right. In that year the city of Budapest celebrated the fiftieth anniversary of its federation, and Dohnányi, Bartók, and Kodály were invited to write suitably celebratory works.

Dohnányi provided a competent, though unremarkable, festival overture, based on Erkel's Hymn (the national anthem), a theme from Béni Egressy (1814-51), and a Credo (*Magyar Hiszekegy*) of recent date and evoking revisionist sentiments; all of which were patently "official". Bartók contributed his *Dance Suite,* an abstract of his views on folk music in general, since it incorporated Rumanian and Arabic influences as well as Hungarian, and a striking example of his individual, direct yet brilliant, style as orchestrator. Kodály produced a choral work; a setting of a paraphrase of Psalm LV by the sixteenth-century poet, Mihály Vég.

The *Psalmus Hungaricus*, written with unusual speed for Kodály in a matter of weeks and only interrupted by a visit to the I.S.C.M. Festival, is a focal work. The choice of subject reveals Kodály's many-sided interests. Devotion to the provincial parts of Hungary and recognition of local traditions led him to a poet who lived in his own birthplace—Kecskemét. Vég belonged to that group of writers, Bálint Balassi and Péter Bornemissza being others, who protested their Hungarian faith in powerful and moving verse during the early period of Turkish rule. Kodály, stimulated by the intensity of religious feeling endemic in his compatriots, has persistently written 'sacred works'. But his exploration of texts has been deep and personal. As Vég wrote with a fervour worthy of the prophets of the Old Testament, so also did Kodály appreciate, and expand, this quality. The Old Testament was, after all, folk-poetry, and most of all the Psalms. Therefore it was natural for him to ally his researches into folk-music with his apprehension of the fundamentals of the psalm. A choral work was a necessary development of his ideals, in that the medium was a community. The words of *Psalmus Hungaricus* were applicable to the period in which the music was composed, but for that matter applicable to almost any part of Hungary's tragic history:

'O . . . hear the voice of my complaining, Terrors of death are fallen upon me, Hide not Thyself from my supplication, Hatred and wrath of wicked men oppress me.

'Better it were to dwell in the desert, Better to hide me deep in the forest, Than live with wicked liars and traitors Who will not suffer that I should speak the truth.'

But finally there is the certainty of a resolution of all ills:

'Forth from the fire Thou suddenly tak'st him, Once more in honour Thou wilt raise him on high.'

The symbolism of the words is clear.

In preparing for the performance of the *Psalmus*, however, Kodály was drawn to another branch of music. 'In 1923', he wrote, 'on the occasion of the first performance of *Psalmus Hungaricus*, I found our only chorus so weakened (it was a few years after the war) that I decided to add a boys' chorus. Their fine singing inspired me to write some short pieces for them, like *See the Gipsy*, and *Straw Guy*, and in a couple of years with the collaboration of my pupils a little literature [for children] came into being.' Thus Kodály turned towards the prospect of music in popular education. His way, let it be noted, was through music to pedagogy, and not through theory to practice.

The *Psalmus Hungaricus* was immediately acclaimed for its purely musical virtues. To see what these are is a matter, in the first place, of analysis.

In the baroque tradition of expressing words through music Kodály employs a rich symbolism. In general the work is permeated by Hungarian gestures, both rhythmic and intonational. Since anacrusis is practically unknown in the Hungarian speech structure, the consistent strong beat beginning is an unaccustomed experience to the English listener (and singer) and a continual hazard to the translator; but within the texture of Kodály's music it holds a certain strictness and extends an austerity appreciable also in the general theme of the text. While this is a limiting factor it is balanced by the subtle play of mensural variations within the individual phrases. These variations are akin to those of speech, but, like all Kodály's recollections of the basic values raised to another, and purely musical, level. The same is true of the quasi-modal organisation of melodic contours. In each of his leading motivs Kodály gives a modal impression, which is not diminished by the admission of chromatic alteration. Thus

30a
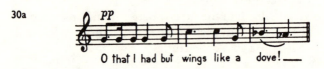
O that I had but wings like a dove!___

modulates into

30b

I would fly a-way___ far in-to the wil-der-ness;

The intention is clearly delineatory—the psalmist is carried into the wilderness, and the listener with him. At the same time, such changes of direction are within the scope of the composer's naturally flexible and colourful harmonic method. Such a rapprochement between a fundamentally diatonic melodic style and a sophisticated harmonic scheme is difficult to achieve (Vaughan Williams never did, relying on more ingenuous practices which, however, are legitimate enough in their own context); but Kodály did achieve it and in so doing did precisely what he wished to do: to bring Hungarian music into the company of European music on equal terms, but without loss of dignity or detriment to personality.

    Kodály, of course, is a pragmatist. His theories regarding

musical expression are tested by their relevance to practice. Music for voices must be vocal. Thus there is a Handelian quality in his larger works, in the vividness of the style, and in the inevitability of the contours. Any single phrase may be said to sing itself. That this is so is due to dependence on the foundational intervals of fourth and fifth, on a diatonic lay-out that limits the use of semitones, but principally on a powerful sense of climax. Examination of the vocal sentences in *Psalmus Hungaricus* shows how in each case the individual phrase develops progressively in energy, continually expanding from the nuclear tonic (or what temporarily serves as tonic) to cover a wider and wider range. Dramatically this procedure is highly effective, as is particularly shown in the violent middle section of the work (between figures 11 and 16), but it is also an emblem of practical wisdom. The disposition of the notes is, in fact, likely to aid the singer.[1]

Within the broad outline of the work detailed descriptiveness is frequent, for Kodály thinks in terms of words-cum-music, so that, I suspect, there is, as in Schubert's case, no frontier between the one and the other. The semantic underlining is in the melody alone, but more patently it is in the harmonic and instrumental textures. 'The voice of complaining' is illustrated in

31

a germinal proposition which plays a powerful part in the *Psalmus*; the 'wings like a dove' shown in a fluctuating sequence of quavers, in which the semitonal move of the previous quotation is used again to a different end; the secret movements of the 'wicked' illustrated orchestrally by a baroque figure set about a minatory bass that reflects and intensifies the already prominent semitonal shift; where David acknowledges his trust in Jehovah

[1] Cf. A. E. F. Dickinson: 'Choral music has its limitations of range in comparison with the power of orchestral music to make its indelible impress of varied mood and texture, but the contact with natural speech endows choral expression with a peculiarly urgent position, potentially, in musical experience, and Kodály understands voices' ('Kodály's Choral Music', in *Tempo*, No. 15, 1946, pp. 7-10).

the music—caught here at the high point of the *naïveté* which Wilfred Mellers notices[1] is characteristic of the composer—as a serenade, the tenor solo being supported by a sequence of enlarged arpeggios.

So far as the chorus is concerned in the *Psalmus* it is allowed only a supporting role to that of the tenor soloist. Part of the reason for this was in the invalid condition of Hungarian choral music in 1923, but part in the appreciation of its dramatic potential. This is no comprehensive subject in the sense that the subjects of the *Passion*, the *Requiem*, the *Messiah*, or even the *Dream of Gerontius*, are. It is limited, it is primitive, it is immediately and emotionally affective. Therefore Kodály uses his chorus dramatically and directly, not as a detached body of philosophic observers. The function of the chorus, accordingly, is mostly homophonic and ejaculatory, but the skill of the composer in the application of choral colour is notable. Thus at the outset alto and basses enter in octaves with this urgent and valuable motiv

32

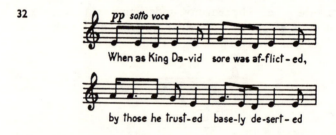

When as King Da-vid sore was af-flict-ed,

by those he trust-ed base-ly de-sert-ed

which is repeated a fifth higher by sopranos and tenors at figure 8, set below the soloist in ample harmonies at figure 14, and developed in duple time in the last section of the work. The exposition of this idea in the low voices only to define the chastisement of the wrath of the Almighty is splendidly effective, as for that matter is the wordless extension of Ex. 31 after figure 12. After figure 21 the chorus, again wordless, build a large climax (the resolution of this into the following paragraph should be noticed

---

[1] 'Because of, rather than in spite of, his technical fluency in the *Budavári Te Deum* he is, in the history of European music, the last great *naïf*'. ('Kodály and the Christian Epic', in *Studies in Contemporary Music*, London, 1947, p. 143.)

as a brilliant piece of technical management), derived from a figure given at the beginning of the orchestral prelude to the *Psalmus* and, in turn, related to Ex. 31.

The overall design of the work, dictated by the exposition of the text, is tripartite. In the first section, of commingled distress and anger, the main thematic material is laid out and at once developed. As has been suggested the development is closely reasoned into an organic pattern wherein the disparate parts are, in fact, interrelated. Kodály has a distaste for loose ends and, obliged by the traditional role of sequence, allows his music to move from one point to another without irrelevant side-issues. The first section of the *Psalmus*, therefore, is tightly drawn, and cogent.

After the serenade section, the chorus reintroduces Ex. 32, in bare fifths, against which the orchestra strikes independent gestures, both contrapuntally and harmonically. From modified Aeolian climate the music moves towards A major, in which the redeemed hero is apotheosised. The climax of triumph is reached, however, not in a tonic but a subdominant triad, which, the third having been altered to minor, is used pivotally to return the work to the atmosphere in which it opened. The last fifteen bars—the *l'envoi* in the poem being of the conventional nature of such endings in sixteenth-century Hungarian religious verse—present a coda based on Ex. 32.

Mellers is right in settling on Kodály's *naïveté*—so long as the quality of this *naïveté* is seen. Kodály's emotions are simple and uncomplicated. His attitudes on social and national affairs are equally simple. He is moved by anger, by love, by Magyar pride; he is intolerant of injustice, chicanery, exploitation. All this is basic; it is also basic to the *Psalmus*, which makes an immediate, unforgettable impact. This, one may say, is Kodály; and this is why his music fails to commend itself to those who, in arguing about the purpose of music, become blind to the fact that it has one. But Kodály is also a highly civilised, intellectual person, whose sense of ultimate control is immaculate. Thus the *Psalmus* also represents this dominant side of personality. It is a highly wrought work of art, an example of classical craftsmanship.

The *Psalmus Hungaricus*, within the recognised choral tradition insofar as it could be listed as 'sacred',[1] was the first great post-war choral work (unless Delius's *Requiem* (1912) or Honegger's *Le roi David* (1921) can be regarded in a higher class, which I would doubt). It released new forces, such as may be seen in other environments in Vaughan Williams's *Sancta Civitas*[2] and Janáček's *Festival Mass*. It also, finally, set the seal on Kodály's reputation as a European composer, which in 1923 was also recognised by the inclusion of the unaccompanied 'Cello Sonata in the summer programmes of the International Society for Contemporary Music, whose Festival that year was held at Salzburg.[3] These early performances depended greatly on the fine interpretative powers of Ferenc Székelyhidy, (1885-1955) the tenor singer, who was a member of the State Opera and professor at the Academy in Budapest.

On 18 June 1926 the *Psalmus* was first performed outside Hungary, at Zürich, when the soloist was Karl Erb. A year later it was given (the chorus singing in Hungarian) in Amsterdam, by the Oratorium Vereenigung Choir and the Concertgebouw Orchestra. On 30 November 1927 *Psalmus Hungaricus* was brought to Cambridge through the initiative of Cyril Rootham, then Conductor of the University Musical Society, and four days later it was performed in London, Frank Mullings being the soloist.[4]

Sustained by the initial success of *Psalmus Hungaricus*, Kodály progressed on many fronts. In the summer of 1924 *Székelyfonó*

---

[1] See A. Tóth, 'Zoltán Kodály', in *Revue Musicale*, X, 9, 1929, p. 206: 'Cette œuvre est-elle une composition d'église? Non, ou du moins on n'y trouve aucune parenté avec la musique sacrée du siècle précédent. Ce qui la caractérise mieux, c'est son accent "biblique", Kodály est d'ailleurs issu d'un peuple abandonné qui ne peut prendre à témoin de ses luttes que son Dieu, au sens où Dostoiewsky dit: "Celui qui a un peuple a aussi un Dieu." '

[2] In which a figure akin to that in Ex. 31 plays a not dissimilar part.

[3] The Duo for Violin and 'Cello was performed at the I.S.C.M. Festival of 1924.

[4] 'In the *Psalmus Hungaricus*', wrote F[erruccio] B[onavia] in the *Musical Times* of January 1929, 'one sees Kodály completely free from the obsession of those moderns who write music as if they hated it. . . . He shows his modernity clearly enough in his treatment of harmony, but there is not a chord in the whole *Psalmus* that should cause annoyance to grammarians. The music is robust and even violent, but so is the theme. . . . Dissonance here is not only justified; it is necessary, since it stands for a world that is out of tune: for a mind distressed.' Cf. pp. 84 and 89 for other early estimates of Kodály in England.

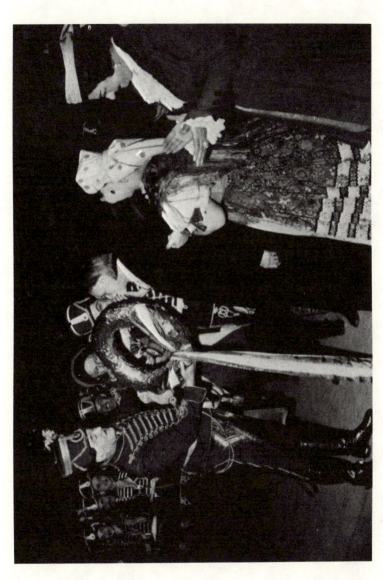

Gala Performance of *Háry János*, 1962: Imre Palló presenting a golden wreath to the composer

'The Viennese Musical Clock', scene from 1952 production of *Háry János*

(*The Spinning-room*), a loosely dramatic arrangement of folk-songs from the Székely region, was performed at the Blaha Lujza Theatre in Budapest. This was the prototype of the more important *Háry János*, and was revised and expanded in 1932. By this means Kodály was determined to invade the field of opera with his ideals; an incursion he felt to be the more necessary in view of Bartók's previous discomfitures.

7

New Ideals

THE EDUCATIONIST

Although Kodály's status now appeared to be assured there were still those who denigrated his efforts. A savage and personal attack, occasioned by a concert given by Kodály's students in 1925, appeared over the signature of Béla Diósy. To this Kodály replied in a trenchant article entitled *Tizenhárom fiatal zeneszerző* (Thirteen Young Composers), which was less an act of self-defence than a *credo* on behalf of Hungarian music—and Hungary.

'What right', he said, 'have you to forbid us the use of our own musical idiom? To prevent us from teaching this idiom also in our schools, modestly, alongside the universal language of music? We allow freedom to every taste within the limits of art. But for how long do you expect us to put up with your attempts to dictate to us the foreign tastes of your foreign soul? To your conservatism, rooted in small-town Germany or international platitudes, I oppose a Hungarian conservatism, nominated by a universal culture. We want to stand on our own feet. . . . We refuse to be a musical colony any longer. . . . We have our own musical message, and the world is beginning to listen to it attentively. It is not we who have invented Hungarian music. It has existed for 1,000 years. We only wish to preserve and foster this ancient treasure; and, if sometimes the opportunity should be granted to us, to add to it.' If this charge was valid in 1925, it is also valid at the present time; and in a wider field. The 'international platitude' is no less infrequent than it was.

It is here that Kodály's new point of departure in 1925 becomes significant. The possibilities of music within education were revealed, as has been shown, by the singing of the boys' choir in *Psalmus Hungaricus* in 1923. In 1925 Kodály had been given further cause for reflection. Walking one day in the Buda Hills—a favourite exercising ground to this day—Kodály encountered a group of girl students from a teachers' training college. Learning at first hand the music they proposed to dispense to their future pupils, he was appalled. His duty was clear: to have phoney 'educational music' abolished, and folk-music established as the basis of operations. His thesis went into epigrams, such as 'Singing and music must be taught in the school in such a way as to instil a lifelong thirst for nobler music. . . . Often a single experience will open the young soul to music for a whole lifetime. This experience cannot be left to chance; it is the task of the school to provide it.'

To realise his intentions in this particular, Kodály launched a two-pronged attack. He devoted himself to the arrangement and composition of suitable works, and he harried the administrators. In the latter direction he made slower progress, and operations were spread over a period of forty years. On 2 April 1925, however, performances of *The Straw Guy* and *See the Gipsy*, by the Wesselényi Street Choir (conductor, Endre Borus) were electrifying. An audience which had assembled for a concert of folk-music arranged by Kodály, and to enjoy performances by the leading artists of the Opera, were enchanted. Kodály had won the first round; and these two choruses became indispensable thereafter. It was at this point that Kodály first began to influence English school music,[1] for in 1925 Hubert Foss visited Budapest in order to take both Bartók and Kodály into the new music catalogue of the Oxford University Press. The two songs named above were the first of Kodály to be published with English text.

At this point Kodály's music began to be noticed in the English journals, which, apart from the single instance of the *Monthly*

---

[1] That similar attitudes to those of Kodály were being brought to bear on British school music at about the same time is shown by an excerpt from an essay ('Music as a Factor in Education') by R. R. Terry: 'But, to my mind, more important than the learning of "an instrument" is the exercise of the oldest musical instrument in the world—the human voice. Not only is it a healthy exercise, but it quickens the pulse, induces mental alertness, and incidentally brings the young mind in contact with things of real beauty as distinct from mere utility. The low standard of musical taste which prevailed in the last century rendered the full exercise of this practice somewhat difficult. The music available for use in schools was of a poor type. . . . Our British folk-songs have now been rescued from oblivion, and nothing better could be given to a class to sing . . .' (reprinted in *A Forgotten Psalter* (O.U.P.), 1929, p. 176).

Musical Record (see p. 203), had hitherto ignored it. The two new school songs were noticed in the *Musical Times* of May 1926: '. . . Both are in a dance-mood, with the "snap" effect we hear, nearer home, in Scots songs, and (in *See the Gipsy*) crush-notes that jump a third . . . the part-writing is straightforward. Lively-minded singers can make these songs go with a swing' (W. R. A[nderson]). In August the first available volume of *Hungarian Folk-songs of Transylvania* was reviewed in a thoughtful essay by T[homas] A[rmstrong]: 'The interpreter of folk-song is always faced with the problem of implications; often in simple melodies there is a high concentration of feeling, and the singer or arranger must either work very simply, in the hope of letting the overtones sound clearly, or he may attempt to extract the inner meaning and re-express them in his own language. The latter is Kodály's way, and it is done with tremendous energy, command, sense of the dramatic, and many moments of beauty. In every number there are striking touches of imaginative setting. . . . The danger of the method is that by saying too much of what is implied, one may repel, . . . at any rate the arranger may overload; and one does feel in the bigger number of Kodály's examples that things have got beyond legitimate latitude. The settings become rhapsodies, based on folk-songs, but grown into a quite different sort of thing: and one remembers how very much more effectively, though quietly, some of Bartók's simple arrangements set off tunes which are quite well able to operate for themselves.'

HÁRY JÁNOS

From here to the opera *Háry János* is an easy step, for *Háry János*, a sequence of folk-melodies arranged, in its freshness and simplicity is, in one sense, also within the territory of juvenilia; to be listened to with the eagerness, and acceptance of wonder, of youth. Because it has this quality, but without condescension, it is, in the broadest sense of the word, popular, and permanently in the repertoire of Hungarian opera. *Háry János* is the obverse of the *Psalmus*. Thus it is gay, but also sardonic; beautiful, but without sentimentality; simple, but worldly-wise; companionable, yet critical. *Háry János* is a comedy, and in realising the elements of the plot Kodály also realises the Hungarian temperament—that part of it that is not shown in the *Psalmus*, but which is its main support.

Háry János was a Transdanubian character who took part in the Napoleonic Wars. His exploits grew to large dimensions and became legendary; they were memorialised in a poem by János Garay. The story (worked into a libretto by Béla Paulini and Harsányi Zsolt) became symbolic. It is not difficult to penetrate the symbolistic covering. Háry, a variant on the eternal theme of Quixotism, is a story-teller whose divagations from fact represent to himself the straight road of truth; a condition noticed by Kodály, who commences his Introduction (as also in the Suite derived from the opera) with a simulated sneeze. (According to ancient, and Hungarian, tradition a story preceded by a sneeze is thereby denoted as fabulous and of doubtful veracity.) The Empress, Marie Louise, wife of Napoleon, falls in love with Háry and takes him to Vienna, despite Háry's long and firm attachment to Örzse, a girl from his own village. Napoleon's minister, who is himself in love with Marie Louise, declares war on Austria. Háry, single-handed, defeats the armies of Napoleon to find Marie Louise more than ever in love with him when he is given a hero's welcome in Vienna. Now confident that true happiness lies in his love for Örzse, Háry dismisses the Empress, returns home with his sweetheart, to spend the rest of his days in recounting and embellishing his memories.

Kodály's music is an admixture of folk-music, other traditional music, and some that is original. That in the first two categories defines the common people, that in the last is courtly, but the antitheses are resolved in Kodály's personal idiom, which, harmonically and instrumentally, enlarges the one and diminishes the other. The folk-music came mainly from Kodály's own researches, but the melody of the Intermezzo (No. 10 in the opera, the fifth movement of the Suite) was taken from a piano method by István Gáti, issued in 1802, and that of the *con moto* of Háry's song, 'Hullo, hullo, brave rider', from a piece ascribed to Bihari.[1] The presentation of the folk material is colourful and imaginative, the programmatic points of accompaniment growing from the text and forming as inevitable parts of the texture as similar

[1] See p. 9.

items in the songs of Schubert. Thus in the love duet between
Háry and Örzse (set as No. 3 in the Suite) the recollected home
landscape is placed behind the vocal line in woodwind cadenzas
against a shimmer of *tremolo* strings and the evocative sound of the
cimbalum. Brilliant scoring illuminates the *Viennese Musical
Clock* (No. 12 in the opera, No. 2 in the Suite), as also the military
music of the French, and that for the Emperor's Court (both of
which are thematically allied). In the case of the Napoleonic
movements, however, Kodály touches the picture with the hand
of a caricaturist, which shows at its most dramatically apt in the
song given to Napoleon after the Funeral March. Thus the original march motiv is transformed, combined with the rhythm of the
Funeral music, and placed behind the Emperor's faded reputation:

33

It was suggested that in *Háry János* Kodály was not far from the
territory of his music for children. His illustrative gestures belong
immediately to that province, while his choral writing (see the

chorus of Ruthenian girls, or the minuet-style duet between Empress and Princess against the background of women's voices) has a particularly engaging quality of simplicity and freshness. At one enchanting point, indeed, children's voices deliver a nursery rhyme:

34

Á-bé-cé - dé, Raj-tam kez - dé, A nagy böl - - cses-sé-get, A nagy e - szes-sé-get, Á - bé-cé - dé.

It is thus seen that the opera ranges widely in reference and in characterisation. But its direction is pointed by a pervasive eagerness, and controlled by an economy of means. On the one side of *Háry János* is Smetana, on the other Vaughan Williams. *The Bartered Bride* has charm, freshness, vivacity, and a certain ingenuousness. *Hugh the Drover* is a fine and earnest endeavour to furnish a new idiom in English opera, but founded on a folk-song style that could never be more than a conscious revivification. Kodály's comedy piece, correcting the prettiness of the one and the moralising of the other, is nearer than either to the realities that Háry seeks to expose through fanciful allusion. It is thus summarised by Tóth, *op. cit.*, p. 2ᵉ5: 'En somme Háry János démontre que Kodály est un poète national, mais dans le sens le plus large du terme: quand il parle la langue de son peuple, l'humanité peut l'entendre. Son "hungarisme" ne lui est pas une limite; il ne borne pas son univers poétique: son regard, pour partir du sol des ancêtres, n'embrasse pas moins le monde entier.'

Háry János has been performed in Germany, latterly at Nürnberg and Heidelberg in the revised text of 1960, in Switzerland, and in America by the Juillard School of Music, but not as yet in Britain—which is a sad omission. On the other hand, the Suite which Kodály made from the opera in 1927 won immediate acclaim, was taken up by all the principal conductors in Europe and the United States, and found its way into Henry Wood's Promenade Concerts in 1928.[1] So far as the audiences were concerned, here was 'modern music' not lacking in progressive ideas, but wholly intelligible—and an antidote to pessimism.

The Suite comprises the Prelude to the opera; the Viennese Musical Clock; the duet between Háry and Örzse (*Tiszán innen, Dunán túl—Beyond the Danube and by the Tisza*), of which the melody is also used in the Finale of the opera; the military music, including the entry march of the French troops, of Napoleon (after figure 5 of the miniature score), and the Funeral March; the Intermezzo, placed out of order; and the entry music for the Viennese Court.

ENGLISH CONTACTS AND INFLUENCES

In the autumn of 1928 Kodály paid his second visit to England, for the Promenade Concert and the Three Choirs Festival performance of the *Psalmus* (for which an English text had been prepared by Edward Dent) at Gloucester. A close association between Kodály and the oldest of the English festivals was promptly formed, and in token of this Kodály keeps a picture of Gloucester Cathedral in his study in Budapest. Kodály approved the English landscape, the architecture of the medieval churches, the particular character of the Three Choirs Festival, and English choral singing. He met Elgar, who entertained him and Mrs. Kodály to lunch, amused them by his high-spirited conversation, and sent them away with a signed copy of *The Dream of Gerontius*.

The 1928 Three Choirs Festival was the first prepared by Herbert Sumsion, who had lately succeeded Sir Herbert Brewer

---

[1] See *The Times* of 31 August, noticing the concert of the previous night: 'The Suite is fantastic and humorous in mood. Between the gargantuan orchestral sneeze with which it begins and the satirical pomp of the final march, the "Entrance of the Emperor and his Court", there is a diversity of adventures. A visit to a show of clockwork puppets provides a delightfully scored movement. This is followed by a "Song", in which the composer has treated his native folk-music in the same imaginative way as Vaughan Williams has treated our own, and with results as lovely. Then there is a grotesque battle-piece, in which Napoleon is defeated by the hero of the tale. This burlesque "1812" Overture stood out, even in this brilliantly scored work, as a particularly skilful piece of orchestration. Kodály clearly knows exactly how to get his effects, and there is no fumbling or clumsiness in his writing. As a conductor, too, he showed a very complete, though quite undemonstrative, control over the players. . . .'

as organist of Gloucester Cathedral. A widely ranging programme had the conventionalities of Brewer and Howells at one extreme and the excitements of Verdi (*Requiem*), Honegger (*King David*), and Kodály at the other. In a lively notice in the *Manchester Guardian*, Granville Hill suggested how the new music came into the Three Choirs ambit 'like a cyclone passing over a smiling plain'. ' "The Hungarian Psalm",' he wrote on 8 September, 'was conducted by Mr. Kodály himself. It carries to extreme lengths the violence of treatment that until recently was considered almost blasphemous in works based on sacred texts. The music shows the same disregard of all conventional ideas of counterpoint. It is, indeed, by the clashing of great harmonic masses and by the employment of a subtle colour scheme, rather than by contrapuntal means, that Mr. Kodály finds expression for his version of the 55th Psalm.

'The savagery of the stanza beginning with the words "Violence and strife rage fierce in the city" is quite as prolific of discordant sound as anything in Honegger's *King David*; but Kodály's music in its most grotesque sections shouts, whereas Honegger's gibbers queerly at you from a distance. A remarkable effect of numbness is secured in the closing pages of the psalm, where sopranos and basses sing long phrases in octaves, the orchestra supplying middle harmonies. Strangely enough, Verdi has anticipated this effect in the "Agnus Dei" in his *Requiem*.

'There are moments when Kodály's work expresses very beautifully the sadness of David lamenting the treachery of his friend. Such quiet moments, however, are rare, and it is the ferocity of its invective that gives the music a strange hold on one's imagination.'[1] The *Psalmus* was given at Worcester in 1929 and at Hereford (where a radical spirit led to the omission of *Elijah* for the first time at such a Festival) in 1930.

Back in Hungary, Kodály projected a festival similar to that of the Three Choirs, the participating choirs to come from Sopron, Szombathely, and Győr. Although this project failed to materialise,

---

[1] Cf. *The Times*: 'Coming as it did after the theatricalism of Honegger's "King David", in which certain of the same words were used, the concentration of purpose in the heartfelt choral chant of the Psalm was doubly effective. Here is a work free from any self-conscious poses, simple in design, yet trenchant in expression.' The soloist in the *Psalmus* was Steuart Wilson.

some progress in the expansion of Hungarian choral music was made in 1929, when a competitive festival at Debrecen brought together 10,000 singers from different parts of the country. After the final, open-air, concert, the Forest of Debrecen resounded with the songs of this vast chorus. In the same year a concert of Kodály's works (five receiving their first performance) for children's choirs was outstandingly successful, and in the town of Győr a competitive festival for school choirs took place. From this time, and until the nationalisation of Hungarian publishing houses in 1949, valuable work was done by the firm of Magyar Kórus in making choral music, both secular and sacred, available for schools and also adult amateur choirs. Magyar Kórus was directed by Lajos Bárdos (b.1899), conductor of the Palestrina Choir[1] in Budapest, and Gyula Kertész (b.1900), a church organist. Bárdos, a composer of choral music and Professor of Theory in the Academy, was, like Kertész, a pupil of Kodály, and later a Kossuth Prize-winner.

To raise the standard of musical education is, in general terms, a worthy ambition. It is, however, to be hoped that those who hold it have some premises on which to build. One common attitude stems from barely veiled *snobbisme*: those who are acquainted, however superficially, with 'the best' are more acceptable than those who are not: hence the cult of 'musical appreciation'. Allied to this is the sentiment that a little music—again from impeccable sources—is a face-saving antidote to more palpably materialist studies: hence the educational intravention of Friday afternoon 'liberal studies'. In England there is a powerful third element. Music in schools—particularly by playing off one school against another or by artful window-dressing—can be tenuously associated with athletics and choral activity related to healthy exercise. In every case the cause of music needs to be argued, for the idea that it is good in itself is hardly cogent; the subsidiary thesis that it diffuses pleasure is even less agreeable. Kodály, faced with not entirely dissimilar situations, was able to answer back from a position of strength. He premised that in Hungarian music, in the practice of music by Hungarians, there

---

[1] Founded in 1916, and directed by Bárdos since 1929, the Palestrina Choir undertook the general choral (oratorio) repertoire, and not only polyphonic music.

was a means of safeguarding and perpetuating the Hungarian spirit. In 1929, in one of many articles written at this time in the fields of musicology and pedagogy (which two fields he saw as one), he observed in respect of folk-song that 'We have no other music that lights up the recesses of the Hungarian soul in a form at once so solid and so enduring'. If this premise be accepted (and what is important is that Kodály accepted it) the way is clear: musical education, as a means of self-understanding, is vital. Behind this, of course, lay experience. On the one hand Kodály recollected the singing of his own schooldays in Galánta, with all that that had meant in effecting a kind of circumscribed but none the less real feeling of equality and community; on the other, the still living, oral tradition of folk music that to him was a guarantee of personal dignity. This, perhaps, is the secret. Kodály's humanism is of a fundamental quality. All affronts to human dignity to him are anathema: most of all affronts to those less able to take care of themselves, children, peasants, and, among nations, the small ones.

Bad music, where there could be better music, bad teaching, where there could be good teaching—those were wrongs which he himself could right. And in so doing, for his view is comprehensive, other evils could be overcome. At the end of the road was the vision of a unity in human relationships, of which music could be at once the catalyst and the outward symbol.[1] Kodály is, as has already been stated, a pragmatist. Throughout his career he has recognised to what extent he could use his own talents to the greatest purpose. Thus, in 1929, he went into action on the limited front of school music: but broader issues were his inspiration:

'Our musical education has meant seventy years of erratic wandering, and that is why it has produced no results. They [the authorities] wanted to teach the people music by ignoring, by throwing aside, what the people know of their own accord. Yet it is only possible to build upon what exists, using the folk heritage as a foundation, otherwise we shall build on air.'[2] What music,

---

[1] See 'Folk Tradition and Musical Culture', Chapter IX of *Folk Music of Hungary*, pp. 126-8.

[2] This backward glance came from the article, 'Let us dare to be Hungarians in our music too', written in 1945.

properly presented, could effect is thus epitomised: 'Often a single experience will open the young soul to music for a whole lifetime. This experience cannot be left to chance; it is the task of the school to provide it.' As for the institutions conventionally supported at public expense and their future, Kodály observed: 'The State maintains opera and concerts in vain, if nobody attends them. A public must be reared for whom music of a higher order is a life necessity. The Hungarian public must be lifted out of its lack of musical requirements. And this can only be started by the schools. . . . It is much more important who the singing teacher is at Kisvárda than who is the director of the Opera House. For the poor director becomes a failure at once, [whereas] a poor teacher can exterminate the love of music for thirty years in thirty successive classes.'

Within this context, then, the songs for school choirs, which Kodály composed in the late 1920's, are of considerable importance. They are of folk-music origin; but the basic melodies are built into the structure of the works as were, for instance, plainsong motivs into that of medieval polyphony. Thus the living quality of folk-tune—which is not seen as merely beautiful in death and meet for embalming—is emphasised. It is in fact a point of departure. Children sing best (and develop a technique) when unaccompanied. With Kodály this is basic. His part-songs, therefore, are freely contrapuntal—the counterpoint being balanced, however, by episodes of homophony—and congenial companion-pieces to those of the sixteenth-century masters. At the same time they are splendidly aware that their own abiding-place is in the twentieth century, which induces the sharp-edged, diatonic, dissonances of *God's Blacksmith*, the plain-spoken rows of triads of *St. Gregory's Day*, the occasional thrusts into bitonality in *God's Blacksmith* and *The Swallow's Wooing*, the plangently repeated motiv that separates the octaves of the *Gipsy Lament*. Such works still remain as a challenge to musical education, to composers, and to young singers: the likeliest to meet the challenge are the latter.

8

The Cause of Choral Music

By NOW KODÁLY was in the prime of life, fully matured as an all-round musician, and involved in music on three main fronts: as scholar, as teacher, as creator. Since Kodály's own works defy the normal categorisation into period, his personal style maintaining a consistency—at least of technique—unfashionable since romantic interpretations inflicted a sometimes unwarrantable schedule of development on the progress of composers, it is only possible to refer to the varying pattern of his activities in relation to his overall interests. In the 1930's he intensified his concern for musical education, began to see the results of his long musicological researches, but also became increasingly conspicuous on the international scene as a considerable and brilliant master of orchestral music. The point at which all functions met was the Hungarian people.

In a period when his more modest fellow-countrymen needed the incentive of a visionary who believed in their capacity and could in some way provide a unifying faith and sense of communal spiritual purpose Kodály came more and more to assume the prophetic role. In the early 1930's the economic crisis that afflicted western Europe caused even greater distress in Hungary than elsewhere. At least one-third of the population, and two-thirds of the agricultural population, was living in conditions of grave poverty. At the other end of the scale was a relatively small group of persons of extreme wealth: feudalism was not yet dead. 'Bethlen's Hungary', writes Dr. C. A. Macartney, 'was emphatically a class state, and in a Europe which then believed itself to be advancing towards democracy, it was a conspicuous laggard; and its handsome façade . . . covered grievous unsolved social problems.'[1] In 1931 Count Bethlen fell from power and

[1] *Hungary: a short History*, p. 220.

was succeeded by Count Gyula Károlyi. Unable to cope with growing unrest and increasing spasms of social disorder, Károlyi resigned after a year, to be followed by Gyula Gömbös. Fascist affiliations, first with Italy and then with Germany, developed as the rulers—under the regency of Horthy—attempted to sublimate discontent in revisionism. With the carrot of the territories lost to Czechoslovakia dangled before them, first Gömbös and, after his death in 1936, Darányi, and then Béla Imrédy, found themselves more and more committed to the policies of Hitler. In due course fascist principles were applied domestically. The Arrow Cross Party symbolised fascism, of which the worst faults quickly became evident, and, inevitably, there was by the end of the 1930's discriminatory legislation against the Jews.

Against this background the integrity and strength of Kodály's ideals stood out. His concern was for the people of Hungary, and the most effective means he could employ to express this was his music. István Széchenyi had once expressed the hope that the 'nine million faithful serfs' of Hungary 'should rise from slavery to a life more worthy of man'. The ideal of the worthy life, enjoyed in an equitable society, and based on a generous belief in the spiritual virtues of the human being, is symbolised in Kodály's choral works, which stemmed immediately from his broadly educational ambitions.

Among Kodály's keenest disciples were the school-teachers of the Székely district. It was in Kolozsvár that Pál-Péter Domokos, inspired by Kodály, founded a choir in 1926. In the Marianum girls' school in the same town another excellent choir flourished under the direction of Caecilia M. Kotsis, and by 1935 the children of the Calvinist school (Benedek Kálmán) joined the Catholics under Domokos, and the Unitarians led by Lajos Ütő, to form a Kodály Choir. Other pioneer choral work was done in Marosvásárhely, where the choirmaster István Nagy found out the stimulating properties of Kodály's works. But it was not until a demonstration had taken place in the capital that choral music could really said to have been launched on a national scale.

In 1934 a performance took place in Budapest which, under the motto 'Singing Youth', began to rally the young to the cause of choral music and to define a movement. Thus Kodály expressed himself:

'All the problems now confronting us can be summed up in the single word: Education. But it must be a reciprocal education. On the one hand, the mass of the Hungarian people must be given the opportunity of appreciating art music of the highest quality; on the other, the devotees realise that there is another, specifically Hungarian, tradition, which has produced work as perfect in its kind, as pure and noble in its art, as the great musical tradition of the west. . . . Choral music is the means by which this aim can be achieved, but only on the condition that the art of choral singing is reborn.'

The focus of this proposition is the chorus *To the Magyars*, a four-part canon, designed for massed voices, composed, in 1936, to words by Dániel Berzsenyi, the inspired, patriotic poet of the Reform Era. Since it was written *To the Magyars* has served as the rally call of Hungarian amateur choral societies. Of the other works for *a cappella* chorus of this period the most important are the *Mátra Pictures*, the *Székely Lament, Jesus and the Traders*, the *Ode to Franz Liszt, Mountain Nights*, for female voices, and various settings of words by Kölcsey and Ady for male voices. It will be seen, taking into account the works for children's choirs, that no section of the choral community was ignored. By the nature of their purpose these choral works were by way of being *Gebrauchsmusik*, and it was, therefore, essential that they should be viable. It is, of course, a distinguishing feature of Kodály that his works lie within the limits of more or less immediate practicability. In respect of music for amateurs it was (and is) imperative that they should both encourage and survive rehearsal under not always ideal conditions. At the same time they should expand common musical appreciation and open up new imaginative vistas both for singers and audience. Kodály broke the long-established conventions in words and musical setting, just as Vaughan Williams dethroned the Victorian concept of the 'part-song' in England. Both composers had in common a basic instinct for folk-music—that transcended a mere knowledge of the subject and substituted a desire to re-live the experience of life contained therein—and a powerful sense of the infinite possibilities of musical colour offered by the medium of unaccompanied voices. 'Music', said Kodály, 'that seeks to proclaim the fullness of life demands the fullness of the human voice'.

Of these works some were deliberately occasional. Kodály has increasingly welcomed the stimulus of the date-line, thus pronouncing his acceptance of the composer as a practitioner in a community and his status as a craftsman after the eighteenth-century manner. The *Ode on Franz Liszt*, for example, was composed in celebration of the fiftieth anniversary of Liszt's death; while *The Peacock*, poetically transmuted by Endre Ady and in that form set by Kodály, was in honour of the thirtieth anniversary of the Socialist Workers' Choir. The great work of 1936, to which later reference will be made—the *Te Deum*, was a celebration of the liberation of Budapest from the Turks in 1686, and was commissioned by the civic authorities.

The best of choral music is illuminating in a particular way. The involvement of a number of singers, usually amateur, automatically provides a sense of community, from which the music itself acquires a particular dramatic quality. Elizabethan-Jacobean madrigal, with its busyness, its wit, its allusiveness, gives a vivid impression of our distant ancestors who possessed these characteristics (otherwise the music of Weelkes and Wilbye and Gibbons would not carry them). So too do the passionate moods of the anguished German Protestants of the century following the Thirty Years' War live on in the choruses of Schütz and Bach. This property of choral music transcends technicality, provided that the movement of life is transmitted through rhythmic vitality.

Kodály was at one time close to the Impressionist camp, but, observing that French music tends most frequently to appeal to the eye and to an *élite* rather than to the musical commonalty, his absorption in folk-music removed him towards a more substantial, realistic, vantage-point. Choral music, in contradistinction to instrumental music, is, by its nature, realistic—by people, with people, and from people. The nineteenth century part-song denied this premise, by relapsing into academical terms, by being conceived abstractly as music—music to give a somewhat etiolated pleasure.

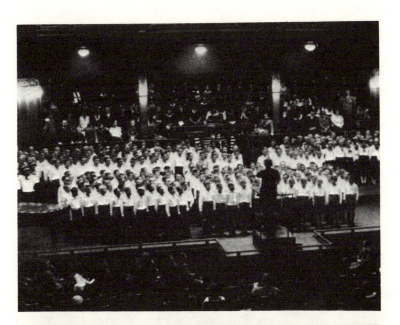

(*above*) Kodály conducts a children's choir, Academy of Music, 1935
(*below*) Visit to Training School for Teachers, Nyíregyháza, 1937

Three Choirs Festival, Gloucester, 1937

The urgency of Kodály's choral works springs in the first place from narrative, in the second from the folk idiom (whether patent, as in the *Mátra Pictures*, or latent, as in *Jesus and the Traders*), and in the third from the composer's determination to treat his material vividly. Programmatic considerations come incidentally.

MÁTRA PICTURES

The Mátra district of Hungary, with its mountains rising to a height of more than 3,000 feet, lies north and east of Budapest and has its own regional life and traditions. The *Mátra Pictures* are based on five folk-songs which (as in *Háry János* and *The Spinning Room*) are arranged in effective dramatic order, the whole, however, presenting a cohesive index to the life of the region. In the first of the songs the life and death of Vidrócki, the bandit who disguises his vocation under that of a swineherd, is told. Like all the songs, this is a set of variations. In the first stanza the melody—the first phrase introduced by soprano and tenor in octaves—is given to the top voice. In the second verse, as night falls, the *cantus firmus* is dropped to the tenors and basses. Finally, and in fragmentation, to the basses alone. There follows a lively middle section in minor rather than modal tonality, in which the pursuit of Vidrócki and his execution by the well-intentioned Stephen Pintér is outlined in intermittent canonic writing. But Vidrócki should not have been liquidated. His crimes were committed only against the rich; to the poor he was a benefactor. The coda of the movement, therefore, is a *Trauerode,* the contraltos sustaining the original melody against an accompaniment of poignant dissonances that, when given space in which to take effect, have a heavy nostalgia.

In the second song the discontent of youth is imaged. The boy would leave the village for the wide world: the girl entreats him not to go, but to stay at home on the security of his paternal half-acre. If he should go then she will call down a curse from Heaven unless he should remain faithful to her. The first verse is given by tenors and basses in unison; the second by sopranos above a deep chordal texture. In the third and fourth verses the little drama is lived out in a simple contrapuntal development that extends the basic melodic line into a freer outline. In the third song, again

contrapuntal, but slender in polyphonic implication, the symbol
of the bird is evoked. The boy has gone away, and is unhappy
in separation from his homeland, so he asks the bird to tell his
sweetheart of his broken heart:

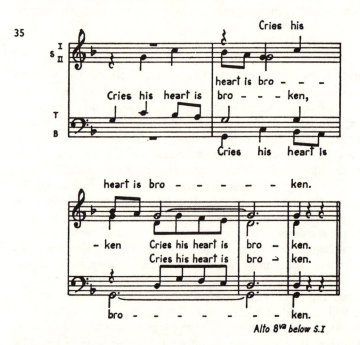

This succeeds to a gentle lyric, an even-tempered and languid
melody lying over the susurration of major triads of C, D, and E
warmed by the occasional langour of an old-fashioned 'dominant
seventh', which extols the peaceful country life. The finale is
a comedy piece—coloured with the bustle of a picture by Brouwer:
the village inn, the scattering hens, the busy virago, her husband,
the chattering girl. . . . All this is conveyed by skilful changes of
and contrasts in speed, by percussive open fifths, by tonal
diversions, by ornamentation applied in quasi-improvisatory
manner; above all by an appreciation of choral sonorities.
Kodály is not given to asking his performers to achieve the
impossible, nor even the improbable. Since, however, he has a

poetic appreciation of the faculties of choral singers he always gives them as much as they can manage within the limitation imposed by once- or twice-weekly rehearsal.

JESUS AND THE TRADERS

Thirty years ago the colour of choral music had been forgotten. Thus—and it is so with Vaughan Williams—Kodály not infrequently provides wordless music. The example of this period is the sequence *Mountain Nights*. If this is a lesson in one direction, then *Jesus and the Traders* is a lesson in another. This is a didactic piece, a homily, that catches the antiseptic austerity of the old Calvinists of post-Reformation Hungary. By a blaze of anger, Kodály condemns not only the money-changers in the Temple, but all those who put profit before people. *Jesus and the Traders* springs from Kodály's deep humanism. The music—and this is where the veristic element is taken over from folk-song—is an extension of the words. There are programmatic factors, which Kodály never fails to employ for their referential value. Some of the descriptiveness of Kodály's style is deliberate: to take the most obvious kind of examples, there are the helter-skelter of the swine of the first of the *Mátra Pictures* which is contained in a sudden rush of semiquavers, and the falling-coin motiv of *Jesus and the Traders*; but more often it is unconsciously contrived. Kodály finds it impossible to think of words and music as separate entities; always the two appear to him as one. Thus experience drives the pen, and contours, rhythms, chords, and counterpoint appear, as it were, from within a text. *Jesus and the Traders* opens, solemnly, in octaves (Kodály has a great respect for the power and directness of choral *ottave*):

As the feast ap-proach-ed

The octaves and the interval of the rising fifth together underline the significance of the occasion. The *incipit* is completed with this natural, and musically logical, termination, which also contains its modal inflection:

36b

It is hardly necessary to point out that the operative, textual, 'up', is thereby enhanced. At this juncture the parts spread out into these characteristic, homophonic, resonances

36c

which, by the process of multiplication, allude to the many-peopled city, and by reduction from discord to concord indicate the atmosphere of the Temple. The transient A flat chord which goes into the cadential G major adds, perhaps, an aura of mystery. The detail of illustration may be ignored by the listener, for the effectiveness of the writing will induce in him an unconscious apperception of the scene, but not, I would think by the singers. Kodály is a composer who often leaves the best of his thought to recognition from within the texture of the music. That is why his choral works of this middle period of his career were so valuable at doing precisely what they set out to do: to stimulate choral singing.

Some of what has been said, especially in respect of particulars, could also be said of Bach. And Bach—the dramatic Bach—is more clearly at Kodály's elbow in *Jesus and the Traders* than heretofore. Thus there is more or less elaborate fugal development, the subject expanding the leap of the sixth already seen in Ex. 36c within a vigorous and syncopated rhythm, when the money-lenders are expelled from the Temple. A theme which is stated in conjunction with the fugal subject is also robust, and exemplifies Kodály's general dependence on fundamental melodic intervals, of fifth and of fourth:

37

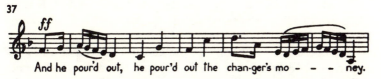

And he pour'd out, he pour'd out the chan-ger's mo - - - ney.

The dramatic crisis is brief, percussively pungent, and harmonically arresting, as the crowd three times shout the word 'robbers'. From across many centuries the cry of the *turba* sounds, and Schütz and Bach would have acknowledged this.

TE DEUM

The greatest of Kodály's choral achievements of these years, however, was the expansive, festal *Te Deum* of 1936.

'Auctor hoc opus a principe civium Budapestinorum rogatus in anniversaria CCL. Oppidi Budae armis recuperati composuit. Opus primo cantatum est in insigni ecclesia coronationis ad B. Mariam Virginem in coelos assumptam occasione gratiarum actionis moderante Victore Sugár die II mensis Septembri Anni MCMXXXVI.'

There is nothing merely academical about this inscription. Kodály used Latin—also in other dedications—as a recognition of the special place of that language in Hungarian history.[1] It will be recalled that in youth Kodály was so captivated by the language that he wrote an essay on the Latin inscriptions in Nagyszombat: this was a class project suggested by an intelligent

[1] Cf. C. A. Macartney, *op. cit.*, p. 112: 'The nation had never renounced the tradition that its official documents were couched in Latin, and since the sixteenth century the debates of the Diet and even the county congregations, and the proceedings of the Courts, had come to be conducted in that language.'

teacher, but among the pupils Kodály was keenest to execute the task thoroughly, and in this way—also helped by liturgical Latin —he came to accept the language as a living expression of thought. The *Te Deum* was first performed in the 'Coronation', or Matthias Church, within Buda Castle. This is the finest medieval building in Budapest, was built by Béla IV in the thirteenth century, rebuilt by King Matthias two centuries later, badly damaged in the recapture of the city in 1686, and subsequently restored in the eighteenth century by two Viennese architects. The church, again severely damaged in 1945, became a repository for priceless works of art. All of this is splendidly transfused by Kodály into terms of music.

The opening homophony of the chorus, derived from Palestrinan method by way of Verdi, is offset by exuberant trumpet calls and exultant figuration in the strings. The triplets of the "Sanctus" are within reach of those which illumine this word in the *Mass in B minor*. "Pleni sunt coeli" is fugal in the manner of Haydn, after which homophony, for the time being in the lower voices, returns for the 'Apostolorum chorus'. In the *adagio* middle section Kodály localises the music by Hungarian rhythms, and by pentatony, varies the tone quality by extensive use of four solo voices, but reaches a climax at the words "Tu ad dexteram Dei sedes", which is both formally and dramatically significant by the recapitulation of the earlier triplets. "Judex crederis esse venturus" is given with tremendous force in octaves. The final section commences with the words "Te ergo quaesumus", and the colouring is dark, and the manner hesitant: but the mood changes, with the words, until, over a pentatonic motiv heavily worked in the orchestral bass, the tonality moves across wide spaces until it reaches the dominant E and the introductory trumpet call. Enough of the opening material accompanies "Per singulos dies . . ." to give the idea of a sonata-style movement (again, a reflection of Austrian eighteenth-century practice). A new theme is introduced for "In te Domine speravi . . ." which is itself laid out *fugato* and then combined with the earlier fugal motiv of the exposition in the final paragraph which, however, ends distantly, *in aeternum*, on a chord of A major given to the high voices.

The *Te Deum* is one of Kodály's most vivid works, touching

the great points in the European tradition of choral music, yet firmly integrated and individual.

Shortly after its first performance the *Te Deum* was heard in Britain, through the B.B.C. Hanslick once said: 'It is very difficult to gain the favour of the English public—and absolutely impossible to lose it.' Kodály was well on the way to proving the point.

9

Scholarship and Art

MEANWHILE the scholarly qualities were finding other outlets, and more tangible consequences of the researches into folk music were becoming evident. In 1937 Kodály published his *Folk Music of Hungary* (English translation, 1960), in which he summarised for general consumption the results of many years of research that had hitherto mostly gone into papers in learned journals. Some four years earlier he had indicated how Hungarian musical history, in large measure devoid of adequate documentation, could only be understood when the references within the field of folk-music were properly explored and explained. The important essay in which he expounded this point of view, relevant not only to problems of Hungarian musicology, was entitled 'Ethnography and Musical History', and was published in *Ethnographia* (Vol. XLIV), in which journal earlier contributions of his had appeared. The idea expressed in this essay had considerable effect on *Musikwissenschaft*, which hitherto had confined itself, under strong German influence, to documentary evidence alone. While Kodály the scholar was absorbed by considerations of geography (in respect particularly of the interdependence of Hungarian and eastern European and Siberian pentatony), of history (so that he was able to recreate the inexactly notated rhythms of Tinódi's balladry), of prosody (showing the connections between sixteenth-century folk-rhythms and subsequent versification), of social change (reflected in the transference of musical ideas from the old Protestant psalters to the 'Beggars' Songs'), and to more modern popular church music, he has ever been at pains to take as his starting-point the actual, and the present. 'The point of departure', he once said, 'must be life, the living present, so difficult to know.' Thus the antecedents of the popular music, of the gipsies, and of the *verbunkos*, that was part of his own upbringing, have been scrupulously analysed. What is more, this type of music has been taken into his own stylistic ambit on equal terms with the 'authentic' tradition.

Among musicologists Kodály, a pioneer, must take high rank. But musicology, indeed music itself, was subordinate to a greater purpose. In the 1930's—when Bartók was setting his sights on the wider world, preparatory to emigrating from Hungary—Kodály fought with all the vigour of which he was capable against the influences that were disintegrating his country. He was once asked what he was doing bothering with Székely folk-songs. His reply—a quotation from a famous poem by Ady—was as follows: 'I should like to take them to every place where "four or five Hungarians are leaning towards each other", that they should not ask "What for?" but say: for this and for that and for everything —life is worthwhile and should be lived.' This vatic utterance sprang from a conviction that the vitality of a people, and the cohesion of a community, depend on language: in broad terms, one language, one people. This led to an effort to improve the use of the Hungarian language, by which means a more intense national unity might be created. At this point the English social ameliorist could be instructed. Hungarian, he said, must be correctly spoken so that 'every mistake in grammar, every turn of foreign speech, every mis-pronounced word is felt to be a betrayal: as if a gap had been cut into the Hungarian border. . . . Hungarian pronunciation has to be learnt, even by born Hungarians. The best way is to have contact with village people who speak well. This would, anyway, do town-dwellers good. That oft-quoted Hungarian solidarity and spiritual union cannot be brought about as long as one layer does not know the other.'

One of the most significant decisions within the field of Hungarian scholarship in those years was that of the Academy of Sciences, in 1933 and 100 years after its first determination, to undertake publication of the available folk-music material. In 1934 Bartók, at the request of the Academy, was released from his teaching commitments at the High School for Music, in order to exercise editorial control. (Between 1929 and 1935 Bartók's folk-song inspired composition, and his *a cappella* choral works indicate his closeness at that time to Kodály's ideals.) But, Kodály collaborating by concentrating his attention principally on the folk-song manuscripts in public collections, the project was long in developing and Bartók's part in it terminated when he emigrated in 1940. Thus nothing appeared before the war which made the situation once again impossible. But by now there had developed from among Kodály's and Bartók's pupils and disciples a considerable body of musicological talent.

Of the younger school of scholars, which came into prominence in the 1930's, Dénes Bartha (b. 1908), Ottó Gombosi (1902-55), Ervin Major (b. 1901), and Bence Szabolcsi (b. 1899) are outstanding. Bartha studied at the High School for Music in Budapest, and later in Berlin. He was for a time librarian of the Music Section of the National Museum in Budapest, and, from 1935 on the staff of the High School, since 1942 as Professor of Musical History. He has also occupied other influential offices. Among his publications, which extended from the work of Kodály, were his *Sources of Hungarian Song Verse from Faludi to Adám Horváth* (1932), *The Musical Notes of Bishop Szalkai from His School-Years, 1490* (1934), *Hungarian Melodies of the Eighteenth Century* (1935), *Hungarian Folk Music on Gramophone Records* (1937). In 1943, in conjunction with Kodály, he issued *Hungarian Music*. Gombosi was also educated in Budapest and Berlin, whence he returned to edit the progressive musical journal, *Crescendo*, from 1926 to 1928. His particular field of research was that of the sixteenth and seventeenth centuries and his work led to a proper assessment, and editions of the music, of Bálint Bakfark and Thomas Stolzer, in which undertaking he was subsidised by the Hungarian Ministry of Education. Gombosi emigrated to America in the early years of the war. Ervin Major, son of a composer, was one of Kodály's composition pupils, and in his extant works (many were destroyed during the siege of Budapest at the end of the war) the influence of Kodály is readily to be appreciated. But it is for his researches into the music of Hungary in the eighteenth and nineteenth centuries that Major—who has taught at the principal musical institutions in Budapest—is best known. Starting with his doctoral thesis— *The Relationship between Hungarian Popular Art-music and Folk-music*—he has proceeded to analyse the Hungarian elements in

Haydn, Mozart, Beethoven, Brahms, and Liszt, and to illuminate the territory of *verbunkos* and *csárdás* with unassailable precision. Szabolcsi also studied with Kodály (on whose music he is an invaluable commentator), and later in Leipzig. Since 1926, when he joined the staff of the musical journal, *Zenei Szemle*, Szabolcsi has been one of the most prominent figures in musical scholarship, not only in Hungary, but in the international field. Szabolcsi is a methodical scholar and, learning from Kodály, he has based much of his research on Magyar music on its philological origins. In 1930-1, in conjunction with Aladár Tóth, Szabolcsi edited the *Hungarian Musical Lexicon*, to which Kodály contributed one essay on folk-music.

The value of Hungarian musical research was enhanced by its highly practical emphasis and frequently by the literary quality of its presentation; this derived from the fact that the inspiration came from practising composers, who felt that in music science and art were indivisible. The influence of Kodály was thus recognised by the *Schweizische Musikzeitung* of 15 May 1942, in reference to *Székely Fonó* (*The Spinning Room*): 'Kodály's exuberant and powerful way of dealing with folk-tunes has won the day. This is no academic display of folk-lore, but the very life of the people illuminated by the strong beams of a "dramatic searchlight" (L.P.).'

THE SPINNING ROOM

The Spinning Room was Kodály's second venture into the theatre—if one excludes the incidental music written for Zsigmond Móricz's (1872-1942) play, *Lark Song*[1]—and he regarded it as an important part of his method. The opera house, which had afforded nothing but failure to Bartók, must be purged of its reactionary impulses; until this, a focal point of musical-social life, was reorientated, Hungarian music would never gain proper parity of esteem. There was, of course, *Háry János*; but this was insufficient. Therefore *The Spinning Room* was contrived. This, a succession of Székely songs arranged, rather as in the *Mátra Pictures*, into a dramatically

---

[1] Orchestral music, and a song with 'gipsy ensemble' accompaniment. The former has remained in manuscript. The song was transcribed and as the last of *Four Songs* (U.E., 1925).

viable sequence, and linked together by some narrative (also taken from folk-lore) was composed in more or less modest fashion, with pianoforte accompaniment, in 1924. Half a dozen or so years later Kodály amplified and orchestrated it. In its new form it was presented at the Budapest Opera, conducted by Sergio Failoni, on 24 April 1932. The work, sub-titled by Kodály himself as *A Scene from Transylvanian Village Life*, was applauded by some, and disparaged by others, to whom it was no theatre piece. A reasonably sceptical view, tempered with respect for its purpose, was expressed in the *Signale*, on 25 May, by Gerhard Krause: it was, he said 'an utterly unconventional work, strictly puritan in spirit, rooted in the very soil and life of Hungary, less popular in its appeal than *Háry János*, but subtler and loftier. . . . It is not easy to apprehend at first contact.'

More than thirty years later one may, I think, conclude that *The Spinning Room* is among the least successful of Kodály's works—at least to the non-Magyar, who is expected to approach it as a representation of Transylvanian village life and as such to find it convincing. What it lacks as an entity is the universality of *Háry János*, who is as much everyman as Quixote or Falstaff. In *The Spinning Room* one feels that the composer has gone on location, collected the stars together, and called up the extras (considerable choral forces are required). One might, taking into account the accompaniment, suggest also that some studio mock-ups have been devised. In respect of plot, altogether too much goes on: an illicit liaison between the 'housewife' and her lover, teen-age love-making (under the ritual prescriptions of folk-lore), death and resurrection singing-games, mummery—the villain of the piece disguised as a flea, gendarmerie exercises, kinder-garten by-play: the lot. In all there are twenty-one movements, songs, choruses, and dances, which hardly lose their separate identities to the compulsions of a plot. *Háry János*, of course, is episodic, but the character of the hero, the general relevance of the text to the human situation, and the blend of Kodály's personal style and that of Hungarian folk-music, give it the commanding consistency of a picaresque novel. *The Spinning Room*, being a contrivance of surrealistic, or symbolist, poems into a realistic sequence, comes apart at the division between action and thought, what is and what is imagined. Thus it is that the *Mátra Pictures*, for instance, more loosely ordered and retained within the realm of what is heard, but not actually seen, are musically and dramatically more impressive.

But *The Spinning Room* has its numerous felicities: the Schubertian figuration of the spinning chorus (No. 4); the Brittenesque realisation of 'Once I went to market' (No. 6), in which, as in the children's music of *Háry János*, Kodály shows the rare genius to interpret the child mind through music that is simple, but not merely naïve; the canonic treatment of Scene 4 that is characteristic of much of Kodály's most direct choral music; the choral variations of Scene 5; the exuberance of No. 12, and of the Finale. The sum of this, however, is perhaps, a cantata rather than a stage-piece. Since the analogies are to hand it is worth remarking that when Vaughan Williams strung together a cycle of folk-songs, in *The Four Seasons*, he kept to the cantata form and achieved a sufficient continuity; but that when he wrote his most folk-conscious opera *Riders to the Sea*—like *The Spinning Room,* a one-act piece—he employed no folk-songs at all.

SUMMER EVENING; DANCES OF MAROSSZÉK, AND GALÁNTA; BALLET MUSIC

If *The Spinning Room* fell short of its objective, the orchestral pieces of this period were, beyond question, masterpieces in their genre. In the 1930's, indeed, Kodály established himself as one of the orchestral masters of his generation. As usual, new departures were stimulated from without. Thus the version of *Summer Evening* now in being was a revision of the work of 1906, undertaken at the suggestion of Toscanini (whom Kodály had met for the first time on 11 November 1928, when Toscanini conducted the *Psalmus* in Milan, and for whose daughter's wedding he wrote the *Four Italian Madrigals* of 1932). *Summer Evening* in its new form was first performed in Budapest by the New York Philharmonic Orchestra, under Toscanini, in the course of its European tour of that year. *Summer Evening,* particularly in its generous treatment of cor anglais, as in its Aeolian and Mixolydian allusions, and its pentatonicism, has its affinities with Vaughan Williams's first *Norfolk Rhapsody*. But, unlike this work of the English composer, it does not disengage itself, harmonically and formally, from the main and accepted tradition of European music. It is, of course, schematic, and the composer's theories are evident. At the same time there are other affinities. In warmth and subtlety of orchestral colouring—small forces are used—and in the growth of climax one is reminded of certain contemporary trends in the visual arts; particularly of the distinctive palette and formal moulding of the painter István Szőnyi. Here one meets a distinctively Hungarian style in painting, partly inspired by the Impressionism developed by the so-called Nagybánya school, partly by the structural and constructivist exercises of the group which was formed in 1909 and known as 'the Eight'.[1] *Summer Evening* is Impressionist, but it is written into sonata form, and, indeed, interfused with fugato. At the same time the mystical element is pervasive. Therefore, because of the characteristics of the orchestration and the shape of the melodies, one is made aware of 'the magic of *nature* and a close spiritual link with the inner life of *language*', which Szabolcsi states as the dual foundation of Kodály's style.

In 1930 the *Dances of Marosszék* also received their first performance by the New York Philharmonic Orchestra, under Toscanini. They were noted in the *Musical Times* (November 1930), as containing "abounding vivacity and a great deal of beauty' (T.A.) and were compared with the *Three Folk-music Rondos* (1926) of Bartók. This work, initially considered as a project in 1923, but put aside on account of Bartók's somewhat similar intention for the festivities of that year, appeared for pianoforte solo in 1927. In this form the brilliance of the keyboard realisation is positively Lisztian, and the intensity of colouring is enhanced by orchestration.[2] The melodies are Transylvanian in origin, and taken from Kodály's researches. Again the manner of presentation is classical, in the sense that the formal design is of the rondo. Three years later a complementary—in more senses than one—work was produced for the eightieth anniversary of the Budapest Philharmonic Society: the *Dances of Galánta*, a transmutation of the *verbunkos* tradition. In the former work Kodály paid tribute to the

[1] Róbert Berény, Dezső Czigány, Béla Czobel, Károly Kernstok, Ödön Márffy, Dezső Orbán, Bertalan Pór, Lajos Tihanyi.
[2] The work is transposed up a semitone in the orchestral version.

distant past: 'My *Dances of Marosszék*', he said 'have their roots in a [much more] remote past, and represent a fairy land that has disappeared.' The *Dances of Galánta*, taken from a Viennese publication of *c.* 1800, contain within themselves the whole of the nineteenth century, and, especially in the highlights of orchestration, memorialise boyhood recollections.

From the two works a ballet, to a libretto entitled *A Rebel's Tale* and written by Zsolt Harsányi (1887-1942), was devised in 1935. Despite criticism that the libretto's realism confounded the idealism of the music, the idea, promoted by the Budapest opera, was not unacceptable, and the ballet, though with various libretti, went the rounds of the German theatres. In 1937 Kodály's independent *Ballet Music,* following Prokofiev's Third Piano Concerto and prefacing Bax's Fourth Symphony, was successfuly introduced to a Promenade audience in London: 'five minutes of boisterous romping with rustic themes, presumably Hungarian. This is real peasant music, but as the peasantry of South-eastern Europe differs from that of Somerset, it comes to us with exotic vividness.'[1]

PEACOCK VARIATIONS

For all their vivacity and exuberance the two sets of *Dances* remain on the far side of what is expected of a "major" composer. With the next orchestral work, the *Variations on a Hungarian Folk-song*, however, there is no doubt as to the composer's stature: this is a piece which takes its place among the important contributions to the variation method. In one sense, of course, the whole of Kodály's output, in the larger sense, is variational: on the twin themes of Hungary and Hungarian folk-music.

The *Variations* were the result of a commission, to compose a work in celebration of the fiftieth anniversary of the Concertgebouw Orchestra in Amsterdam. The première, conducted by Mengelberg, was on 13th November, 1939, at the Concertebouw, and this was followed by performances at the Hague and in Rotterdam. The theme was a melody collected in the County of Somogy, which stretches from the western end of Lake Balaton towards the Yugoslav frontier. Formerly a territory of large

[1] *Musical Times,* September 1937.

estates and contrasting peasant poverty it is a region distinguished
on the one hand by a wealth of folk-lore and folk-art, and on the
other by the paintings of the impressionistic József Rippl-Rónai,
a native of Kaposvár, the county town. The theme which Kodály
selected (from *Hungarian Folk-music Recordings*, 1937) is of some
exceptional interest. It lies within the folk-song repertoire of the
Mari people who, separated from Hungary some 1,500 years ago,
now live within the U.S.S.R. When Kodály conducted the
Variations in Moscow in 1947, an old Mari song-collector in the
audience called out, 'That melody I too have taken down.' As
might be expected, the melody is of primitive structure: it derives
from the words of the ballad in that each of four six-syllable
lines in the stanza has six principal notes. These belong to the
pentatonic scale and are treated with the freedom of the speech
rhythm. Each, however, is decorated by free ornamentation
by the folk-singer. The melodic unit of the first line (phrase) is
reflected, with slight modification, to provide the second phrase.
The third phrase is as the first, but transposed down a fifth; the
fourth is a further repetition, with the cadence modified to induce
finality. The melody is reduced by Kodály to its essentials—inevitably, to suit it to its orchestral purpose, and thus it stands in
'cellos and basses. The tonic D is emphasised by bassoons, horns,
and by timpani interpolations during the rests:

38

With this opening may be compared that of the Symphony. The
initial paragraph concluded, another is commenced by a strongly
functional G sharp, which the kettle-drum maintains against
canonic evolution of the thematic formula by clarinet and bassoon;
but before this is ended the upper strings and upper woodwind

Kodály at home

In a Budapest classroom, 1958

proceed to point the significance of the drum notes by stating a chord of E major, from which further expansion of the formula, through a characteristic kind of *organum* in the strings in counterpoint with the horns, follows. This leads to a climax in the dominant, in which harp *glissandi* and brass chords participate. This preludial section concludes *piano*, the G sharp being again featured in the strings, against a drum D which is supporting a cadential decline of trombones in thirds: all of which find their way again to the dominant. Now the theme is given, in the oboe, over vagrant strings, which like the horns at this point are muted, and harp. Although the outlines of melody

are clear, the atmosphere is softened, first by the unexpected B flat pedal in the double-basses, second by the triadic mutations in the strings:

This, though firmly held so far as rhythmic organisation is concerned, is evocative of landscape—on a summer evening; not least of all in the concluding chord—a complex of three superimposed major thirds surrounding the by now long-held dominant of the oboe:

At this juncture it is, perhaps, worth inquiring into the validity of the style. There, in eighty bars, Kodály has stated the material out of which the variations are to follow in all the amplitude of a gigantic variation *per se*. As has been seen the melody itself is there—in two forms, the one simple, the other less simple. This, *mutatis mutandis*, is, as Kodály has elsewhere shown, in the nature of folk-music. There is, as throughout the work, sufficient of pentatony to keep the ear attached to the basic thesis. But there are excursions into subtleties, tonal and contrapuntal, that lie far away from the elemental qualities. Now, folk-music is undoubtedly ingenuous—by non-folk-music standards; but its implications, through verbal allusiveness and even melodic melisma, are anything but simple. Kodály is a keen analyst, but also a synthesist. Folk-music is a collective inheritance, but an individual responsibility. Having drawn on the tradition—and the authentic tradition must be guaranteed—the individual folk-singer will breathe new life into it. Kodály was no mere *imitator* of an atrophied idiom, but a *creator* within the terms of reference imposed by history and environment. Once again we return to environment, to place, to atmosphere. Kodály observed one day of French musicians that 'they must see music'. Some part of what he implied is stimulating to the visual sense. In short, in a folk-song meditation —which is what the introduction to the *Variations* is—he restores what is lost through transplanting. In rather another way Elgar's *Introduction and Allegro* may be scrutinised for its reflections on landscape and personality through its Welsh allusions.

The variations which follow the large exordium, are both extension and commentary: extension, because the foundation melody, ever-present, is adapted and modified through a sequence of mood phases; commentary, because these mood phases, seen to be endemic in the natural function of folk-art, direct the varying, rhythmic, harmonic, and instrumental patterns. In the first the distant enchantment of the conclusion of the introduction is fractured by the energy of a figure, later to play an important role in the *Concerto*, divided between strings and woodwind, that surrounds the main theme, curtailed and energised, in the trombones. Semiquavers run straight into the second variation, where quick-tongued, high-pitched, diatonic clusters in the woodwind set off the ornamented, and free, gloss on the melody in lower strings and bassoons. In variation 3 the character of the first is recollected, and the purposeful figuration of the strings and woodwind is impressed with a sequence of powerfully expanding chords in the brass. This section ends abruptly in Hungarian manner so far as the rhythm is concerned and on a chord based on D and comprising the familiar sounds of the open strings of the violin.

After a pause the mood is marked *poco calmato* and syncopated chords in woodwind and horns move against two brief, but impassioned, refrains in the first violins, in octaves, which follow the original tune contour. With bass instruments playing a more significant role the general idea is carried forward into the next variation, the whole of which is now marked *appassionato*. This movement is bigger and climactic, but linked to its successor rhythmically, in that the triplet figuration which had been introduced markedly by the horns is continued. The scene, however, is, once again, tranquil. Around and above a pedal—taken over after four bars by the kettledrum which thus assumes the importance it enjoyed at the outset—is a beautifully worked-out, because pellucid, canon:

At the end of the movement, of which the temper is, perhaps, as of a 'Scholar Gipsy', the tonality of D, which has persisted throughout, is heightened and enriched by a long major chord. This also terminates the first main part of the work.

Variations 7 and 8, the key signature changed to two flats, but the pentatonic character of the melodic outline retained, are dance movements, ingeniously flavoured (see, for example, the use of brass in No. 7 and the writing for double basses and

'cellos, and for clarinet and piccolo in No. 8). The rhapsodic
element originates in folk-music and is a characteristic of Kodály's
style. Variation 9 carries on where the second movement of the
Háry János Suite left off. The melody, much embellished, is
written for violas, 'cellos, and one solo bass (the precision of the
scoring is in keeping with the methodical manner of the composer). Above it is a chord pattern, colour-washed by first violins,
div. à 4. Here a Delian sequence carries a derivative melody—in
brief:

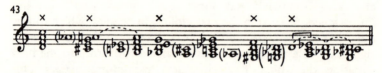

The texture, it will be seen, leaves no loose ends, nothing being
irrelevant. Above this flutes and clarinets exchange demisemi-
quaver groups. This, again, is a movement demanding visual
imagination. The quality of dance is now resumed in a brilliantly
contrived *orientale* for orchestra without brass, in which piccolo,
flutes, and oboes in fifths appear canonically against bassoons at
two octaves' distance, all of those backed by pizzicato strings. This
terminates a second main section of the work, which, like the
first, maintains an overall unity of its own within the greater
unity imposed by the theme and by the architecture of the
Variations as a whole.

A dramatic mood change is indicated by the choice of B flat
minor (shades of Schumann and Brahms in the harmonies) for the
next variation, in which, as in the two succeeding variations, the
theme is indicated only allusively. The tone colour is marked
by the prominence of cor anglais. In variation 12 the tragic mood
is carried above a consistent tonic pedal and expanded rhetorically,
apparently extempore and in reflection on the improvisations of
gipsy music, to a gigantic climax: this movement leads to a
correlated funeral march, and then to a kind of shepherd's song.
This, on the slopes of optimism, leads to another vigorous dance
movement. Variation 16, commencing with an emphatic A flat
(corresponding to the G sharp of the introduction), paraphrases
the principal melody and acts as a prelude to the Finale.

The first part of the Finale, *vivace*, deals intensively with a more metrical version of the original theme (an authentic variant, in fact):

44

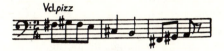

This is whipped up to a high degree of excitement and ends over a pedal figure

45

the relevance of which to the whole work is readily apparent, especially since after thirty bars the last quaver is modified by a natural in order to strike the D major *Andante Cantabile* in which the main theme is proudly given—*nobilmente* one might say—in the strings. Thereafter is a coda, inspired, as the *Te Deum*, by uplifting brass.

As the fulfilment of Kodály's aspirations and intentions, as a work of evident organic growth and creative energy, the *Variations* stand out not only among modern Hungarian but also modern European music.

The words of the folksong (with additions by Ady), both pertinent and allusive, run as follows:

> The peacock flew to the County Hall [beneath which was the jail, hence the point] for the freedom of many poor young men.
>
> Proud and delicate peacocks dazzle [even] the sun with their feathers;
> They proclaim news of new things that are to be.
>
> [They signify] new things that will come at the end
> [Of] new struggles: these [shine in] new eyes
> And smile up to the sky.
>
> New minds stir the old Hungarian trees
> And await, expectantly, new Hungarian wonders.

Are we foolish? Have all of us lost our way?
Will our beliefs turn to reality?
Will our Hungarian words give new meanings?
Or will Hungarian life remain, as of old, sorrowful?
Will the flame strike [and consume] the old County Hall—the
symbol of ferocity?
Or will our souls stay longer in subjugation?

It is small wonder that such texts, created out of long discontents, should be regarded with official suspicion, and that in the fulness of tyrannical oppression Kodály's orchestral apotheosis of the folk-song should come under interdict.

It is not impossible to appreciate a baroque ancestry in the *Peacock Variations*, and the same impulses that led Bach to expatiate on chorale motivs are present, in occasional figuration, in melodic adornment, in the implicit relationship with a text.[1] In the work produced at the same time as the *Variations*, the *Concerto for Orchestra*, other baroque methods are apparent.

CONCERTO FOR ORCHESTRA

The *Concerto* takes over the main tonality of the *Variations*—D, fundamentally Dorian, and comprises three sections: *Allegro risoluto*; *Largo*, Aeolian in flavour and with a key signature of three sharps; and *Tempo primo*, the latter section being, broadly speaking, recapitulatory. As John Weissmann[2] points out, Kodály faced particular problems when composing for instruments: 'His idiom, and generally that of Hungarian music, is essentially vocal in character.' This, perhaps, is the point at which Kodály separates himself from the main body of twentieth-century composers: it is also the point at which the main strength of his music lies. The *Concerto* maintains its vocal connections in the intervallic relationships within melodic gestures; in the particular, private, logic of minor phrases, or lesser note-groups, in the individual instrumental parts—all of which will be found basically singable; in the essentially choral-type middle section. The counterpoint of this section, fluent and often even voluptuous, is

[1] Cf. the free arrangement of the same song for male voices in *The Peacocks* [*sic*] (Budapest, 1937; English version, 1957).
[2] 'Kodály's Later Orchestral Music (1)', in *Tempo*, No. 17, 1950, p. 16 *et seq.*

inevitable in the way that that of the Italian High Renaissance (modern Hungarian music carries a good deal of the tradition of *bel canto*) is voluptuous: apt for voices, but also for instruments. Within his own terms of reference, Kodály's problem was not a great one. Vocal music was fundamental, but not necessarily antithetical to instrumental music. From the outskirts of song was the melisma, which could easily expand into a subsidiary, accompanimental, figure which could in turn meet the improvisations peculiar to Hungarian instrumental music: thus, in every orchestral work, his treatment of the woodwind is noticeable. In the same way the harp could, as in the *Concerto*, idealise the cimbalum. Incorporated within these possibilities was also the other vital, national, element: the dance.

It is, then, with the physical thrust of the dance that the *Concerto* begins:

46   Allegro risoluto

f (strings in octaves)   stacc.

This, in the formal manner of folk-song, is repeated a fifth higher. The originating material, broken down into its component parts, is developed, extended into more patent Baroque rhythmic derivatives, and dispersed mostly between contrasting strings and woodwind. From the syncopated bass that shows at the fifth bar stems a second subject, given to the horns

47

and then repeated by them above a correlated theme in the 'cellos. This builds to a large climax, with trills in the high woodwind and sextuplets in the violins—characteristic features of Kodály's technique in scoring for brilliance, and turns into a brief restatement of Ex. 46. At the end of the section a sustained G sharp above the dominant A again recalls the *Variations*. The *Largo* is carried on this large and evocative theme

48

which throws out a rich contrapuntal texture,[1] submits itself to variation treatment, and again reaches to a climax. In the final section all the previously heard material is restated, but with still-developing energy that enhances canonic, fugato, stretto, devices, and enriched harmonies, which are all reduced into a compelling coda which finally and triumphantly incorporates Ex. 46.

As a synthesis of ideas the *Concerto* is remarkable, not least on account of its formal clarity. Like the *Variations*, this is a masterly piece of musical planning: the more so because its architecture is more apparent to the ear than to the eye. It can never be said of Kodály that he does not hear what he writes.

The *Concerto* was again a commission, from the Chicago Philharmonic Society, to celebrate the jubilee of its foundation. By the time the work was completed war had broken out and that Kodály, as was intended, should conduct its first performance was impossible. The première did not, in fact, take place until 6 February 1941—the score having been taken to America by Bartók, who finally left Hungary at the beginning of 1940.

[1] Cf. W. R. Anderson in *Musical Times*, November 1946; '. . . a meditative, slow middle part in rich string style, like a modern rethinking of Tudor feeling, in that happy blend of harmonic and contrapuntal writing that he commands.'

10

Renaissance Models

DURING the Second World War the fortunes of Hungary touched their lowest point. A government intent on revisionism, but unwilling to adventure too far in the dangerous company of Hitler, found itself impaled on the horns of a dilemma. To enlarge the Hungarian territories, however, was an obsession, and thus it was that a strong pro-Axis line was adopted—though not without a show of unrest that unseated Béla Imrédy. After him Pál Teleki took over the premiership, and, steering a more direct course towards disaster, imposed stricter controls on Jews and on members of left-wing organisations. In 1940 the so-called Second Vienna Award restored to Hungary almost half of the lost territories, and the Government signed the Tripartite Pact a few months later. It was still the hope of the ruling classes in Hungary to avoid war—and when its imminence seemed inevitable Teleki committed suicide. Thereafter Horthy, speculating on a possible Allied victory, endeavoured, first through László Bárdossy, and then through Miklós Kállay, to engineer secret bargains with the Western Powers, while still maintaining convenient relations with the Germans, on whose account the Hungarians were fighting on the Eastern front. In January 1943 the Hungarian Army was virtually destroyed at Voronezh. A year later Hitler, well aware of the duplicity of the Government in Budapest and of doubtful loyalties in the country generally, compelled Horthy to impose on his people a completely collaborationist régime, under which all supposed enemies of the régime, and the greater part—about 80 per cent.—of the Jewish population, were removed. On 15 October 1944 the eastern part of Hungary was occupied by the Russians, with whom Horthy tried to arrange an armistice. But, controlled by Germans, he was impotent to reject their order to withdraw from such negotiations. Ferenc Szálasi, leader of the

Arrow Cross Party, took over the Government. Under the
stubbornness of German resistance, Hungary was subjected to an
attritional campaign of retreat, and Budapest was all but destroyed.
During the battle the Russians invested the ancient city of Pest, but
were compelled to fight for the conquest of Buda, across the
river, for almost seven weeks. During this time the inhabitants,
bombarded all round the clock, lived in cellars. Kodály took
shelter first in the air-raid shelter of a Convent School in Propheta
Road (*For St. Agnes's Day* was composed in memory of the Mother
Superior of this House), and then in the basement of the Opera
House, where he worked on the score of the *Missa Brevis*. Perhaps
this work, set against the background of the period in which
it was written, is the supreme example of the composer's faith.

'Faith' is a large and complex word. When applied to Kodály it
may only be used in its most extended sense. Working from the
centre outwards, Kodály has always been distinguished by a
faith in himself, and in his powers, but which stops short of
arrogance and is irradiated by humour; by a faith in the Magyar
destiny that would be described as mystical were it not applied
to the practical circumstances from which, in fact, it derives;
and by a generous appreciation, uncircumscribed by dogmatism,
of the Christian tenets that have, throughout history, inspired his
race. To say that Kodály is an individualist is the one side of
truth; the other shows him an individualist concerned for the
effect of his individual actions on the communities of which he is
part. At times such a man is liable to be swimming against the
current: what matters is that he is a good swimmer. In this
instance the metaphor is less than metaphor.

Kodály, an international figure of acknowledged eminence,
stayed in Hungary throughout the war. He had, prior to its
outbreak, made his declaration on basic issues of 1938, when
combining with Bartók and others to demand equality of rights
for citizens. Later he and Bartók declaimed against racial intoler-
ance; alas, without result. Under the political conditions of the
times, in so far as he was able, Kodály simply continued on the
pedagogic, and prophetical, course he had set himself. He taught
at the Academy of Music until 1942, both in composition, and
in the appreciation of folk-song (on which he had previously

lectured in the University), and supervised the work of the school singing-teachers now formed into an Association. Being in one way a fundamentalist, he devoted himself, in an almost Johannine manner, to his own *Logos* theory. Thus in 1939 he adjudicated in a competition, sponsored by the University, for 'correct pronunciation', and continued so to do in subsequent years. Epigrams relative to this topic are self-explanatory. 'The language', he said in 1935, 'is the creation of millions, and it lives more truly the more people use it consciously.' In 1941 he put language as a source of regeneration: 'speech, pronunciation, is only an expression of, is dependent on, a new type of Hungarian culture, which is what we should be striving for'. In 1943 Kodály participated in a Committee appointed by the Academy of Sciences to study the Hungarian language, and eight years later he was president of a philological congress.

In 1940 the theme of a new national ethos was stressed in a lecture. 'If we really desire a new life for our country—and who is there who does not?—then we must seek regeneration through our music as well.' In the next year there appeared the first volumes in what has later been built up into *The Choral Method*. It was in 1941 also that Kodály failed to be elected a Member of the Academy of Sciences. Political forces were, as for many years, eager to destroy a reputation by stealth. In 1943, however, Kodály was made a Member of this body. By this time he had passed his sixtieth birthday, had retired from his official teaching post at the Academy of Music,[1] and had been publicly honoured in many ways.

An excellent *Festschrift*, a symposium of learned essays, was issued in Budapest in honour of the occasion, with Government backing. Through the circumstances of the times, however, many who would have done so were unable to send contributions. At Kolozsvár, in the Székely district, Kodály was especially honoured on account of his long connection with the region and the *Dances of Galánta,* the *Te Deum, Háry János,* and the Second String Quartet (played by the Budapest String Quartet, led by Sándor Végh) were all included in the season's programme.

[1] Kodály was succeeded at the Academy by János Viski (1906-60), one of his former pupils, and sometime head of the Conservatory in Kolozsvár.

The most rewarding tribute, perhaps, was that of the National Federation of Choral Societies, whose well-being had depended so much on Kodály's interest and works: they declared a Kodály Year. Such demonstrations move and a little surprise Kodály, but serve to renew in him a sense of past or present obligations, above all the obligation to preserve both humanism and humanity. It was under this obligation that in the worst days of oppression Kodály, apparently occupied in his professional commitments, took such steps as were open to him to succour the persecuted: through his intermediacy, Jews, and others, were enabled to escape. Six months after the Russian army had expelled the German forces from Hungary the Kodálys, their home heavily damaged, went to stay in Pécs at the invitation of the municipality. From Pécs they moved to Dombóvár as guests of László Péczeli, a teacher of Hungarian literature and German in a secondary school, and his wife, a teacher of singing, long devoted to the music of the master.

The record of these years is in a number of choral pieces, in which Kodály recreates the synthesis of idea and music that distinguished the choral music of the later Renaissance. It is part of Kodály's argument that Hungary, through force of circumstance, missed out on large tracts of the Western European tradition. Thus, in so far as he can, he fills the gap, but not by archaism. His *a cappella* works are comparable with those of the sixteenth century—favouring Venice or south Germany rather than Rome—and adopt similar procedures: which, since the glory of the medium lies in the conquest of its limitations, is but common sense. Further, Kodály, like his great predecessors, wrote with a sense of urgency. His works were to be performed, were, so far as possible, to be taken in the stride. Of the works of less than epic stature of his later life there are none which cannot be read at sight with a reasonable hope of success by an averagely good amateur choir.

A CAPPELLA WORKS

The *Hymn to King Stephen* was composed in 1938. Although mainly homophonic, this piece depends on contrapuntal incipits and on the free variations set above or below the initiating cantus firmus. In the *Battle Song* of 1943, the words being by Petőfi, a double-choir is used with dramatic force. This brilliant and exciting exposition of pride in the traditional bravery of the Hungarian people, tempered with the memories of past disaster and the need for sacrifice, is of the order of the valorous music heard centuries before by Sidney. It is a study in vital rhythms and in sonorities that range far, but with certain direction. This, for example, is a sharper harmonic edge than is associated with the composer:

But the acridity is applied within the boundaries of choral competence. In the same year a fine setting of *Psalm 121* appeared, and here the mood and the lay-out recall Schütz, who too could urge a wealth of emotional experience into small compass. By dividing the parts, Kodály, as is his habit, manages to put two choirs into one, the effective contrast being between the lower and upper groupings. Another Petőfi setting of the same period was the rather simpler, *To The Transylvanians*. All these works, their texts having relevance to the national situation, were apposite to the times; but they are not bound to time, nor even to place. The music is timeless, but also referential.

These choral works lie at one end of the spectrum: at the other are the exercises which Kodály designed more or less at the same time to ensure that in due course there would be a sufficiency of singers able to perform the larger things. The world might be disintegrating. Kodály, with concern for those who must ultimately reintegrate it, began to expose the fundamentals of correct intonation in the philosophic belief (otherwise directly promulgated) that perfect harmony in music was an aid to a similar condition in human affairs. The introduction to *Let Us sing Correctly*, in which one vocal part learns immediately to adjust itself to a second, is characteristically down-to-earth: '. . . The "C-major-scale-method" is the enemy of correct singing. Every interval must be memorised separately, and each in its particular characteristic tonal function, not fitted together as steps of a scale. Those who try to sing the longer intervals by climbing up the scale will find them but slowly and vaguely. The scale will sound correct only when its 'pillars' are established in advance, and true "pillars" are the notes of the pentatonic scale . . .' There followed *Fifteen Two-part Exercises*, in which what has been learned in *Let Us sing Correctly* is put to a severer test in free, and varied counterpoint. Of greater importance are the four volumes of *Bicinia Hungarica,* in which there are almost 200 miniature masterpieces; perhaps the finest vocal pieces ever to be devised for the use of schools. In the *Bicinia Hungarica* are folk-songs, each deftly arranged in a fluent counterpoint that runs out of the originating melody according to the principle of melodic genesis that characterises Kodály's manner of invention. There are arrangements of psalm- and hymn-tunes, of classical provenance, and original settings of texts taken from the classical Hungarian poets. There are also excerpts from the *Kalevala* epic. In these works Kodály provides an imaginative, and inspiring, background to the Hungarian child's acquisition of the history of his own people: with the advantage that it is non-polemical. Some years later, when the English edition of *Bicinia Hungarica* was in preparation, Kodály turned a nice compliment in the prefatory notice he was writing: 'I am', he said, "now very pleased to return to the English what I learned from them, and was able to adapt to our own needs in Hungary.'

In this period of intensive educational effort Kodály also issued a primary stage sight-reading manual, of 333 graded exercises. Beginning with two-note melodies, guided by the sol-fa system—in which Kodály puts as much faith as an old-style Welsh precentor, and working through a nicely graded progression of patterns of gradually increasing difficulty the pupil can hardly fail to achieve some sort of practical skill, and, since everything that Kodály puts down on manuscript paper is to be seen as music and not merely a pedagogic implement, immediate contact with a great composer.[1] That is, if the teachers are on their mark. For obvious reasons that was a grave problem in 1943 and so it was for the most of another decade. But Kodály was building for the future—with an impatience at frustration of his plans that he does not ever easily conceal.

MISSA BREVIS

In 1942 Kodály composed a work for organ, and this, an 'Organ-Mass' was given its first performance in St. Stephen's Cathedral by Sebestyén Pécsi (b. 1910), organist at the Basilica and later a professor of organ.[2] In 1944 the composer, who had in the beginning added liturgical extracts to his manuscript, transformed the *Mass* into a choral work, with accompaniment for organ or orchestra. In the early part of 1945 the *Mass* was performed in an improvised concert-room in the Opera House, where the Kodálys had lived during the past weeks while the work was being completed. The dedication was to Emma Kodály 'in anniversario XXXV'.

The *Mass*, in the basic key of D (minor-major), begins and ends with an introduction and a postlude, the latter entitled *Ite missa est*. The relationship between voices and organ (orchestra) is similar to that in the beautiful *Pange Lingua*, of 1931, with the latter maintaining and enriching the choral texture, but adding occasional and significant independent figuration. In the close connection between the principal vocal and instrumental lines the manner of late Renaissance instrumentation is again recalled. Indeed, in so far as the *Mass* is the least obviously national of Kodály's large-scale works and in its predominantly contrapuntal character, it is the one which most clearly shows the influence of the polyphonic era. But the polyphonic impulse may be felt to have reached Kodály through an assimilation of *seconda prattica*, as in Monteverdi. A striking feature of the work is the way in which the colour of the harmony is affiliated to the contrapuntal inclinations of the voices, to the general intention of melody, or to particular rhythmic tendencies. For instance, the last bars of the

---

[1] See p. 190, for reference to Kodály's terms for giving an autograph to the young.
[2] See List of Recordings, p. 220, entered under Chamber Music.

Introit move thus towards an original kind of non-categorisable cadence, which leaves the opening chord of the "Kyrie" as a natural corollary:

50

Kyrie

Another excellent example of harmonic progress which grows out of a general situation is the dominant seventh chord (based on F sharp) which prefaces, and resolves into the chord of G major (second inversion) assigned to the opening of the "Cum Sancto Spiritu" section of the "Gloria." From here to the end of this movement there are more examples of the so-called dominant seventh chord than in almost any other work of the twentieth century. Their placing, their resolution, and their contrasting fundamentals demonstrate that a composer can just as readily discover new paths leading from the nineteenth century as from the fifteenth. As a composer Kodály is eminently practical, and theories of procedure are not allowed to obtrude. It is because of this that the *Mass* is an original contribution to the literature of liturgical music. It combines Kodály's known affections, so far as styles are concerned, into a comprehensive whole that escapes the pejorative 'eclectic'.

The Introit builds at once on a diatonic accumulation of D, A, E, G, A, E, G—sounded successively but sustained and then resolved into a D minor triad. In bar 12 this figure, with its ecclesiastical overtones of association, commences:

51

This, which looks towards the first movement of the Symphony, is found in augmentation in the "Kyrie" (at first above a tonic

pedal), and at the end of the "Agnus Dei". In the Introit, which
grows from Examples 50 and 51, the second idea is shown at one
moment more or less rhapsodically and in the orchestral version
is given to the solo clarinet. The "Kyrie", mostly in two parts
(alto and bass), and above the pedal, is relatively austere and dark
in colouring. On the other hand "Christe eleison" is assigned
principally to high voices—three solo sopranos being employed—
and the chords are intensified through ingenious, but minimal,
movement of inner and lower parts. Since the final "Kyrie"
section, developed from the opening of the movement, concludes
with a *tierce de Picardie* the tenors are ready to go directly into the
exultant tonality of D major:

52

The shape of this phrase, subjected to rhythmic variations,
provides material for figures which are set into the accompaniment
during the progress of the movement; while the mediant serves,
Haydn-wise, to switch to the tonal centre of F sharp major, or to
F sharp minor. "Qui tollis", indeed, commences in this key and the
words are set for alto, tenor, and bass solo voices. At the words
Quoniam tu solus sanctus the opening motiv is returned, but
extended to a triad—the unexpected triad of D sharp major, from
which point the music moves to the final, climactic, Amens,
and to D major. A similar sense of economy of thematic material,
of fluent development, and of form, distinguishes the Credo—
also inaugurated by a diatonic statement, parented by plainsong
(s s l s f s r) and folk-song (s d' r' f' r' d f s s). The central section
of this movement is remote, in E flat minor, and with the word
crucifixus movingly set in a high register, wherein suspensions
and passing notes underline the significance of the word. From
this point the parts move downwards to a dark cadence at
sepultus est, the last chord again being a *tierce de Picardie*, preparatory to *Et resurrexit* and the return of G major.

The "Sanctus" is closely worked about a four note incipit—
d r s f—which, in diminution, underlies the disparate triads of the

"Hosanna". The final chord being a second inversion of D major the music is poised for the "Benedictus", when the alto commences, in D major, but, after two bars, slips into the mediant key of F sharp, in which the final "Hosanna" section ends (again on a second inversion, beautifully laid out for soprano and alto above the pedal bass), after a review of the striking triadic sequence of the first section. But this is looked at from the other side, as it were; from F sharp rather than from D. In the "Agnus Dei" material from earlier movements is employed and the process of recapitulation is carried into the "Ite Missa est", where the main Credo motivs form the basis. In the vocal score the movement is shown in its original form, without voices, as a postlude, and it would seem preferable to use this rather than the version with words, which, at this point are superfluous, and were added eventually to suit the conventions of concert performance.

The first British performance of the *Mass*, together with *Jesus and the Traders*, was given in a broadcast by the Belfast Co-operative Choir in October 1945. In 1948, conducted by the composer and now scored for orchestra, it was given at the Three Choirs Festival, at Worcester, and was repeated at the Gloucester Festival two years later: since which time it has formed a regular part of the English choral repertoire.

11

Reconstruction in Hungary

THE WAR being over Hungary, ravaged by battle and impoverished through the depredations of alien forces, began the long and arduous process of reorientation—under the aegis of the U.S.S.R. and the successive governments of Ferenc Nagy and Mátyás Rákosi. The rebuilding of an economy, the reordering of industrial and commercial method, and of society itself, were in accordance with the demands of the new united Communist and Social Democrat parties and the strategic requirements of the Russians. The changes in Hungary, for so long a country controlled by fascist principles, were revolutionary and unwelcome to many. Education was affected to this extent: that the domination of religious bodies was removed (although religious instruction was permitted), and with it the caste system that had previously obtained. For the first time in Hungarian history all children went to school (before 1945 about 10 per cent. of Hungarian children did not go to school), and general schools, under Government supervision, were instituted. There was an expansion of post-general school (i.e. high school) facilities, an increase in university and technological education, and much new ground was broken in the field of adult studies—vital in a community where there were still those who, through past lack of opportunity, were illiterate.

It was the beginning of a new era, and Kodály accepted the challenge. For him there was little change, for the ideal of what Hungary should be always lay ahead, in the future. A new type of government could hardly be less responsive to his urgings than its predecessors, and, conceivably, since new precepts of equality were bruited, it was possible that musical education could take shelter under these precepts. Kodály was a member of no political party, but his record as artist and citizen was unassailable, and if a choice had to be made between the labels 'reactionary' or 'progressive' it was clear which should properly be pinned to him. In 1945 he was made Chairman of the new Arts Council, President of the Association of Musicians, and a member of the Council of the Academy of Music.

Thus invested with authority, Kodály seized the opportunity to plan a consistent method of musical education, such as would assist in the general regeneration of his country. In 1945 he published a paper which announced, yet again, his thesis: 'Our musical public education has meant seventy years of erratic wandering, and that is why it has produced no results. . . . They wanted to teach the people music by ignoring, by throwing aside, what the people knew of their own accord. Yet it is only possible to build upon what exists, using the folk heritage as a foundation, otherwise we shall build on air.'[1] But Kodály was not one who, holding authority, contented himself with platitudes and the statement of vague aspirations. Progress must be planned. 'Every thinking music teacher', he wrote in the Preface to *24 Little Canons on the Black Keys*, 'realises the faults of the old methods, but still continues to use them. If music is to become common property and not only the privilege of the few, we shall have to look for new ways.' In 1945 a new set of eight song-books (in collaboration with Jenő Ádám) was issued as a first pedagogic step, and was universally used until its supersession by a new

[1] At the same time, but quite independently, Sir Henry Wood was advocating methods in respect of English general musical education that were similar to those initiated by Kodály. Thus:

'. . . This is so urgent a matter that I cannot speak too strongly regarding the method of approach in many instances. Children must be taught in a specialised manner, and I hope that the day of the semi-amateur school music-teaching will soon be ruled out. . . .

'. . . I could wish that the method I suggest with regard to training school orchestras could be adopted for singing classes in schools. If these children were taught to sing the daily hymn with good diction and intonation, and the little class-ditties treated in the same method, I am sure it would create a love for this very health-giving exercise, and would be a means of bringing back the voices and singers we need so much. One professor could manage several schools in a given radius, and as a specialist would justify the expenditure, and at the same time relieve the school teacher for duties to which he or she is specially suited, and would, I think, institute a love for singing and orchestral playing to the lasting benefit of the future adult generations.' 'Children's Orchestras and Choirs', in *About Conducting*, London, 1945, pp. 116 and 119.

series in 1948; in these books the sol-fa system, hitherto hardly known by Hungarian educationists, was shown as the necessary foundation for effective singing. At the same time the young pianist was brought into the pentatonic scheme by the *24 Little Canons on the Black Keys* and the *Children's Dances*, also 'for the black keys': both consanguineous with Bartók's *Mikrokosmos*. More importantly Kodály in 1945 inaugurated his first specially devised music course at Pécs, an ancient Transdanubian city with relics of Roman and Turkish occupation; this being an experiment which was to grow into a significant, and unique, department of Hungarian education. In 1948 the scheme was tried at Békéstarhos, but was discontinued by doubting officials in 1950. In that year, however, the tentative scheme was expanded into the first fully organised General School of Music and Singing, which was established in Kecskemét. This—promoted with admirable celerity in view of the fact that the reorganisation of education had so far had only five years in which to settle down—was, as the name suggests, a school belonging to the established pattern for children between the ages of six and fourteen. Since the foundation of the first of the General Schools of Music—for which parents may opt, and the demand increasingly exceeds the supply—about a hundred have been established in various parts of the country, and, tentatively, some six or seven secondary schools of music have been set up in recent years. In a General School of Music, the Director of Music being its head-master, and a general teacher acting as second-in-command, a normal curriculum is followed, except that more music tuition is available. In the first class (since singing is the foundation of all musical experience) there are six singing lessons weekly. In the second class recorder-playing and group music-making is obligatory, while in the third class instrumental music is optionally introduced. The purpose of this special course is not primarily vocational, but to infuse a broad strain of musical culture into the community as a whole. In fact—and this is inevitable—there is now a proportion of professional artists, and students in the Academy of Music, who have passed through this course. It was the prospect of hearing an ex-General Music School pupil in the passing-out examination of students of the Opera School of the Academy that drew Kodály to the Opera House one evening in the summer of 1962: his pride in this development is, justifiably, considerable.

As he has so often said himself, his work in the general field of education is Kodály's principal devotion. In this commitment, which has obstructed his advance as a composer *par sang*, he is unique. As to his achievement (to be appreciated outside of Hungary through a small number of recordings) there are many witnesses. Of these two may be quoted. First, Tibor Kozma, Professor of Musicology in Bloomington University, Indiana, U.S.A.:

'The results must be heard to be believed. When they are understood, their true meaning should be shouted from the rooftops. The point is not that ten-year-old children sing, often sight-reading, Palestrina, Schütz and Kodály choruses of complicated harmonic and contrapuntal problems with the utmost clarity, precision and correctness: such feats were accomplished before through dedicated training of hand-picked youngsters. The point is that this is done as part of a general school curriculum, with "average" children without exceptional musical gifts. The very word "sight-reading"—this paralysing bugaboo of music-makers everywhere—has lost its meaning to these children. They would no more think of "sight-reading" a page of music than of "sight-reading" a newspaper. They simply *read* it; they would consider themselves illiterate if they could not. While traditional musical pedagogy the world over is laboriously bringing up a crop of outstandingly competent instrumentalists and singers of a highly specialised training for whom there may never be an outlet as their fellow citizens seem to be more interested in high-fidelity phonographs than in music, Kodály's life-work converts a whole nation into connoisseurs of music, into an audience of which artists have vainly dreamt for generations.

'What we see here in the making is, if its potentialities are permitted to mature into fulfilment, an entirely fresh departure, a completely new beginning in the history of music. It contains the promise of a truly democratic musical culture in which quantity and quality may at last be reconciled. This promise of a future in which the torn body of music may yet be whole again, in the creative as well as on the social level, makes Zoltán Kodály only one of the most meaningful phenomena in twentieth-century music.'[1]

Second, from *The Times* of 15 April 1959:

'On our last visit to the Hungarian capital, we again had the opportunity to hear the Children's Choir of Radio Budapest; this time, however, they sang only music by Bartók and Kodály, and the whole private concert which was *a cappella*, consisted of pieces the technical difficulty of which simply staggered the imagination. Among other things, were were introduced to the series of two- and three-part vocal exercises which Kodály has written as part of his training course for the elementary schools. The most difficult of these are, incorporated in . . . *Tricinia*, 28 three-part exercises. Not only is the music a fabulous mixture of Palestrina, Gesualdo and the harsh, dissonant austerity so characteristic of Kodály's later style. ("Like the winter wind over the Hungarian plain", was a colleague's comment); but the children sang the most advanced enharmonic modulations in perfect pitch.

'The music, moreover, is often written in the old soprano, mezzo-soprano, and alto C-clefs and in keys running up to five flats. We know a good many professional musicians who would find some difficulty in negotiating *a prima vista* this combination of old clefs and enharmonic modulations of dazzling complexity.'

During this post-war period Kodály's wider interests in musical education increasingly bore fruit. 'Formerly', he said, 'we had good *bourgeois* audiences, a public which was rather well educated. They're gone. Then we got a very bad public, and what I am trying to do—if one can say it—is to elevate the general public's taste. And so I started at the only level you can start, in the schools.'[2] The new public began to be built up from the schools, but also through the new generation of teachers, and through the newly developed institutes of adult education (variously named, but serving this purpose). Through this medium, and by adapting and revitalising already existing bodies, a great new active public has been encouraged towards music through participation. In the City choir in Budapest (in which many teachers are members), the civic choir in Pécs (to which music students in the Conservatorium are admitted), and the Kodály choir in Debrecen, standards are high, and the rehearsal discipline—three times a week—severe. The Festival movement, under the aegis of the Institute for Folk Arts, and taking its first inspiration from the eighteenth-century choral tradition of Debrecen, includes 100,000 singers, which are dispersed into some thirty or forty festivals in all parts of the country. The general musical director of the Festival movement is Zoltán Vásárhelyi, and the principal conductors Lajos Bárdos and Imre Csenki. Kodály has been involved in this activity since its inception, and from time to time has participated in the festivals not only as patron but also as conductor.

Imre Csenki, formerly a student of the Academy of Music in Budapest, was Director of the Debrecen College Choir immediately after the war, and in 1948 took that Choir on a tour of Switzerland. In 1950 he became conductor of the newly found State Folk-Ensemble, a co-ordinated team consisting of choir, folk-orchestra, and dancers, recruited after a countrywide search for talent and added to, from time to time, from amateur ranks. It was for this body that Kodály composed his *Kálló Folk Dances* in 1951, the first performance being on 4 April of that year.

OCCASIONAL PIECES

The Kálló Dances, first described at the end of the seventeenth century, but not noted until 1895, belonged to Nagykálló, one of the towns of the north-eastern county of Szaboles-Szatmár. Kodály arranged them for a quasi-folk-ensemble—chorus and a brilliant instrumentation comprising E♭ clarinet, two B♭ clarinets, cimbalum, and strings. The result is exciting, not least of all in the tonal unity that is accomplished by the assimilation of harmony by rhythm and orchestral colouring. The sophistication of the former, which would appeal to the eye and to the ear in close analysis, are felt as no more than inflections of plain speech. These dances, temperamentally allied with those of Galánta and Marosszék, but bolder, more strident in texture, more improvisatory, are the meeting-point of the two traditions, of the folk and of the gipsies. Having argued at one stage for a judicial separation Kodály thus reunited the natural, complementary elements in Magyar popular music. In commencing with one interpretation of 'popular', Kodály ends with another: the *Kálló Folk Dances* are enormously popular. In the *Soldier's Song* of 1951, a piece for male voices, Kodály again shows a happy application of the common touch, by adding side-drum and trumpet to the vocal ensemble. The trumpet is at first concerned with a commonplace signal borrowed from the old (and hated) Austrian Army, and then one, more optimistic, from the Rákóczi song. Immediately these appear to tincture the score with a Stravinskyan insouciance and an engaging impertinence in dissonance, but to the initiate they provide the necessary allusions. This makes a fine piece for a musical festival (competitive): but the British male voice choir— once one of our minor musical glories—is almost a thing of the past; assassinated by bad music and negligence. As a practical matter, it is worth pointing out that Kodály in general prefers three-part writing to four for a male ensemble, thus giving a clarity and flexibility that is often missing in this medium.

During this period Kodály continued to write numerous choral works. Some, like the setting of Sándor Weöres's *A Song for Peace,* the variations on the *Marseillaise* contained in *A Hymn to Liberty,* and the arrangement of Petőfi's *National Ode,* for the Ensemble of the Hungarian Army, were *ad hoc* pieces, reflecting current hopes and aspirations which, though officially inspired, had deep roots. A fine setting of *Psalm L* renews older links, with the *Genevan Psalter* (see also *Bicinia Hungarica,* IV, Nos. 117 and 118), and with that part of Hungarian literature that derived inspiration from the asperities of Calvinism, for the words Kodály used were those of Albert Molnár (1574-1634). The setting of *Psalm CXIV* is an allied work, distinguished by vigorous counterpoint and by an organ part that contains manual roulades borrowed from the Kálló climate and pedal exertions of an entertaining literalness. The mountains skip

 53a

and the earth trembles

53b

and the organist must heel and toe with an alacrity some long time forgotten. Such ingenuousness is out of fashion in organ accompaniments, unless in those of Britten. In 1955 a larger work, for baritone solo and *a cappella* choir, appeared: the *Hymn of Zrinyi*. This, 'dedicated to the faithful companion of my life at her sick-bed on our 45th anniversary', was given its first performance . . . by Imre Palló and the Hungarian Radio Choir, conducted by Zoltán Vásárhelyi. The *Hymn of Zrinyi* returns to the spirit of the *Psalmus Hungaricus*: it is, at the same time, an injunction to the artist not to relinquish his responsibilities as citizen and patriot.

HYMN OF ZRINYI

Miklós Zrinyi (1620-64) was the grandson of one of Hungary's famous heroes in the struggle against the Turk and the Austrian. Zrinyi also fought against the Turks, and inveighed against them and the Austrians in his literary works. As a military leader, Zrinyi succeeded in defeating the Turks at Szent Gotthard, near the Austrian frontier, but his victory was cancelled by Leopold I, who did a deal with the Turks in the Peace of Vasvár and recognised the acquisition by them of Transylvania. It was an old story and one of the reasons for Hungarians insuring against the frailties of the sword by the power of the pen. In *The Peril of Sziget* Zrinyi, modelling a poem after the manner of Tasso, added notably to the epic literature of his country. In a pamphlet, *Medicine against Turkish Opium*, he went ahead of his time, and in a practical direction, promoting the idea of a national army recruited from the peasantry. It was from this work that Kodály drew the text of the *Hymn of Zrinyi*.

The *Hymn of Zrinyi* begins with a fable. The baritone soloist narrates how when Sardis, in Persia, was invaded a soldier discovering King Croesus made as to kill him; at this point the King's son, silent since birth, cried out:

The narrator continues, but points the analogy and the cry of the prince is transformed to 'Hands off [save] the Magyar', and the harmonic pattern is changed to a clearer definition of three major triads (in second inversion). The verbal phrase is repeated at frequent intervals throughout the work, and the music to which it is set varies according to context with striking harmonic relevance.

After the exordium the solo voice contemplates the misery into which the nation has fallen in a freely flowing quasi-recitative, above which three parts—at first sopranos and altos, then sopranos and tenors, lastly sopranos and contraltos again—move in self-commiseration. The soloist, complaining that he alone is insufficient to save his country, alerts the people, foresees a great catastrophe, the shape of which is shown by the chorus in a brief, Bachian outburst culminating in a fiery chord of F sharp major. In the next paragraph the lower voices, commencing in urgent imitation, detail the depredations of the Turkish invaders. For a moment the possibility of finding refuge elsewhere is considered, but rejected. The first act concludes with a Latin phrase, *Hic vobis vincendum vel moriendum est* ['Here we must conquer, or perish']. A half-close in F sharp minor is also the conclusion of the tonal scheme that has emerged from the Aeolian beginning.

In the next main section the people are reminded of their heritage of valour, but the solo voice chides those who have allowed this national reputation to sink low and the cause of disaster is analysed within the body corporate:

55

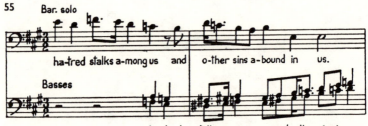

Against a mainly wordless choral background in which the
general lyrical quality is punctuated by 'Hands off the Magyar'
the narrator looks optimistically forward in the premise that 'we
are no worse than any other people'. Outspread chords, each
containing a seventh piled on a seventh, give poignancy to the
recurrent idea and a fine, Phrygian close ends the passage.

There follows a mainly contrapuntal account of cowardice—
the people scatter, or sit still, crying out for pity, and finally are
tempted thus—the voices in unison giving force to the phrase:

56

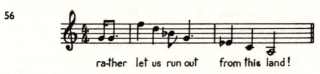

There is, it is said, a desert in which perhaps the Spanish King
will allow settlement; against the narrator the voices other than
the basses fall momentarily into a Spanish idiom, and a sensuous
chord (C, E flat, F sharp, G, A) holds out enticement. But the
temptation is defeated, the solo voice recalls the *Song of Deborah*
and fresh courage is discovered. The tonality moves towards
D major and a fine irradiation of sunlight comes with a supertonic
ninth chord (the sopranos now reaching a high B) as preliminary
to a perfect cadence. This is the starting point for a splendid
fugue subject

57

which, treated Handelianly, brings the whole work to a magnificent ending.

As in *Jesus and the Traders* and the 'choral drama' *Annie Miller*, Kodály allows the music to grow out of the words, with an underlining of their significance by rhythmic and harmonic means rather than by phrase shapes alone. In this work the varied texture of the voice parts, from the technical point of view an aid to the singers, is also conducive to a dramatic interpretation. Freed from precise formulation of a musical pattern dependent on repetition of motivs Kodály gives a prose character to the *Hymn*, but assures musical coherence through a scheme of tonal logic. This is *a cappella* music; that it should remain secure is an important consideration. This Kodály effects through his disposition of tonal centres.

A prophetic work, the *Hymn of Zrinyi*, has the vatic quality of Bloch—a quality more rare in music emanating from a more settled order of living—and, at the same time, the hard objectiveness of Bach. Zrinyi himself was both participant in and critical of the national situation and so too is Kodály. Since, in the history of a nation, time is a matter of little significance, the message of this work is always apt. Its truth is as absolute in 1964 as in 1664. But the end is in hope, in a nine-part chord of D major.

12

Realisation of Scientific Aims

IN SEEKING to establish a new social order in post-war Hungary the idealists (and there were many) were, from time to time, disturbed by conflicting political dogmas. Rákosi was followed by Nagy, before the former once again took control, only to be dismissed for a second time in favour of Gerő, whose brief reign ended in the disastrous outbreaks of 1956, at which point János Kádár became Premier. It was against a background of conflicting loyalties, prejudices, and suspicions that Kodály conducted his own ameliorating campaign. It required vast resources of faith, and of humour. Kodály in the narrow sense is uncommitted to particular and unreasonable dogmas whether of Church or of State, but he is persistent in applauding intentions that, in his view, are founded on principles of equity and justice. An advocate of reform he prefers gradual, evolutionary, processes; and deplores lip-service. On political matters he has expressed himself with a judicious detachment, but never without concern for the perpetuation of Hungary's noblest traditions nor for the welfare, in all departments, of his fellow-countrymen. Throughout his life Kodály has been consistent, disapproving exploitation—whether of men or of nations, inhumanity (of which he has witnessed more than most), and stupidity. It is the latter defect, especially when allied to authority, that incenses him most, and it would be difficult to find one who suffers officious fools less gladly. Because he has remained constant, because he has palpably stood out as Hungary's best-known representative in world affairs, Kodály has remained impregnable and unassailable.

On the occasion of his sixty-fifth birthday Kodály was made a Freeman of Kecskemét and was awarded the Grand Cross of the Order of the Hungarian Republic by the Minister of Education. A year later he was honoured with the Kossuth Prize. In 1952 he was awarded a second Kossuth Prize, the title of 'Eminent Artist', and a further State decoration. His seventieth birthday was otherwise distinguished by Járdányi's *Vörösmarty Symphony* which was composed for the occasion.

In the meanwhile Kodály had been rejoicing in the ambassadorial functions which had been prevented during the War. In 1946-7 he visited France, Switzerland, Britain, the United States, and the Soviet Union. In New York the League of Composers announced a concert in honour of Kodály at which Andor Földes played his transcription of the *Háry János* Suite, the *Dances of Marosszék*, and the *Children's Dances on the Black Keys*, with the manuscript of which Kodály arrived in America. In the Soviet Union, where *Háry János* excited great enthusiasm, Kodály approved the recognition attended to the artist and the thoroughness of musical education. Two years later he conducted further performances of his works in Sweden, Austria, and England—the *Missa Brevis*, orchestrated for this purpose, now taking its place in the repertoire of the Three Choirs Festival (at Worcester, and in 1950 at Gloucester). In the autumn of 1950 there was an outstanding production of *Háry János* in Zürich, conducted by Victor Reinshagen. During this period of activity Kodály was, however, most deeply engaged in the affairs of the Academy of Sciences, of whose Committee of Musicology he became Chairman in 1951. In this year the first volume of the *Corpus Musicae Popularis Hungaricae* was published.

CORPUS MUSICAE POPULARIS HUNGARICAE

This was the beginning of the fulfilment of the wish to preserve the body of Hungarian folk-music that had inspired the founders of the Academy of Sciences far back in 1832, and of the long-held ideals of Bartók and Kodály. Bartók had gone away in 1940 and his death in 1945 had drawn eloquent words from his colleagues on various memorial occasions. In the first place Bartók and Kodály collected the folk-music of Hungary. Then, (having made use of it within their own compositional practice) they considered how best it could be issued. Discussion on method took place over many years, and it was found desirable that a new and logical system of classification should be employed. In general—as in Britain—folk-music had hitherto been fortuitously assembled into volumes unified, if at all, by a regional principle (e.g. county songs), or a functional principle (e.g. as British sea-shanties), but with no reference to structural organisation. In their original outline for a *Corpus Musicae Popularis*, drafted as far back as 1913, Bartók and Kodály were inspired by Ilmari Krohn's method of classifying folk-song material for the Finnish Literary Society (Kodály had himself analysed Kalevala melodies as far back as 1906, made comparisons with Hungarian melodies, and, of course, introduced the poetry of the Kalevala into his own works). Thus they planned the reduction of all melodies to a common terminal note and the consequent division of material into groups possessing common melodic or rhythmic formulae. In 1924 Bartók evolved another system in which the most ancient melodies should be grouped together, then those—of nineteenth-century provenance—which might be described as modern, and finally any which did not fall into either of these groups. When the first volume of the *Corpus Musicae Popularis* was, thanks to long-delayed official support, a publishing practicability Kodály, now assisted by a considerable team of researchers and benefiting from later musicological and ethnological conclusions, prepared as the pilot volume that entitled *Children's Games*. As Kodály explains, the arrangement is necessarily other than in folk-songs proper, because the child's song is based not on line structure but on a constant 2-bar unit. Melodic range is also smaller ('the children's songs end where the adults' songs begin: about an eight-tone range. But even this range of tones is not fully utilised, in fact the vast majority of children's songs consist of five or six tones . . . not filled by different types of scales but by the very same scales, the do-hexachord, the descending *la* to *doh* section of the basic scale'). Despite the difference between children's and adults' music the final classification in each case is musical rather than literary. There is, however, this compromise that within particular groups songs of similar verbal significance are placed together. The order of *Children's Games*, then, is as follows, with each major division broken down into further detail:

(1) songs with a tonal range of *m, r, d,*
(2) hexachordal melodies beginning with *s,*

(3) adult melodies transferred into children's melodies,
(4) melodies of foreign derivation.

As this work proceeded it became clear that other types of folk-music required similar and extraordinary treatment. The second volume to be published centred on the traditional festival days—New Year, Twelfth Night, Carnival, St. Blasius' Day, Sexagesima Sunday, Shrove Sunday, Shrove Tuesday, St. Gregory's Day, Palm Sunday, Easter, Whitsuntide, Midsummer, Harvest, Advent, St. Lucy's Day, Christmas, together with the *Regös* songs[1] (derived from primitive rites which passed into minstrelsy), and the 'name-day' greetings songs. Volume 3 contains Wedding Songs, Volume 4 Courtship Songs, Volume 5 dirges—the only prose songs in the Hungarian tradition, susceptible to improvisation and discovered as a category by Kodály,[2] and Volume 6 Vocational Songs.

From the scientific aspect the work done by Kodály and his collaborators in the *Corpus Musicae Popularis* is incomparable. But Kodály—who paradoxically disapproves the combination of musicologist and composer in one person—has an enthusiasm which allows no musical material merely to remain of documentary interest.

'He for whom the treasury of folk songs is not a dead museum, but a living culture arrested in its development, will browse through these unpretentious little melodies with the excitement of continuous discovery. There is throbbing life in them, for the imagination and invention of the child develops the four simple basic forms into a thousand and one patterns.'[3]

On the one side of the *Children's Songs* are the *333 Sight-reading Exercises,* in which aids to musical literacy the principle of arrangement according to musical behaviour is similar to that in the *Corpus Musicae Popularis*; on the other side is the charming, late set of songs for infants (without accompaniment), entitled *Kis*

---

[1] See 'Children's Songs and Regös Songs in *Folk-music of Hungary*, p. 69 *et seq.*
[2] See *Folk-music of Hungary*, p. 76 *et seq.* This section of the *Corpus Musicae Popularis* was founded on Kodály's early researches in northern Hungary. Much of the material was ready for publication in 1924, but Kodály himself held up publication pending further research into unsolved problems.
[3] Preface to *Children's Games*, Budapest, October 1951.

emberek dalai (1962, English edition, 1964). Thus again the extension of the musicologist into the teacher, and the teacher into the creative artist, may be appreciated.

Kodály's humanism is stirred by current conditions, but nourished by Magyar pride. He sees himself less as an individual artist in his own right than as one link in a strong native cultural chain. To be with Kodály is to live in the present, but also in the past as though it were present. The power of his exegesis derives from the same quality of *Erlebnis*: it is the quality which he appreciates outside of Hungarian literature in the writing of Scott, and in British literature in general. All the work devoted to the *Corpus Musicae Popularis* has been under the compulsion of bringing the living past into the living present. In point of time, the most heroic days in the Hungarian way to freedom are relatively recent, centring on the mid-nineteenth century. In 1952 Kodály paid his respects to János Arany (1817-82).

Arany, who, as will be seen, died in the year in which Kodály was born, was an outstanding figure in the Hungarian literary development. Born of peasant stock Arany,[1] the close friend of Petőfi, wrote epic poems of which the most famous related the story of the fourteenth century legendary character Miklós Toldi. Depending on folk lore and on colloquial vocabulary, Arany did much to strengthen the texture of nineteenth-century poetry. Together with Petőfi, Arany aimed at a democratisation of literature, both in content and appreciation, and a talent for political satire gained for him both friends and enemies. Like Burns (still an inspiration to many Hungarian intellectuals), Arany had an acute ear for folk-poetry and, also like Burns, he recognised the indivisibility of words and music within this province. After his death, Arany left a manuscript collection containing 148 tunes. This was a miscellany, of authentic folk-material, but also of pseudo-folk-song such as was promulgated in the nineteenth century, and of melodies composed by Arany himself. 'If', said Kodály, 'this had been published in [Arany's]

---

[1] Arany was for some time a teacher in the Reformed School at Nagykőrös: for the centenary of the Protestant Teachers' Training college in this town Kodály composed *Cease your bitter weeping* (for S.S.C.), after the original song by Andrew Horváth de Szkhárosi.

lifetime [it] might have exerted considerable influence on the development both of music and of poetry. . . . If he was able to derive inspiration for such poetry as his from a mere handful of songs like this, how much greater inspiration should the poets of our own day be able to discover in the huge collections now available.'[1]

Other scholars followed Kodály's example, and among later publications of national and musicological importance are the editions of Ádám Pálóczi-Horváth by Dénes Bartha, of medieval hymns and sequences by Benjámin Rajeczky, of sixteenth century melodies by Kálmán Csomasz-Tóth, and the extended works of Bartha and Somfai on the music of Haydn (especially in respect of its Hungarian content), and János Maróthy on European folk-song in general.[2]

[1] See *János Arany's Folk-song Collection*, Budapest, 1952, and 'János Arany's Collection of Melodies' in *Papers of the Department of the Hungarian Academy of Sciences*, 1953.
[2] See B. Szabolcsi, '*La situation de la musicologie hongroise*', in *Studia Musicologica* I, Budapest, 1961, p. 9 *et seq.*

13

An International Figure

By now KODÁLY was revered as a patriot *sui generis,* his modest flat in the famous Népkőztársaság útja which leads to the Heroes' Place, one of the landmarks of Budapest. It has afforded Kodály some wry amusement that during his life in Budapest the name of his street has been altered four times, a symbol of the troubled times through which he has driven his own *Laufbahn.* As an official musician laureate, Kodály sat on numerous committees—including the Bartók Memorial and the Mozart Committees; supervised the folk-music department of the Academy of Sciences, where he has engaged in similar musicological activities in neighbouring countries and succeeded Vaughan Williams as Chairman of the International Folk Music Council;[1] undertook various lectures and broadcasting engagements; and sat on the Praesidium at musical festivals. In 1957 the Government instituted a National Music Council, of which Kodály was appointed President. And in the same year his unique services to the nation were again recognised in the bestowal of a third Kossuth Prize.

More informally, he exercised a general and benign influence

[1] Cf. 'I have collected the choral themes for school use from among the pearls of the thesaurus of Hungarian folk songs.

'These themes, by the way, have spread beyond the frontiers of Hungary. It is an interesting fact—although not just by chance—that they will become the common treasure of teachers and children in a country whose musical culture has inspired me many times during my life.

'That country is Britain, where I had the opportunity to study the teaching of singing at school in 1927.

'I was able then to get acquainted with those British composers and musicologists who, simultaneously with but wholly independently from us, followed a similar course in this folk song research.

'It is a special honour for me today to be able to fill the late Vaughan Williams' place as the Chairman of the International Folk Music Council—as he was with Holst the leader of that movement in Britian.' (From an interview in *New Hungary,* December 1962.)

over education, whether in the schools for which he continued to augment his works within the now comprehensive *Choral Method,* or in respect of particular groups or individuals. So far as composition was concerned he wrote an accompaniment to Petőfi's *National Ode,* for the Ensemble of the People's Army, and a number of choral works, which included settings of poems by Mihály Vörösmarty (1800-1855), the greatest of the poets of the Reform Era and the author of the famous *Appeal to the Nation.* This, issued in 1837, ranked among the notable essays in patriotic literature, and Vörösmarty's fearless exhortations to his fellow-countrymen to strive for their independence were at an early stage written into the faith of Kodály.

At the end of 1956 the Kodály's were out of the capital staying at Galyatető (in which spa there was lately established a 'holiday home' both for the intelligentsia and the workers) in the Mátra country. While they were there the troubles took place in Budapest. A year after the celebration of Kodály's seventy-fifth birthday Emma, now greatly advanced in age—ninety-five, it was said—was taken ill. On 22 November 1958 she died.

For some months Kodály was unable to settle to consistent work, but the old patterns of self-discipline again asserted themselves. The Symphony—a familiar legend by now in Hungarian musical circles—was looked at afresh and the intention to complete it formulated. And then, on 18 December 1959, Kodály remarried. His second wife was Sarolta Péczeli, a nineteen-year-old student of the Academy of Music, and daughter of the family that had given hospitality to the Kodálys in the first months of 1945. A vivid, lively person, the present Mrs. Kodály —whose linguistic mastery is outstanding—is a charming hostess and a devoted protectress of the master's affairs. It was at this time that Kodály gladly accepted a commission from England, to contribute to a European Song Book edited by the Countess of Harewood and Ronald Duncan. He, Britten, and Poulenc, all made settings of Shakespeare's 'Tell me where is fancy bred' from *The Merchant of Venice.* In the summer of 1960 Kodály was again able to visit England, primarily in order to add an honorary Doctorate from the University of Oxford to his other distinctions. From Oxford Kodály went to Birmingham and to Keele

University, for a concert by the B.B.C. Midland Singers, on 13 May. A fortnight later he was again in Oxford to conduct the *Te Deum* at Merton College. On 3 June he was in London, to conduct *Ballet Music*, two songs from Op. 5, *Kádár Kata*, and the *Peacock Variations*, with the London Symphony Orchestra. At this concert Sir Arthur Bliss, from whose apostrophe one sentence is to be found on the title-page of this book, and Colin Davis also conducted.

While in Oxford he delivered the Philip Maurice Deneke lecture at Lady Margaret Hall on 3 May, the title being *Folk Music and Art Music in Hungary*[1] In this lecture Kodály gave an indication of his artistic philosophy, which, perhaps, goes far to showing the extent to which his life and art are, in a rare degree, one:

'Simplicity and clarity', he said, 'do not exclude profoundness. Indeed, many times the most profound works are the clearest. Hungarian taste looks for the essence of a work and will always break away from one in which the emptiness is covered by complicated decorations. Hungarians do not like ceremonies; however, they know how to give a proper form and shape to everything. They prefer to cut rather than to untie the Gordian knot. Therefore in Hungary only those masters of German music have a real appeal who grew up and were educated on Italian culture, from Schütz to the Vienna Classics, and to a certain extent to Brahms. The sobriety in Hungarian taste is afraid of all those who try to express German "profoundness" without a Latin culture of form.

'Sobriety is art? The most sober masters are among the greatest. Profoundness should not be sought in complexity, but is to be found in simplicity. Dante, Palestrina, Mozart were sober as all great "impeccable poets". Also Arany was sober, therefore perhaps a bit more Hungarian than Petőfi. But Petőfi is also sober in his epic poem *Childe John* and in so many other works of his.'

The high point in sobriety in Kodály's own works is the Symphony, which as now, having been all along encouraged by

[1] Reprinted from Kodály's English script in the Winter issue of *Tempo*, 1962-3, p. 28 *et seq.*

the Italian Toscanini, promised for completion for 1961. His love for the Italian culture was heightened in the summer of 1962 when he was invited to receive his decoration from the Accademia Santa Caecilia, of which he had previously been made an honorary member. Sobriety underwrote Kodály's consistent way of life. Whatever his official engagements he continued to swim each day in the Lukács Baths (an activity viewed with both awe and amusement), and to walk in the hills. It was with great reluctance that the former activity was, on medical advice, given up in 1960, when Kodály suffered a heart attack. Happily recovered from this, however, he went energetically forward towards the great celebrations that marked his eightieth birthday.

14

The Symphony

THERE ARE TWO FALLACIES to be disposed of. The first is that near octogenarians should be creatively exhausted; the second that a composer may only enter the ranks of the great with a set of symphonies. It is, of course, unusual that a composer should appear with a first symphony in his eightieth year, but then Kodály is an unusual composer. It has already been seen that he has been active in so many ways that the amount of energy and time available for composition has been less than is the case with most post-classical composers of similar rank. The contrast between the creative artist and the man of affairs has, however, had this compensation, that the wells of imagination have not been dried up: Kodály, whose activity in any case makes mockery of his years, is yet prolific in musical thinking and ideas appear to run with pristine ease. The notion that symphonic writing is in some way obligatory—a proposition derived from German music-philosophy and, therefore, not readily acceptable to him even if he were to consider it—has no place in Kodály's attitudes. There are other priorities. Some time after his Symphony had appeared Kodály answered the question as to why he had taken so long to accomplish it in a radio interview. 'I was,' he said, 'busy with more important work: I had to educate a public.'

That the Symphony exists is in part due to the belief that a public, up to a point, has been educated, for, no less than his other instrumental works, it is aimed at Hungary and complex with the theses that had hitherto found other outlet. At the same time it takes up from the first part of Kodály's career, when he might have seemed to be heading for a more exclusive course. Nostalgia is a word that comes to some pens. 'With the assurance of a personal and familiar language', writes John S. Weissman in his admirable, analytical, essay,[1] 'whose inflexions were formulated as decidedly in his early music as in his later compositions, he conjures up visions of distant landscapes and far-off days, pondering on the memories of a world that is gone for ever.' This is superficially satisfying, but at odds with Kodály's temperament, for his attitude to time is, paradoxically, outside of temporality—a point which has already been made, but deserving of restatement in this context. Naturally the past holds significance, but not in the sense that all that was was necessarily best: virtue is a constant in human affairs, and it is the essentials of human action within the framework of time and place that matter: not time nor place in themselves. In linking up with his own youth insofar as his symphony was concerned Kodály was, in fact, protesting his faith in a continuity in humane values.

The Symphony bears the inscription: *In memoriam Arturo Toscanini'* . . . *is etenim saepenumero me adhortatus est* . . .' It is an open secret that Toscanini proposed that Kodály should write such a work at about the time when *Summer Evening* was in process of revision.

The first impulse towards a symphonic motiv came suddenly one day when Kodály was travelling on a tram-car in Budapest and was inscribed on the back of a ticket. At home the beginning of the present first movement was put down in pencil (see illustration on back cover). Thereafter for many years such sketches as were made joined the mass of 'work in progress' on the composer's desk, always tending to find a place only at the bottom of the pile. After the end of the war further progress was made and by the early 1950's two movements were known to be complete. The movement that was causing concern was the middle movement. In 1958 the death of Emma prevented consistent work for some time, but a commission—always an incentive—brought Kodály back to the project. By this time Kodály's Symphony had become as familiar in local legend as Sibelius's Eighth. However, when the Swiss Festival Orchestra were importunate, Kodály resolved on conclusive measures. There was, nevertheless, one further impediment, when he was seriously ill in December 1960. But in May

[1] 'Kodály's Symphony: A Morphological Study', in *Tempo,* No. 60, Winter, 1961-2, pp. 19-36.

1961 the work was announced as completed, and on 16 August 1961 the first performance took place, under the direction of Ferenc Fricsay—once a pupil of Kodály—at Lucerne. Within eighteen months something like fifty performances of the work were given in different parts of the world. The first English performances were in Birmingham and London on December 7, 1961, and then the Three Choirs Festival, faithful to early loyalty, included it in the Gloucester meeting, where it was played by the L.S.O. under Herbert Sumsion. The first U.S.A. performance was by the Cleveland Symphony Orchestra, under George Szell, on January 4, 1962. By February 1963 the work was so well set in the English repertoire that it could be played twice on the same night in one county, Yorkshire; at Leeds by the Hungarian State Orchestra, and at Bradford by the Hallé Orchestra under George Weldon. All of this poses a series of questions. Why can this work accommodate itself so amiably to the present? What degree of respect should contemporaneity compel? To what extent is musical personality independent of style? What, indeed, is a symphony?

The Symphony, answering the Schoenbergian observation that there was still life in that key, is in C major. It is scored for moderate orchestra—3 flutes (the third alternating piccolo), 2 oboes, 2 clarinets, 2 bassoons, 4 horns, 3 trumpets, 3 trombones, and tuba, timpani, triangle, cymbals, and strings. Its duration is half an hour. There are three movements, thus the symphonic structure is returned to the pattern employed by most of the early classical school in the relaxed overture-symphony. The tripartite division of larger musical works, however, appeals to Kodály, and precedents lie in the Second Quartet, the *Serenade*, the *Variations*, and the *Concerto for Orchestra*. The manner is simple, encourages directness and compression, and is aesthetically convincing.

The first movement (*Allegro*) begins with a long paragraph in C major, which serves a dual purpose; having the directive qualities of a *praeludium* and anchoring attention on the significant tonal and melodic properties of the whole work, but also stating and developing its own argument. As in the 'Prelude' to the *Háry János* Suite and the *Variations* the opening music, being sited

in a low register, is evocative, and on the borders of mystery.
Here the 'cellos and basses announce the principal theme, above
a pedal note (another Kodályan device) on one of the timpani. By
thus giving the melody in virtual isolation (*cf.* the opening of
Summer Evening, and of the 'Kyrie' and 'Gloria' of the *Missa
Brevis*) the primacy of melody is acknowledged. Able thus to
concentrate the ear is encouraged to appreciate the rhythmic
subtleties that counter the elemental contours. The opening of the
first subject is, in fact, as follows:

The features of this are the interval of the fourth, the pentatonic
scale, the spring of the rhythm, marked by off-beat accentuation,
and the manner in which the melody, while turning back on itself
between tonic and dominant, suggests a prospect of continuous
progress. Scale and intervallic motivation are allied to, and derived
from, the processes of folk-song, as also is the four-line stanza
into which Ex. 58 is built. But at this juncture the antecedents in
folk-song are irrelevant, for it must be felt that any composer of
similar quality and with a similar intention would arrive at a not
dissimilar conclusion by the light of nature. Tchaikovsky, Sibelius,
Elgar, Bruckner are cases that spring to mind. The punctuation of
the rhythm and the frequency of the fourth in different rhythmic
situations illustrate the interest which Kodály can generate from a
simple statement. A somewhat similar treatment of fundamentals,
and an analogous stanza structure, in *Bicinia Hungarica IV*, No.
138, shows to what extent the opening of the symphony stems
from the composer's natural mode of musical thinking.

At bar 12, a new point of departure marked by a unison by two
horns, leads to a transposition of the *incipit* a major sixth higher.
A bassoon, joined soon by violas and a clarinet, is added to the

string bass, and the melody is in fact treated variation-wise. There appear these rhythmic modifications:

59a   59b

After the tonic pedal by the drum has ceased, the single line of melody is lifted yet higher, to centre on the dominant of C. The whole of the strings are involved, as also some woodwind and horn tone, while the timpani, concerned with repetitive tonic and dominant, and more injected semiquavers (*cf. Concerto*), also help to increase the sense of expectation. This is raised to a higher degree by the continuous uplifting of the orchestral *tessitura* and by the episodic employment of a series of consistent quavers. At bar 46 a fissiparous gesture gives a bitonal and canonic representation of Ex. 58. At this climactic point the complete orchestra appears, the upper instruments in C major, the lower, having been led by a G suddenly acquiring the character of a leading note, in A flat.

The woodwind now alternate with the strings in a gloss on the germinal motiv in a tonality near A major, but, so far as the strings are concerned, placed over a double pedal of F sharp and C sharp. Modification of the existing material leads to a less stringent atmosphere in which flute, oboe, and clarinet rhapsodise (at bar 90 note the flexible triplet in the first clarinet) above a string texture which takes leave of the first subject and—without other instrumental colouring for the last eight bars—furnish a connection to the second subject.

This is shown after two and a half bars, during which the key of A major is indicated and the strings are reduced to violas, 'cellos (with a tonic pedal in the new key) and basses. The violas maintain a pulsating figure of their own which gently embellishes the dominant, while the basses play a four-note ostinato, which also develops a life of its own. But it is the clarinets which are entrusted with the main theme of this section. The treatment of the clarinets, mostly in thirds, is familiar from Kodály's previous scores (especially *Summer Evening*), and the affiliation is with landscape:

The harmony is an extension of melody, and each chromatic inflection, Bach-wise, adds as much melodic, or contrapuntal, point as harmonic. The subject itself, like the first, leaves from a long note, while the shape of the arc succeeding the first note has previously been hinted at, as in bar 12 and in and after bar 21. After transferring the subject to the divided strings, against a restatement of the viola pattern in the horns it is lightly disposed across the orchestra with references to A flat major and to the quaver movement encountered in the opening paragraph. Here, however, the quavers appear primarily as a 2 against 1 counter-theme to the persistent, but enlarged, ostinato. Indeed, broken down into four-note fragments for the oboe (bars 158 and 159) the quavers show themselves as a diminished version of the ostinato. In the meantime the A flat has been swinging towards the idea of being G sharp, so that the firm key of A major can be re-stated. At this point the sentiment is again relaxed, into a fresh idea which rides thus engagingly

with a discreet backward glance at C major. Also re-asserted, although it has never entirely disappeared, is the motivating interval of the fourth. In bars 4 and 5 there is also continuation of a feature developed in Ex. 60.

The middle section—the 'development' in conventional terminology but here as in general a misnomer since the whole movement shows perpetual organic growth, with new shoots issuing from firm branches throughout—is prefaced by a drum roll on the dominant of C major. Bassoons and 'cellos and basses carry forward the main rhythmic impulse of Ex. 61, above which a chorale presentation of the same idea is given by homophonic brass. Ex. 58 is thus extended in an oboe solo—in a manner which shows the close relationship between that and Ex. 60, above a held G flat in the basses—and a clarinet answer to this, set above a more direct version of Ex. 61, now in two horns. The interpolation of quavers, the sharper percussive edge of crotchet chords in the strings, heightened by quiet contributions by triangle and cymbal leads to a canonic devolution of the middle part of the first paragraph of the movement, into which also is set the pattern of Ex. 61 by trumpet and trombone. The climax of this section is the 'Grand Pause' that fractures an impetuous line of contrary quavers in widely separated treble and bass.

The end section of the first movement begins with a generous discussion of Ex. 58, fragmented and then reassembled. At first the cutting edge of high strings in octaves, above a tonic pedal now rustically deployed, recalls the atmosphere of Galánta; at this point the music most nearly touches the mood of folk-dance, which relationship is enhanced by the ingenuousness of a chromatic counter-subject in the horns:

In this calculated rejection of inhibitions, the kind of gesture to attract the affection of the uncommitted listener, is the temper of a century and a half ago, with which time Kodály has his own, private, connection. Ex. 58 is soon shown again, in its first shape, in the bass and centred on A flat. Further expression of the same theme in oboe and flute places further stresses on the tonality, but the prevailing dominant is reiterated and under-written by rhythmic energy. The recapitulation of Ex. 60 is slipped into C flat major, whence a typical Kodályan move returns it to C major. After a newly coloured version of Ex. 61 a brief, ebullient coda brings the movement to an end.

Thus the formal properties of the sonata are observed with a professional rigour, but also with a certain detachment. That is to say formalism is subsidiary to a degree of palpable expressionism, which, however, is independent of programme. The spiritual affinity with Haydn is close. In the central movement this affinity is heightened, by an unexpected transference to the tonal centre of G sharp, which, by allusion, imparts its own gravity, and by the use of variation form. Kodály, taking the hint from the improvisation of folk-music, is persistent in his employment of variation form, of which, indeed, he is one of the greater masters. In this connection he, like Brahms, avoiding decorativeness, perceives and exposes the mosaic of patterns that lies beneath the top surface of a melodic line.

The first statement of the melody of the slow movement

is prefaced by a five note introduction by the horns, who, starting on E flat lead to, and merge in, the initial A flat—G sharp. Thus the association with the main contrasting key centre of the first movement is demonstrated, and the structural relevance of the new tonality underlined. In its relaxed metre, rhyming structure, strict pentatonicism, and its range over an octave—beginning on the upper and ending on the lower note, Ex. 63 is indistinguish-able from a folk-melody. It is presented with the utmost simplicity, the only addition to what is shown above being a pizzicato lower octave in the basses to mark the punctuation. In his addiction to unisonal writing one is in mind of Kodály's *dictum*: 'In its choice of intervals, Hungarian folk song agrees almost entirely with the two peak-points of melodic evolution, that is to say, Gregorian chant, and the melodic style of Palestrina. In both cases, we are confronted by a unison melody-style conceived without the necessity of vocal harmony. Despite its polyphony, Palestrina's melodic line never belies its monophonic character.'[1] The second statement of Ex. 63, violas, 'cellos and basses divisi, is a complex *organum* pattern and so, for that matter, is the third, where violins, like the rest of the strings muted, take over the melody against a sliding row of triads.

The semi-tonal juxtaposition of triads continues in the lower strings and the clarinet—so often used by Kodály in idealisation of vocal improvisation—moves, in a sequence of rising fourths, towards a rhapsodic passage which is completed by the flute. This then serves as text for a commentary by oboe, flute, and violins, which, after some interesting polytonal observations

leads to a clear, if decorated, amplification of Ex. 63, with C sharp as the temporary tonic. A canonic interlude, started by the two flutes, and continued by the oboes, leaves the melody, in augmentation, with the second horn: the more enlivening pattern of

65

<hr />

[1] *Folk-music of Hungary*, p. 67.

An open-air lesson at Békéstarhos

Sketch for finale of *Symphony*

is maintained while a wide melodic curve, built up from an exaggerated inversion of the main theme, is described in the upper register. After the climax of this section—resolved through the final extinction of semiquavers in the upper strings—is passed, a highly coloured variant, in which the wood-wind interchange arpeggios (as in the *Variations*, the *Concerto*, and the *Dances of Galánta*) the opening atmosphere is recreated in a brief, allusive, coda of fourteen bars. In the last two bars G sharp is cancelled in favour of G natural, over which clarinets and bassoons sound the tonic as well as the dominant of the fundamental tonality.

The interval of the fourth thus given is the direct lead to the finale of the Symphony, the exordium of which is an exclusive display of the virtues of this interval. This introduction is, so to speak, a clear statement of dogma. So too is the splendid theme which the horns deliver as the principal motiv of the movement:

65

One would be hard put to it to invent a tune which better expressed the conviction that open-air exercise is one of the best safeguards of health and reason. The melody is, of course, a near neighbour of that which dominates the first movement. In this way the ternary character of the Symphony is shown. More importantly, however, the rhythmic shaping of the melody puts it firmly into the indelible popular tradition: the tradition, that is, of the highways. This is the strength of Kodály's situation, in that his view of folk-music is all-embracing, and includes a natural sympathy for the bastard 'folk' music that at the outset of his career impeded the prospects of the authentic strain. It goes back to what he was brought up to. The heredity of Ex. 66 may, therefore, be traced as far back as József Bengráf, one of whose *Magyar Dances* ran thus:

67

The characteristic syncopation is in the *Dances of Galánta,* but also in Bengráf, Kauer, Bihari, Doppler, Müller. In short Kodály's third movement principal subject could fit into almost any period of Hungarian popular music over the last two centuries. In this sense it lies outside time and gives its own answer to those who are bound to a rigid convention by a wrong conception of contemporaneity.

True to form (and to tradition) Kodály repeats his theme in the strings, but enlarges it and introduces the semiquaver movement predicated in the extract from Bengráf. There follows yet another statement, this time with the note units somewhat re-arranged and in E major. At bar 50, when the E major section begins, there is one of those exhilarating canonic episodes which Kodály introduces with the zest of Haydn or Berlioz, or, for that matter, Erkel.

After the principal motiv has been stated and developed secondary material appears. The rhythmic verve is carried over, but the contours of melody are narrower:

Against these, and arising from 68c, are first, a rising scale passage and then a $s\ d_1\ d_1$ figure. In accordance with Kodályan practice this latter also develops is own personality and by extension to an octave interval and the acquisition of a preliminary *acciaccatura* affords a degree of levity in the bass—akin to the 'capricious humour' described by Waldbauer in the last movement of the Second Quartet—where it anticipates the powerful entry of the first two bars of Ex. 66, in the dominant. This theme next appears (at bar 217) in the horns, *piano*, in B major; then at a closer interval, in the clarinets in G, where the character of a development section is assumed. The last main section of the movement, prefaced by a rich sequence of perfect and diminished fifths, arrives in the brass when Ex. 66—its head-note left behind—is announced by the brass and in the tonic key. The recapitulation, alluding to tonalities on the flat side, is regular in order, but prolific in invention. In the coda the interval of the fourth is resumed as the main melodic feature, and, before the final peremptory chords are flourished, in horns and trumpets. It cannot be said that Kodály overlooked that his final commission for a symphony was for a festival.

It is this that provokes further consideration of what a symphony is. Fundamentally—and the point is easily, and even disastrously, overlooked—a symphony is an entertainment. Kodály, faithful to one part of French culture, is aware of this. It has the inner content of good humour that was expected in the first climactic period of the symphony at a Parisian *Concert Spirituel*. It travels some part of the way with the robust zest of Telemann, or the first Stamitz, carrying also something of the sophistication that those masters developed. Stamitz, if one may paraphrase Peter Gradenwitz, made a new audience by his symphonic expression: the bourgeois audience—which was not quite what his Parisian partner, La Pouplinière, expected. Kodály's aim, more deliberate in this respect, is similar. The principles underlying the work are classical in that they embrace integrity of melody, contrast, colour and civilised argument. Thus, in one way, Kodály circumnavigates the stormier works of symphonic expression and, on the whole, misses out on the elementals of Beethoven and his successors. Being a good teacher Kodály refuses to preach. As a symphonic writer he has little to say about 'Fate', about the 'heroic', about the 'soul', about 'God', or 'Destiny'. On this side the later symphonic tradition has been heavily laden. On the other side Kodály does not look to a symphony to be developed as an exercise in abstractions, or in stylistic adventuring. The *Kunst der Fuge* was one thing with Bach, the concerti another; the former was not directed at the audiences at Zimmerman's Coffee-house on Friday evenings, the latter were. Kodály appreciating that Bach was no square, and sees no reason why he should be. It also may be pointed out that Bach at the end of his life (the same goes for Handel if the case is examined thoroughly) was, so far as his children and their contemporaries were concerned, pursuing archaic practices. Kodály's style is resolutely a system of its own—to be examined in more detail at the next stage. If it does not now appear, as it did to Cobbett a generation back, 'wildly passionate' it certainly still deserves this tribute from that writer: '. . . none but the unimaginative can fail to be moved by the intensity of feeling displayed by the composer, who is revealed as one of the most remarkable tone poets of the present time'.

The Symphony is a *credo* in the sense that it contains in its form and feeling the philosophy of its composer in respect both of music and the purpose of music. It is Hungarian, but it is not bounded by a territorial frontier. It is comprehensive in allusion (even though the composer himself admits intimate and personal references) and its musical nature shows its affinities with the main symphonic tradition. That is to say, it is mature music, intellectually powerful, and unified in design. It carries optimism, which is more convenient for the present than pessimism, or nihilism. What does it miss? Tragedy. Of that Kodály, the witness of more than most, has spoken elsewhere. There is a place for a symphony which, in the Shakespearian sense, is a comedy. One is reminded of Friedbert Streller's applause for Prokofiev's intention in writing the "Classical" Symphony: 'The work should not be a museum-piece, but fresh, living music.' *Lebendig* is a good word to apply to Kodály's Symphony in all its aspects.

15

The Composer

OF KODÁLY it can justly be said that had he not achieved distinction as a composer he would have done so through other means. There are not many musicians of whom this may be said with comparable confidence. The reason, as has been amply shown, is that Kodály has regarded himself primarily as a custodian of the Hungarian ethos, most of all as crystallised in the Magyar language: it is not because he was, as is sometimes suggested, born to greatness. Indeed, part of Kodály's greatness lies in his rejection of the idea of a particular personal worth, in his acceptance of his role as a citizen *inter pares*. Most of his compositions stem from this rule of life—which is why they are as they are, and why, comparatively speaking, they are few in number. To evaluate this content requires an assessment of their style, and a judgment on the particular qualities of the style, together with an estimate of the value of the relationship between these and its intrinsic nature. That is, presuming that one may still be permitted to see such a duality in unity, to argue that manner is the outward sign of matter. At least, in this instance one is relieved from having to protest too forcefully, since Kodály himself is a guarantor of the traditional views that (*a*) music can, by allusion, create an awareness of extra-musical circumstances, (*b*) it can, therefore, exert moral force, (*c*) it can, nevertheless, preserve its own, purely musical, status, and (*d*) it can best do all of these if the composer is on terms with his public—even if that public needs bringing to the point of co-operation.

'A general musical consciousness will only be found in Hungary', he wrote, 'when the one-fifth minority accepts the musical feeling of the four-fifths majority, which is still regarded with a certain contempt. If it is not built on this foundation, it will be rootlessly diffused in general world culture or irretrievably lost in the semi-culture of internationalism'. That is the point at which we start—a statement of aims by the composer. In one sense the aims are limited, the public being a particular public. Kodály's music is local, but, as we may hope to prove, local without being parochial. Mr. Donald Mitchell expresses one attitude when he writes: 'To read Bartók's generous evaluation of Kodály . . . one would think Kodály a modern master of equal importance. But he is not; one knows that for sure. And there are good musical reasons for one's certainty. One does not need to deny the common ground that both composers share. But while Bartók was avowedly a nationalist, he was also something more than that, and something more important. The discovery and reaffirmation of folk-melody was a matter of concern to both composers. But while for Kodály we feel that it was primarily a card of identity, the basis of a cultural mission, for Bartók it was also a means of maintaining vital melodic invention in the face of his century's and his own rhythmic and harmonic innovations, which increasingly tended, as the history of modern music shows, to relegate melody to an inferior role. Thus Bartók's "nationalism" was bound up with the main stream development of twentieth-century music, and Kodály's is not. One attaches no blame to Kodály in any sense, but perhaps regrets the sacrifice that musical patriotism exacts. History teaches us that patriotism is necessary, and we rightly celebrate the indispensable patriots; but it is no less historically true that patriotism is not enough. It has got to produce a great composer.'[1]

What constitutes a 'great composer' is, no doubt, definable—but only *post hunc*. Among the living one may only state the likely runners and then hedge one's bets: the more so in a period which is not one in which musical culture is generally regarded, as it was in the nineteenth century, for instance, as possessing a special *mystique* and, therefore, a secure status (even if the musician lacked similar elevation). The side-walks of music are strewn with the names of the formerly successful—whose reputations were once thought firm: Telemann, Salieri, Mendelssohn, Spohr, Goetz, for example. Of these some reputations fluctuate uneasily, while others are convenient subjects for special pleading,

[1] Review of Eösze's *Zoltán Kodály* in *Musical Times*, January 1963, pp. 34-5.

and special interests. As to ultimate election to the Pantheon the twentieth century shows no certainties. If, on the other hand, the claims of possible candidates were canvassed, Britten, Shostakovich, Stravinsky would be among the inevitable entries. Of these the one most bound up with what may be termed the 'main-stream' development is Stravinsky; but it is arguable that the more bound up he has become the less and not the more valid is his musical argument. The other side of the argument is that his music has become 'more interesting': but to whom? As to nationalism none of these three composers has been unaffected by nationalism of a sort. In each case—as in that of Wagner—the national has, in fact, become international.

In the mid-twentieth century two band-wagons have been constructed, on to which young composers have been quick to jump according to their passports. Serialism is anathema to one half of the world: 'socialist realism' to the other. Absolute commitment to immutable dogmas is to Kodály nonsensical. In all cases he regards the suppression of the inquisitive spirit to the dictates of stylistic fashion as deplorable and antithetical to the proper function of a composer; which is to communicate. Of course, Kodály has his own principles, but these he would regard as the underlying principles of music, and applicable to all environments when the necessary adjustments had been made. It would seem, perhaps, that he has an unexpected ally. In one of his celebrated Reith Lectures, Professor G. M. Carstairs said: 'I suggest that the creative artist's role in the future may be to keep alive the sense of significance in local and national traditions, and so to combat the deadening effect of uniformity. . . .'[1] If this be so, then Kodály remains where he began, in the van of progress.

At one period of musical history all composers were concerned with 'local' traditions, in the sixteenth and seventeenth centuries, for instance. These local traditions nevertheless, were neither dead nor untouched by other local traditions. Thus the general polyphonic impulse informed separate schools, each of which, however, was outward-looking. The same with the Baroque. Of the earlier Baroque composers, Schütz, although inspired by

[1] *This Island Now*, London, 1963, p. 101.

Venice, was essentially Saxon: so too his later compatriot, Bach. And both completed their careers by appearing to their younger contemporaries as conservative—at any rate in style. The later eighteenth century saw a spurious form of internationalism (exemplified in the symphonic music of composers of the second and third rank, from Wranitzky, Moravian, to Kelly, Scottish). From this the greater composers, Haydn, Mozart, Beethoven, Schubert, broke free. An academic counter-revolution, though now German rather than Italian in origin, induced a new sense of conformity which nearly killed British, and Hungarian music— the music, that is, that 'kept alive the sense of significance in local and national traditions.'

Later in the day Vaughan Williams and Holst, and Kodály and Bartók, arrived on the scene to try to establish what those traditions were. A comparison between these two pairs of latter-day 'nationalists' has often been made, with the first in each group being assigned to one classification, the second to another. Vaughan Williams and Kodály are regarded as rather less worthy as composers than Holst and Bartók.[1] The truth is that the two Englishmen are complementary, and so are the two Hungarians. Regarding the latter, each saw the same landscape, but at different times of day—or night. Bartók's *Music for Strings, Percussion, and Celesta* (whose third movement Lawrence Gilman described as a 'mystical nocturne') is Hungarian and great music; but neither less nor more so than the *Psalmus Hungaricus*. This distinction may be made: that Bartók, despite his origins, gravitated towards intrumental music, whereas the mature Kodály, although a master of orchestral virtuosity, thought in essentially vocal lines.

---

[1] Cf. *The Times*, 15 April 1959: 'Popular as is Kodály's music with the people, the musical snobs (especially outside Hungary) have long decided that Kodály's music is Bartók made palatable for the average concert-goer; and thus comparison between the two composers can easily turn into the superficial sort which the half-educated make about Handel *v.* Bach, Haydn *v.* Mozart, or Mahler *v.* Bruckner, wherein Kodály, Handel, Haydn, and Mahler always emerge with the short stick. But it will not do, for example, to say that *Háry János* is a "poor man's Bartók" a remark which was heard recently at a diplomatic reception in Budapest. In writing *Háry János*, Kodály set out—and we quote one of the master's pupils—"to show the man in the street that he could hear pure Hungarian folk-music and love it as much as the pseudo-gypsy stuff which was palmed off as genuine Hungarian in the nineteenth century". And the sold-out houses to which Kodály's *Háry János* plays show that the composer has succeeded brilliantly.'

This, *vide* Donald Mitchell above, is present-day heresy; but Kodály, using always the vocal melody as fundamental to musical comprehension, will, no doubt, be ultimately discovered to have followed the one tradition without which music cannot survive as a meaningful experience. That is not to deny the extension of other possibilities; merely to observe that when the bath-water is turned out suitable care should be taken of the baby.

It hardly needs saying that Kodály has lived through an era of disequilibrium: he is almost unique in being a composer of equilibrium. (A striking example of his stability is his composition of the *Serenade* as referred to on p. 65.) This is why he occupies a key position in the music of his own country. On the other hand, he is not a guardian of the *status quo*. In fact, the reverse is the case. This is not a rebel tamed, but a critic whose acumen does not lose its sharpness. He rarely makes a point which does not go home. In the end then he achieves precisely what he set out to achieve: that was to recreate Hungarian music and yet to assure it a place in the wider community of music.

In his Preface to *The Revolt of Islam*, which was once regarded as a work of shattering modernity, Shelley made it plain that the most effective medium for the expression of original thought is that which came most naturally. 'I have', he wrote, 'simply clothed my thoughts in what appeared to me the most obvious and appropriate language. A person familiar with nature, and with the most celebrated productions of the human mind, can scarcely err in following the instinct, with respect to selection of language, produced by that familiarity.' On the question of originality he observed: 'I do not presume to enter into competition with our greatest contemporary poets. Yet I am unwilling to tread in the footsteps of any who have preceded me.'

Music grows out of musical experience. Thus inevitably it is rooted in what is, terminologically, not unfamiliar. The art of independent composition comes when the young composer feels the *materia musica* to be at his finger-tips. At this point he has a technique—a technique which enables him to provide music for singers which can be sung, for instruments which can be played, rather than music that might be sung or played. The wise composer, at the outset of his career, is primarily concerned with

such practical details. It is, of course, fair to assume that whatever
he writes, if he has talent at all, will be found strange by some,
difficult by others—generally because of prejudice against the
living on the one hand and an indifferent standard of sight-reading
on the other. What is termed 'individuality', and is later assessed
as a separate entity, arises from the act of composition wherein
are compressed the composer's predilections for this or that
sonority, his choice of tessitura, his mathematical perception of
the rhythmic permutations possible within even the simplest
metrical schemes, his selection from and reintegration of established values. The stock of established values is increased
naturally by every composer of substance (those who fail in this
contribution—and this failure may be disguised during a working
career that, for reasons extraneous to intrinsic qualities, appears
prosperous—fall into desuetude), so that a composer will always
be aware of new possibilities. Whether he makes use of them or
not is up to him. The virtue of his own work is not necessarily
affected either by acceptance or rejection. Kodály, clear from the
outset as to the relationship between what he wanted to say and
how it should be said, has, in contrast to his most illustrious
contemporary, Stravinsky, rejected neologistic formulas. This
was not due to any ostrich attitude—for 'new music' has had few
more sympathetic sponsors, still less in recent years to a 'political
approach' (as was, unworthily, suggested in an article in *The
Listener* concerning the Symphony[1]), but to the conclusions of an
independent judgement (Kodály being agreeably determined to
oppose such ideas on logical grounds if he feels that opposition is
necessary) and a realisation that his own methods of expression
were adequate to his own needs, and by no means rigidly
delimited. The Symphony, after all, is in C major; by its existence
it shows how this most familiar of tonal sensations can hold its
place.

   'The guiding principle of all his work is still a balanced tonality.
Yet he speaks in a language that is itself new, of things that

---

[1] 'One suspects a misguided attempt to simplify a never very complex style, with
the intention of reaching the widest public, either for personal reasons, like Bartók,
or owing to the political climate, like Shostakovich' (Deryck Cooke, 10 January
1963.)

hitherto have not been spoken of; thus proving that the principle of tonality is still a legitimate one.' So wrote Bartók in 1921, and thus emphasised the strongly classical side of Kodály's musical character. Eleven years later he observed: '. . . [that Kodály's] music created the same atmosphere as folk-music. For only then could he be said to have really learned the musical dialect of the peasants, only then could he be as much at home with it as a poet is with his native tongue.' This is the romantic side of Kodály, from which Bence Szabolcsi starts in this definition of Kodály's style: 'Kodaly fühlte sich von Anfang an zur weiteren Diatonik and Pentatonik hingezogen und ging einen planmässigen Weg von der ungarischen Landschaftsromantik der *Sommerabends* bis zur eurasiatischen Farbenskala der *Pfauenvariationen* und zur palestrinischen Melodienwelt der *Orgelmesse*. Inzwischen wurde aber gerade sein heroisch-lyrischer Sprechton zum charakteristischen Zeichen der ungarischen Bewegung, das in der Cellosonate, im *Psalmus Hungaricus* und in der Vertonung alter Dichter gleicherweise an die Intonation der ungarischen Jahrhunderte anklingt und aus volkhaften oder geschichtlichen Denkmälern ein nationales Parlando von völlig neuer Atmosphäre schafft.'[1]

An examination in greater detail of Kodály's method reveals how this 'new atmosphere' has come about.

Despite the efforts of those of his predecessors who foreshadowed his ideals, Kodály found the Hungarian musical ambience of the first decade of the century heavy with Teutonic overtones. Post-Brahmsian seriousness, combined with Wagnerian heroics, established a general academic ponderousness that ran respectably in harness with the paintings of Liezen-Mayer, Sándor Wagner, and Benczur, all artists schooled in Munich. The immediate antidote to this alien influence was first found in

---

[1] *Bausteine zu einer Geschichte der Melodie*, Budapest, 1959, p. 212 (this book is dedicated to Kodály): 'From the beginning Kodály felt drawn to a broader diatonicism and pentatonicism, and progressed methodically from the romantic, Hungarian, landscape of *Summer Evening* to the Eurasian colour-range of the *Peacock Variations* and the Palestrinan scheme of melody of the "*Organ*"-*Mass*. Meanwhile, however, his heroic-lyric speech inflection merged into the characteristic gestures of Hungarian idiom. This shows in the '*Cello Sonata,* the *Psalmus Hungaricus,* and in settings of the old poets, recalling the Hungarian intonation of centuries. Out of monuments of folk-art or of history he shaped a national mode of expression with a completely new atmosphere.'

another. Thus, again as in the visual arts, and to some extent in literature, French Impressionism became the catalytic agent. The element of light that Kodály and Bartók thus learned to apply immediately brought their music more into accord with the Hungarian landscape, and the Hungarian temperament, which itself is nearer to that of the French rather than the German.

Lightness has these ramifications. There is lightness of texture, economy in fact, which Kodály practised in the orchestration of *Summer Evening*. Consequent upon this is the perception that clarity depends on space and spaciousness. Thus in the early piano pieces chords are allowed to linger, and, in Debussyan manner, are widely spread. In *Summer Evening* the extension of the string parts (violins *div. à 3* in high register) is notable and gives a soft brilliance hereafter to become a feature of the scoring. Complementary to this is the distinctive use of high, and mobile, woodwind. These gestures, related to the vocal style through their *melismata*, give a kaleidoscopic mood, which, borrowed from the realm of painting, communicates itself to harmonic method also.

The exponent of the feeling of the Nyugat encountered, however, the student of philology. Pure aestheticism was then disciplined by reason, and given direction. The word led back to its roots, and therefore to those of folk-song. Kodály concentrated on the significance of melody, and melody became the foundation of his style. It is easy to urge that Kodály's melodic style is founded on the patterns of folk-music. That folk-music, of various kinds, is an important element is undeniable, but, for the most part, the impulses have been used unconsciously rather than consciously —as, for instance, in the *Concerto*, where the opening seems directly to spring from a Transdanubian shepherd's pipe tune. Sometimes it is best to by-pass folk-song and observe how Kodály has, in fact, faithfully reproduced the shape and inflection of the Hungarian language merely through a perception of the musical values inherent in the words themselves. So much was pointed out to me by Szabolcsi, and, in particular, the music on pp. 67 and 68 may be cited to demonstrate the semantic properties within melody at which Kodály aimed. For him music is explicit; It is a means of communication; it is informative. To achieve his purpose, then, he needed to form a vocabulary in which the references were clear, the lines of tradition apparent, and the syntax unexceptionable. Accordingly, the starting-point was melody, and at the root of all Kodály's teaching is the necessity to cultivate melodic independence and fluency.

Kodály (comparing himself with Bartók) lays claim only to exploring a relatively small terrain, but also to having dug deep. His first melodic antecedents are in the classics, especially Haydn and Mozart, who formed the staple fare of the chamber-music activities in Galánta and Nagyszombat (Brahms he did not come to until his student days in Budapest). The summation of this first experience is in the Symphony, where the melodic motivs are flexible, sensitive, refined, and susceptible to elaboration and development. Partly through early experience of Erkel—a master who was at first decried because of the 'Italian' character of his melodic writing—Kodály was drawn to appreciate the emotional properties of pure melody. Even at his most declamatory (cf. *Hymn of Zrinyi*), therefore, there is always present a voluptuous quality (Kodály himself might permit the term 'exotic' in so far as this music is here looked at from the outside) that allows no neutrality in performance. The ecclesiastical influence, both Catholic and Calvinist, was also strong, the former extending from *bel canto* to polyphonic method, the latter towards the economies of folk-song. Folk-song was used referentially by Kodály, and the main mark is intervallic. Fourths and fifths play a dominating role in his melodic outlines, and tonal direction is often affected. But in both instances the resultant melody was placed in such a context that it accommodated itself naturally to the main stream of musical development. The manner in which this is accomplished in, say, the *Háry János* Suite is one reason for the durability of the item in the concert repertoire. The melodic idiom is (or was) unfamiliar, but it is so directed that it sounds familiar.

Rhythmically, Kodály moves across a relatively wide sector. On the one side is the ebullient beat of *verbunkos*, on the other the contemplative *senza misura* of the rhapsodic type of folk melody. The former again renews the gestures, and innocence, of Haydn; the latter reaches over into the Baroque. The way in which Kodály synthesised apparently disparate elements is indicated in an enlightening essay by András Szőllősy.[1] Of the melodic structure of the early *Adagio* for violin and pianoforte he writes that 'the expansive declamation and structural ornamentation which is an organic part of its idiom continue an instrumental tradition whose origin may well go back to chamber music of the Baroque age, with its broad-flowing slow movements'. At a later point Szőllősy commenting on the importance and individuality of Kodály's ornamentation (in slow movements, especially) observes that while ornamentation 'is an integral part of folk song in practice it is not part of its structure'. Kodály perceived the significance of the improvisatory qualities that were part of the organic growth of folk-music.

Szőllősy emphasises another factor of importance. 'With Kodály', he wrote, 'harmony is never an end in itself; but is always the result of the movement of the melody.' In effect, this draws attention to Kodály's intuitive handling of harmonic problems. Within the framework of a general harmonic propriety (in an old-fashioned way, Kodály staked out his ground, especially in extended compositions, and predetermined the main points of tonal repose in accordance with an intelligible scheme of classical priorities) he allowed his melodic shapes precedence. French Impressionism left him with a good many allusive possibilities. These may be seen conveniently indexed in Op. 11, the *Seven Pieces for Pianoforte*. In the first of these pieces, for example, are these atmospheric effects: the tonally conscious sustained note (or octave) set above, and at a distance from, a melodic contour thrown into an apparently ambiguous tonality, which, however, is released from ambiguity by its general relationship to the sustained upper voice; the emancipated dominant seventh, free to remain in interrogatory isolation or to move forward; the augmented triad; the secondary seventh. The movement to and from these particular points is controlled by the imaginative structure of the music on the one hand, or by the inevitable logic of the part-writing on the other. In the *Székely Lament* (No. 2), the same elements, are more rhetorical. The triads stand against whole phrases of melody and strong dissonantal probabilities are indicated, while the incorporation of inessential notes, born out of

---

[1] 'Kodály's Melody', in *Tempo*, No. 63, p. 12 *et seq*, reprinted from *Kodály Művészete*, Budapest, 1943.

appogiature, give asperities that are often partly mitigated by the
spacing of the chords. A rich harmonic sense is enhanced by an
affection for *organum*-like passages, sometimes of consecutive
fifths but sometimes of whole triads.

It is said that Kodály's style has remained virtually unchanged
over a lifetime. This is true: the harmonic range of the Symphony
or of the later Shakespeare settings, or of the *Hegyi-Mari Népdal*
(1960) is basically that of the pieces of forty or fifty years ago.
At the same time Kodály is never quite predictable. The vocabulary is familiar; but the ordering of the details is variable according to context. An intriguing example of Kodály's originality in
handling the commonplaces of harmonic convention is the
'Qui tollis' section of the 'Gloria' of the *Missa Brevis*. Here is a
pellucid musical statement in which every chord is readily
analysable, but in which each constituent note either depends on
the melody or derives from the behaviour of its own individual
antecedent in a contrapuntal sense. As a contrapuntist, Kodály,
who is unwilling to show only an academic ingenuity, resembles
Handel in preferring the gestures to be inconspicuous. Thus the
fugato writing of the *Te Deum*, the closely woven polyphony of
the 'Sanctus' of the *Missa Brevis* or the correlated middle section
of the Concerto, the canonic interludes in the last movement of
the Symphony, make their point without requiring explanation or
discussion. The finest demonstration of contrapuntal assurance,
however, is the magniloquent *A Magyarokhoz* (*To the Magyars*):
the subject of this great piece is as follows:

69   Maestoso energico

The canon is worked out by four groups of voices and concluded by a superbly placed, 'mixed' cadence, of which the harmonic context is

70

and in which the last chord splashes over into ten parts.

It is characteristic of Kodály that his writing—and this is both strength and weakness—exudes a *joie de vivre*. Essentially, although more aware than most of the tragic issues of life, he is on the side of those who interpret life as comedy rather than tragedy. Music being to him an image of life must, therefore, mirror the potential fullness of life rather than its emptiness. Thus in the conjunction of sounds he lays stress on the effulgencies of harmony and of instrumentation. Thus the inevitable reduction of counterpoint into chordal textures of extraordinary warmth, and emotional satiety; the antiphonal scoring that contrasts choruses of strings, choruses of woodwind, and choruses of brass; the enriching effect of middle-part horn motivs, of frequent pedals, or harmonically suggestive reiterations in the orchestral bass—as, for example, in the middle part of the *Dances of Galánta*.

In technique Kodály is among the sophisticates: there is (within the limits imposed on himself) nothing that he cannot do supremely well, to the extent that practically no note in any of his scores can, with advantage to the texture, be altered. His scores are admirable examples for him who would achieve lucidity. Yet, paradoxically, it is this lucidity, at which Kodály arrived, precociously and almost effortlessly, at the beginning of his career that has proved his Achilles' heel. Vivacity, humour, sobriety, pride, reflectiveness, in the truest sense, piety, and also pity: these qualities are evident. What seldom shows is anger. Kodály has all the virtues of a great dramatic musician, but controlled by the urbanity that has conversely enabled him to use his talents to the greatest purpose within his own community. It is, thus, in the *Psalmus Hungaricus* that he rises to the height of his powers. For this—the perfect fusion of melody, harmony, timbres,

(*above*) Leaving Budapest for England, 1960
(*below*) Lecture on English music at British Embassy in Budapest, 1961

At the Erkel Theatre, 1962: Professor and Mrs. Kodály and the Minister of Culture, Mr. Pál Ilku and Mrs. Ilku

verbal inflections, and musical rhythms, all dedicated to the highly emotive idea behind the poem—does indeed strike harshly against the complacencies of history, or of society, that are Kodály's chiefest enemy.

After a recent performance of the *Psalmus* in Budapest (and how difficult it is to feel the veracity of the work when it is divorced from its own language) Kodály remarked that thirty and forty years ago it was considered as both 'modern'—in the pejorative sense—and almost impossible to sing. With satisfaction he noted that its technical difficulties by now seem to have dissolved. In respect of the other comment it is to be observed that with such a work considerations of date become irrelevant: it is among those things that are ageless. To have produced one piece that is unique is more than most can achieve. Kodály, in fact, may be credited with two works that can be put down as permanently contemporary, the other being *Háry János*. Among the rest, no doubt, time and change will play their havoc. The last person to worry about this is Kodály himself.

He would claim that through his music he has opened windows on the new worlds of musical thought; that he has shown the value of music as music; that he has helped to protect the humanities and to uplift personal and national dignity; and, insofar as his works, beloved at home, are esteemed throughout the world, that he has done something to build a bridge between the stronger parts of the cultures of east and of west. There is also the bridge between the past and the present, exemplified by the historic and social antecedents of the music and the stylistic derivations on the one hand, and the adaptation of styles to a personal instrument and the dedication of this to a particular end on the other. Of the painter Tivadar Csontváry, Hans Hess said: 'In a time of laws and machines we occasionally like to be reminded of a golden age that has passed whilst working for the golden age to come.' That is the significance of the music of Kodály.

16

Influence of Kodály and Trends in Contemporary Hungarian Music

'THOSE TRAINED IN "Kodály's School" are fortunate, because it exerts an incalculable influence on the whole later development of a mind. Many would have been discouraged or would have given up had not Kodály guided them, showing them how to work, teaching them perseverance, self-confidence, and self-recognition. Everybody could learn from him that only with purposeful work and complete proficiency in the craft can talent lead to the desired aim, and that clever gestures are no good without serious, introspective, ascetic work. In this respect Kodály's merits are immeasurable.' The writer was Mátyás Seiber (1905-1960),[1] himself one of Kodály's most talented pupils, whose untimely death was a source of great grief to the master. Consideration of Kodály's influence as a teacher of composition calls for a review of the last half-century of Hungarian musical history, and should be undertaken under the reflection that he, like all of his generation educated by German, or German-orientated professors, was indeed the first teacher who was Hungarian, *pur sang*.

WEINER, JEMNITZ, LAJTHA

Of the composers of the generation of Bartók and Kodály who helped to plot a new course for Hungarian music three deserve some attention: Weiner (of whom some notice has already been taken), Sándor Jemnitz(1890-1963), and László Lajtha(1892-1963). Although Weiner was strongly conservative in outlook, and was deeply attached to the nineteenth century, he was acutely critical of musical textures and had a keen ear for lucid timbres. If he often recalled Mendelssohn, it was the Latin affinities of that

[1] 'Kodály the Master', in *Crescendo*, Budapest, 2 November 1926, No. 3; reprinted in *The New Hungarian Quarterly* Vol. III, No. 8, 1962, pp. 22-4.

composer that he reflected. A good illustration of Weiner's gifts, additional to those quoted on p. 60, is the Suite *Csongor és Tünde* (1912), taken from the incidental music for Vörösmarty's fairy-tale play of that title. If Vösösmarty recalled one *Midsummer Night's Dream* so did Weiner another. Jemnitz lacked the certainty either of Weiner or Lajtha and when young largely absorbed the methods of the once-fashionable Reger. (See, for example, his *Introductio, passacaglia, e fuga* (1918).) Without the discrimination of Bartók, Jemnitz swallowed the principles of Teutonic expressionism to the full and proceeded from Reger to Schoenberg, with whom he studied for a time. Primarily an instrumental composer Jemnitz found himself at variance with the prevailing climate of thought after the Second World War and, reconsidering his principles, simplified his style. Of his later works the *Seven Miniatures* of 1948 hold their place in the current repertoire. As a journalist and writer Jemnitz made further contribution to modern Hungarian musical thought by his exposition of a wide variety of compositional impulses. Lajtha is altogether a larger figure, and, in some respects, worthy to be classed with Bartók and Kodály. He was strongly Francophile and was devoted not only to the music of Debussy but also to that of the French Classical era. His own music, the best of which may be found in his eleven string quartets, is fastidious, colourful, and self-evident. He was a prolific writer and his output includes eight symphonies, a ballet, and a film score for T. S. Eliot's *Murder in the Cathedral*. Lajtha became acquainted with Bartók and Kodály in 1910 and also immersed himself in folk-song research, which affected his personal melodic idiom. Lajtha helped to establish the International Folk Music Council and in later years played a considerable part in extending the field of Hungarian musicology. As a composer he was acclaimed in America (his Third String Quartet was the result of a commission from Mrs. Coolidge) and in France. At home he was unable to compete quite successfully with Bartók and Kodály, lacking the variety of the one and the purposefulness of the other. None the less, he was awarded a Kossuth Prize in 1951. Possessed of great strength of mind, wide interests, and personal charm, Lajtha sometimes lacked tact, and his duels with authority were sometimes fought on the wrong ground.

THE FIRST GENERATION OF KODÁLY'S PUPILS

Those who were born at the beginning of the century became students at a critical period in Hungarian music. As has been seen opposition to all that Kodály stood for was at its height precisely at the time when he composed the *Psalmus Hungaricus*, which then became a symbol in more ways than one. For the aspiring student it was the spur to conviction: if this was what the new outlook could produce then it was to be honoured. Among those who came under Kodály's direct influence at this period were Seiber and Ferenc Szabó (b. 1902), who diverged in different directions, each bearing with him contrasted aspects of Kodály's philosophy. Seiber,[1] like Sandor Veress (b. 1907), whose reputation was established outside of Hungary, while retaining many of his Hungarian characteristics, explored every phase of contemporary music to fashion a style that was intellectually secure, but also musically impressive, and became a British composer whose stature is unlikely to be diminished by the passing years. Szabó, whose political interests drew him into working-class activities as a young man, emigrated to the Soviet Union in 1931, returning to Budapest, where he was appointed to a leading post in the Academy, in 1945. Szabó's music with Kodályan influence in its reminiscences of folk-song and in its diatonic substance, is, so to speak, a plain man's guide to modern music; fluent, unperplexing, attractively uncompromising. Not surprisingly Szabó's most popular work—*Emékeztetö* (*Memento*)—was created from a film score. An heroic, nationalist work, it is a symphony in five movements, of which the sections are entitled: *Introduction, The Noble Huntsmen*; *Sadness of the suppressed people* (with some expressive two-part counterpoint); *Rebels*; *Burial* (a fine essay based on the *verbunkos* idiom); *Young Lovers*. In *Ludas Matyi*, ballet and suite, Szabó cleverly pictures a roguish character, somewhat similar to Vidrócki of the *Matra Pictures*, in his successful exercises against his masters. Having discovered a style Szabó has maintained it resolutely, and successfully, but it is to be doubted whether it will stand up to the assaults of the criticism of tomorrow. At the same time it may well be represented that there

[1] Kodály's high regard for Seiber was expressed in his combative essay, 'Thirteen Young Musicians', in *Budapesti Hirlap*, 14 June 1925 (see p. 82).

will always be an appreciative public for such generous statements of musical goodwill as the *Felszabadult Melódiák (Free Melodies)* of 1961.

In some respects similar to Szabó György Ránki, whose *1514*—a programmatic piece for piano and orchestra descriptive of the peasants' uprising led by György Dózsa—belongs to the new nationalism, differs from him in his ability to capture the facets of Hungarian humour. Ránki, indeed, deserves an honourable place in twentieth-century music for his particular skill in disposing of a relatively limited technique to the best advantage. In Ránki are echoes of Mussorgsky, Rimsky-Korsakov, and Prokofiev, and his talents are most effectively displayed in the Suite from his Hans Andersen opera, *The Emperor's New Clothes* ("Introduction and Alla Marcia grotesca"; "Balletto"; "Scherzo"; "Intermezzo"; "Finale burlesca"). If Ránki may be seen here as heir to the tradition of *Háry János* the impact of Weiner, in the economy of texture, and of Bartók, in respect of appreciation of individual instrumental capacities, will also be noticed. Even more does the spirit of these two composers communicate itself to Ránki's chamber music, among which *Pentaerophonia* (1960), three movements for wind quintet, is conspicuous. The opening of the *Rondo* from this work (the outside parts only are quoted) gives some clue to the carefully wrought but care-free, quality of Ránki's method:

71   Allegro vivace

As will be seen Ránki, like Kodály, has a feeling that the tonality of C major is by no means yet exhausted. In passing it should be mentioned that Ránki is one of the few composers who can follow the Kodály method in pedagogic music and, within the limits of unaccompanied two-part writing, produce something that is both viable for twelve-year olds and yet individual in its own right.[1]

CROSS-FERTILISATION AND THE TEACHING
OF SIKLÓS

In the development of instrumental music the teaching of Albert Siklós[2] (1878-1942) has proved of value, and among his pupils were Endre Szervánszky (b. 1911) and Endre Székely (b. 1912). The former, professor at the National Conservatory from 1941-8 and subsequently at the Academy, has kept within sight of Bartók but has pushed on resolutely in directions apparently unfamiliar within the new traditions of Hungarian music. Szervánszky, however, is a born experimenter and his mature works are the result of selection and rejection, of conscious endeavour to rationalise, if not to nationalise, the raw material of contemporary musical thought. The *Serenade for Clarinet* (1954) is an interesting adaptation of traditional manners (not even forgetting gipsy music) to present circumstances. With this work the composer has extended his reputation to England, France, and Switzerland. In later works, especially the *Six Orchestral Pieces* (1960) Szervánszky deals with Webernesque abstractions in a somewhat solid manner. Székely, who has been occupied in amateur choral music, has also written an ingenious *Serenade* for clarinet, as well as a variety of other instrumental, and choral music.

It was inevitable that the young composers of the first three decades of the century should look beyond Kodály if their feeling was for orchestral music, for he came to this department relatively late in life. The sharp edges of Bartók's method and the careful teaching of Siklós, infected with external influences,

---

[1] See *Szabadság*, in *Énekeskönyv*, VI, p. 92.

[2] Siklós was a pupil of Koessler and although an adherent to older manners in composition had a brilliant understanding of instrumentation, which he communicated as teacher and as author.

such as that of Hindemith which particularly touched Pál Kadosa (b. 1905), were, therefore, significant and complementary influences. Of the now senior composers of Hungary, János Viski (1906-60) occupies a central position. A pupil of Kodály, he was among the first wholeheartedly to adopt Kodály's general principles, which also carried through into valuable pedagogic activities. Viski is closely bound to the fundamental contours of folk-music, but the romantic qualities stemming therefrom are, as in the case of his master, meticulously controlled by a neo-classicism that supports in particular his inclination to concerto. In composing concertos for violin (1946), pianoforte (1952), and 'cello (1955) Viski has successfully conveyed the outlook of Kodály into fields (as yet) unexplored by him.

KADOSA AND FARKAS

Of those who came to maturity before the outbreak of the Second World War Kadosa and Ferenc Farkas remain as powerful and independent voices. Kadosa, represented in the I.S.C.M. meetings of 1933 (Amsterdam) and 1941 (New York) by his *Concert Music for Piano and Orchestra*[1] and his Second String Quartet was first remarked as a brilliant exponent of the new neo-baroque techniques. But economic figuration and contrapuntal asperities, which gave a strong and earnest character to his First Symphony (1942), were relieved from aridity by the undercurrents of Magyar rhythm. Nearer to Bartók than to Hindemith, and for some time taught by Kodály and Arnold Székely, Kadosa yet managed to preserve an impressive independence. After the end of the Second World War Kadosa became for a time President of the Association of Composers and so far as his personal style was concerned reviewed its possibilities in the light of newly fashionable ideas. His last four symphonies (1949, 1957, 1960, 1961) and his Third Piano Concerto (1955) are more expansive, more genial, than earlier works in these genres; he has taken vocal music into consideration, with works ranging from settings of Petőfi to the opera *Huszttikaland* (*Adventure in Huszt*); and he has extended his list of pianoforte compositions—he is in fact a prominent pianist

[1] For an appreciation of this, together with assessments of Veress and Szervánszky, see 'Hungarian Music of 1949' in *Musical Times*, June 1949.

—to include several anthologies of pieces for children. At the same time he has lost none of his intellectual power, nor his early faith in the validity of epigrammatic motivation. An interesting demonstration of his late method is the *Pianoforte Trio* (Op. 49/d), published in 1961, which makes no concessions, but is attractive in its quiet way.

In contrast to Kadosa is Ferenc Farkas (b. 1905). A pupil of Weiner and Siklós, he went to Rome, there to study with Respighi. The pull of Italian music has been increasingly felt in Hungarian music, and nowhere more strongly than in the works of Farkas, who is also a professor at the Academy of Music. Farkas is eminently conservative in idiom, his melodies springing from Gregorian and *bel canto* origins, are worked into fluent counterpoint, or carried forward by spaciously orchestrated diatonics, but sensitivity to mood guarantees an agreeable eagerness of expression and Farkas, more than Respighi, is versatile, and his versatility depends on an awareness of rhythmic values. Thus his comic opera, *The Magic Cupboard* (1942), and ballet, *The Sly Students* (1949), have gained regular places in the theatre, while his various oratorio works have valuably increased the choral repertoire. Of these *Szent János Kútja* (St. John's Fountain) and *Cantata Lirica*, both based on poems by the Transylvanian writer Jenő Dsida, are notable for their fine lyric quality. Sometimes, as in the middle of the latter work, Farkas shows himself to have arrived at the same point as Kodály, but by a different route:

Above this melody, clearly susceptible to the movement of the language, is a high counter-subject for the violins. A later work, *Cantus Pannonicus* (1959), set to the Latin text of Pannonius, is, perhaps, more conscious of national characteristics and covers a wide range of emotion.

EXPANDING SYMPATHIES

Of the succeeding generation the most conspicuous figures are Gyula Dávid (b. 1913), Rudolf Maros (b. 1917), András Mihály (b. 1917), Rezső Sugár (b. 1919), and Pál Járdányi (b. 1920). In these composers, all but Mihály who studied chiefly with Kadosa pupils of Kodály, there is both an end and a beginning: an end because they carried conformity with the blue-prints of the master to their logical conclusion; a beginning because under their aegis fresh impulses are to be perceived. It was never Kodály's intention that Hungarian music should become cannibalistic, feeding on itself. But the conditions that obtained during the war and the succeeding years made it inevitable that for a time Hungarian music should be more or less self-subsistent and self-supporting. The development of a new national consciousness and a new social order had a marked effect. If experimentation became more hazardous the loss that this implied was balanced by a new dignity in the social status of music. It was in meeting this that the main challenge to the rising composer lay.

Dávid, an orchestral player until 1945, and since that time conductor at the National Theatre (1945-9) and of various other ensembles, is a highly proficient technician whose talent for orchestration is seen at its best in his dance movements and his *Symphonietta* of 1961. Dávid's output includes three symphonies and a viola concerto. Maros has led a more adventurous life. After the completion of his studies, he worked in Pécs until recalled to Budapest, as professor of composition in the Academy, in 1950. For a decade Maros followed the proprieties of folk-song idiom, illuminating his scores, however, with a lightness and verve derived, perhaps, from Lajtha. Especially attracted to wind instruments, Maros produced a superbly deft Quintet (*Preludio, Notturno, Scherzino, Aria, Postludio*) in 1956. Appropriately, this was entitled `Musica leggiera. Another work of this period of some practical importance was the *Wedding Dance of Ecser*, like Kodály's *Kalló Double-dance*, commissioned for the State Folk Ensemble. In the last half-dozen years or so, however, Maros has devoted himself to the task of writing Hungarian music with techniques more commonly practised further west. Thus in the *Ricercare*

(1957), the *Five Studies for Orchestra*, and the ballet *Miner's Ballet* (1961) he investigates the properties of serialism.

If such *avant-gardisme* is regarded with a certain reservation, this derives from an innate conservatism in the Hungarian temperament. Force of circumstance has usually contrived that in respect of major cultural movements Hungary has arrived late. It is, however, sometimes possible that such enforced tardiness has enabled some artists to avoid blind alleys. This is particularly true of Hungarian painting in the twentieth century, which has produced artists like László Bartha and József Németh, whose capacity for synthesising apparently divergent ideals is equalled by remarkable painterly skill. If Maros attempts similar synthesis, in terms of music, so too does Mihály, whose Violin Concerto of 1959, takes free flight from Bartók on the one hand and Berg on the other. A dynamic first movement, freely and atonally dissonant, yet zestfully scored, is succeeded by a lyrical slow movement underwritten by strong tensions. The finale, more or less fragmentated, is held together by the solo violin. In *Souvenir et avertissement* and *1871—Cantate*, Mihály continues his explorations into relatively uncharted territory, but now involving chorus.

This is a far cry from the music of Sugár, whose talent is best exposed on a broad canvas, whereon may be set the heroic images of the national tradition. Sugár took as his point of departure the chamber music of Kodály, and his earlier works included two quartets and two trios for strings, but his reputation depends principally on the oratorio *Hunyadi* (1952). This, a striking piece of popular exposition, concludes with a final chorus, mixed voices with a children's choir, which is in its way a noble piece of musicianly writing.

Hunyadi represents the attitude to music which was officially encouraged a decade ago—and which may still be seen to permeate the *ad hoc* styles prevalent in the lower reaches of popular (using the word in its correct sense) music. That there was a considerable push in this direction from ideological sources is undeniable. Whether the effects of such pressure are less helpful to creativeness than establishment neutrality, or the powerful forces of philistine indolence, is an open question. The Hungarian composer in present circumstances has an open mind and if he may sometimes be seen to cultivate provincialism it is because the national tendencies of Hungarian musical thought have led in this direction for 100 years. What Erkel tried to achieve is now seen in its culminating phase. If 'realism' had not been thought up as part of a dogma, it would still have been necessary to apply it to musical progress in Hungary during the last three decades. The responsibility of Kodály is, of course, clear. It was not unfitting, therefore, that he should have been celebrated in 1952—the year in which Sugár's *Hunyadi* had its premiere—in Járdányi's *Vörösmarty Symphony*. Based on poems by the poet of that name, this work attempts to convey the moods and aspirations of the period of the War of Liberation. The symphony, unashamedly descriptive, is a compendium of folk-song and *verbunkos*, but strongly moulded and scored with the felicity that marks most contemporary Hungarian orchestration. It was once enthusiastically proclaimed that Járdányi had, in this work, 'solved the problem of Hungarian symphonic style based on the musical traditions of the nation'. Later reflection leads to the conclusion that the necessity for such solution has been built up (and not only in Hungary) as a kind of prestige symbol and is, therefore, a non-musical concern, or, alternatively, that Kodály himself has shown the direction which symphonic music might follow.

Pál Járdányi (b. 1920) is among Kodály's more notable pupils, the one whose function most closely resembles that of his teacher. His musicological researches have value and he belongs to the editorial board of the *Corpus Musicae Popularis Hungaricae*. He has also written a study of the musical habits of rural communities. Thus his approach is regulated by a knowledge, not only of folk-music, but also of folk. When he uses folk-music idiom, therefore, he does so in a full-blooded manner, applying to it the common-sense attributes and imaginative perception of his master. It is not so much where a folk-song has come from that is important, but where it is going to. Járdányi's ability to engender popular enthusiasm is to be seen in his orchestral works, of which the best, most evocative, examples are *Tisza mentén (By the River Tisza)* and *Borsodi Rapszódia (Borsod Rhapsody)*. But Járdányi's expressive proclivities are contained by a counterbalancing, Bartókian economy. Thus his *Missa Brevis* (1940), uniting Gregorian and Hungarian melodic traditions, is for two-part chorus; his *Sonata for Two Pianos* (1942) is a resolute statement of musical austerities; while his string quartets and trios are intimate works in which a strong musical personality is nonetheless evident. In a later work, the *Fantasia and Variations on a Hungarian Folk-song*, for wind quintet, he shows a fusion of his interests and characteristics. A fine work, with native rhapsodisation and rhythmic ebullience as its foundation, it displays the composer's continual preoccupation with contrapuntal development within a freely-ranging, often astringent, harmonic framework. At this point two main streams in contemporary Hungarian music meet and Járdányi and Mihály, Kodály and Bartók, are seen to be not far apart.

EMIL PETROVICS AND A NEW OPERA

At this point one picks up the most talented of the youngest of Hungarian composers (those whose respect for the Kodály-Bartók tradition is judiciously tempered by a zest for exploration of contemporary values in the wider sense): Emil Petrovics. Petrovics, in his middle twenties, was still a student at the Academy when he recognised the musico-dramatic possibilities of *C'est la Guerre*, a political play by Miklós Hubay (b. 1918) centred on the brutal realities of life in Budapest in 1944. In one act *C'est la Guerre* is a *tour de force*. Petrovics, whose orchestral virtuosity is of a high order, synthesises dodecaphonic elements with Bartókian figuration, and folk-music shapes with expressionistic gestures derived from *Sprechstimme* on the one hand and *bel canto* on the other: but the pace of the music, being adjusted to that of the action, is the compelling virtue of a piece that shows the way to new frontiers. *C'est la Guerre* has its place in the regular repertoire by the side of the other popular operas of the newer tradition by Ránki, Szabó, Gyula Hajdu (*Kata Kádár*), and Zoltán Horusitzky (*Sigismund Báthory*). The present vitality in Hungarian operatic life, of course, derives almost entirely from the pioneering of Bartók and Kodály.

*   *   *

MUSIC AND THE COMMUNITY

It is commonly accepted that the arts are in some way or other vital to the well-being of a nation. On the one hand there is the public relations aspect, on the other a deeper psychological understanding of the requirements of human nature. The striking feature of the present Hungarian situation is the extent to which the latter is accepted by the musical fraternity, and by a large section of the educational community. The perpetuation of a musical tradition is not accomplished by vague demonstrations of good-will, nor by the vagaries of chance. Vision requires administrative extension. This is where the influence of Kodály is most significant. Having ideals, he has also had the rare talent to see how these ideals could become effective. One returns again to the project nearest to him: the general schools of music. In them the children are directed towards music, because their musical talent is already apparent, but by no means exclusive. Music is not an end in itself, but a part of balanced life. The enthusiasm of teachers is supported by that of composers, and the tradition of music for the young once started by Mosonyi has in later years been carried on and extended by many composers: Veress, Resző, Bárdos, Pődör, Lendvay, Szokolay, Harmat, Karai, and others, in the field of choral music; Gárdonyi, Szelényi, Kardos, Országh, and Sulyok are among those who have supplied practicable, and graded, instrumental music. While such music is naturally variable in quality, it is important to note that the standard does not fall below a reasonable standard of genuine musicality. At the same time musical education is comprehensive so that while national music is prominent in the class curriculum so also is that of the important schools of the past, with Morley and Purcell as firm in the affections of the young as Haydn, Mozart, and Beethoven. From this will come not only the Hungarian composers of the future, but also their audiences.

17

The Master

ON HIS SEVENTY-FIFTH birthday Kodály was awarded a Kossuth Prize for the third time. Five years later, on 2 December 1962, he received the highest honour in the gift of the State, the Magyar Népköztársaság Érdemrendje (Order of the Hungarian People's Republic). Otherwise there has only been one other recipient of this decoration, the Prime Minister of Hungary. The Master's eightieth birthday gave rise to celebrations which can rarely, if ever, have been paralleled in relation to the life-work of an artist. It was not only that Kodály was honoured as a composer, though naturally his compositions were the focus of attention, but that his status as a citizen was acknowledged. At a time when many tribulations seemed past, and when the auspices for the future were fairer, the figure of Kodály more than ever before was symbolic. Respected by the old, admired by those of middle years, known to all, his chief triumph was to have conquered the hearts of the young.

Hungarian children are not very different from other children: they go to school with equal willingness or unwillingness; they enthuse in their sports, and become football fans; they are alive to the attractions of film and television; in their teens they practise such corybantic exercises as 'the twist' (which Kodály one day inspected, but considered over-praised); but among their autographs that which is most prized is of Zoltán Kodály. To obtain this there is a procedure. On application, the candidate waits until Kodály has found paper and pencil. With amusing deliberation, he puts down a brief phrase in sol-fa. After a successful exhibition of reading at sight—perhaps in the street, or during the interval of a concert—the autograph is forthcoming. The process, simple, and affecting in itself, is another indication of Kodály's powers of communication, both as a person and as a composer; the two being one. Towards the end of 1962 a series of events was organised in Budapest to represent the comprehensiveness of Kodály.

First, he was shown in the context of the Budapest Festival Week, an annual display of modern music, in the company of Honegger, Milhaud, Petrassi, Prokofiev, Shostakovich, Stravinsky, and also contemporary Hungarians, in the programmes given, under Miklós Lukács, by the Budapest Choir and the Philharmonic Orchestra. On 15 October the Kodály Year was inaugurated by a programme in the Academy of Music. (Since the city's chief concert hall, by the Danube, is not yet rebuilt after its almost total destruction in the war, concerts must either take place in the large hall of the Academy, in one of the theatres, or, in summer, out of doors.) In this programme were included the *Háry János Suite, Kádár Kata* (baritone and orchestra, after the version for the film of that name, of 1950), the *Dances of Galánta*, and the *Psalmus Hungaricus*. The latter work, as sung invariably without copies by the Budapest Choir, is established as a kind of national hymn, and written into the national consciousness in similar manner to Handel's *Messiah* is respect of the British people of two generations ago.

On 21 November 1962 the first phase of Kodály's creative career was recalled by a recital of chamber music, in which some of those who had first performed them were invited to participate. Imre Palló, the first Háry János, to whom one book of ballads had been dedicated, sang five ballads, Miklós Szedő four songs from Op. 1, Endre Rösler, a younger singer, three *Lieder,* and Erzsébet Török a number of folk-songs; László Mező played the unaccompanied Sonata for 'Cello and members of the Tatrai Quartet the *Serenade*.

On 2 December a choral concert by amateur bodies took place under the aegis of the Institute for Folk-art—an admirable body which underpins a great deal of provincial activity with organisational efficiency and artistic sympathy. A week later in a radio concert György Lehel conducted the *Peacock Variations* and also a new and honorific piece.

This latter, *Kodály-köszöntő: Tanítványainak variációi a mester témájára (Tribute to Kodály: Variations by his Pupils on a Theme of the*

Master), was based on the opening theme of the third movement of the First String Quartet. The contributors—each with one variation—were, in order of appearance: Béla Tardos, Zoltán Horusitzky, Viktor Vaszy, Zoltán Gárdonyi, Antal Doráti, Jenő Ádám, Pál Kadosa, Géza Frid, Gyula Dávid, Ferenc Szabó, György Ránki, István Szelényi, Rezső Sugár, Pál Járdányi, Jenő Gaál, Rudolf Maros, Gábor Darvas, Béla András, Zoltán Pongrácz, Imre Sulyok, and Lajos Bárdos. The arrangement of the variations in order, their editing, and the finale were the responsibility of Ferenc Farkas. Some of these names have already been mentioned, of those who have not some are not, in the strictest sense, practising composers. Thus the whole work (each variation lasting one minute), with its motions between academic propriety, national idiom, virtuoso scoring, and fringe Webernism is, perhaps, no more than an attractive curiosity. At the same time as an exhibition of sheer compositional competence it is not unimpressive; and one is obliged to wonder what other teacher of composition in the present century could produce twenty-two pupils capable of constructing a similar homage-piece, clear in intention and execution, and patent to the listener. This set of variations was given its first public performance, by the Hungarian State Symphony Orchestra, also under Lehel, at the Academy of Music on 2 May 1963.

Of the contributors to the *Kodály-köszöntő*, all but Doráti and Frid were resident in Hungary. A second set of variations on the same theme was made by Doráti (Rome), Frid (Holland), Ödön Pártos, now Director of the Conservatory in Tel-Aviv, Tibor Serly (U.S.A.), and Sándor Veress (Switzerland). This work was broadcast from Vienna on 16 December 1962. On the same day there was in Budapest a new production of *Háry János*, by Kálmán Nádasdy, to replace that of 1952 which had qualified by now for superannuation.

It was on 10 December that the most official recognition of the Kodály Year took place. The Ministry of Culture together with the Association of Hungarian Musicians arranged a large choral concert—with five children's choirs and five adult choirs—in the Erkel Theatre, at which the *Psalmus* was again performed and the Minister was present. An introductory address was delivered by

Bence Szabolcsi, who was also responsible for the editing of *Zoltáno Kodály: Octogenario Sacrum*. This volume, of wide musicological interest, contains three essays directly relevant to Kodály studies—'Die Welt des Tondichters Kodály', by L. Eősze, 'Kodály and Chamber Music', by Colin Mason, 'Kodály und der Realismus', by Antal Molnár—as well as Szabolcsi's introduction, entitled 'Kodály and Universal Education', and an admirable list of Kodály's works.

The last celebration of 1962 in Budapest was on 21 December, when the Municipal choir combined with the professional symphony orchestra maintained by the State Railways: the programme included the *Te Deum*, the *Dances of Galánta, Kádár Kata*, and the *Peacock Variations*, Outside of the capital, ancillary events were too numerous to mention, but a charming addition to the Kodály literature was the booklet, excellently illustrated, issued by the municipality of Kecskemét, which not only took pride in its early association with the composer, but also in its continuing support for the principles which he propounded.

In Britain the B.B.C. (whose record in promoting Kodály performances is excellent) noted Kodály's eightieth birthday in 'Music Magazine' and surrounded that day with a plethora of performances. The Hungarian Embassy also held a pleasantly commemorative evening. In the United States the most ambitious tribute was planned, for radio, by the University of California; while the Austrians—to whom Kodály has long been congenial—arranged a concert, the high-light being the *Te Deum*, in the Mozartsaal, in Vienna. The Government of the U.S.S.R. sent two of the staff of the Embassy in Budapest to Kodály's flat, armed with appropriate and warm-hearted felicitations in Hungarian, a handsome volume of pictures, and bottles of champagne and vodka.

This, then, was how Kodály reached the age of eighty. But milestones are to be passed. We may now see Kodály on the next stage of his progress.

There is the danger that such a man as Kodály becomes a legend in his lifetime. There is nothing more distasteful to him. His enthusiasms are as wide as ever, his energies still remarkable, and his priorities judiciously regulated. He confesses to feeling no diminution of response, of interest, no alteration of fundamental attitudes; the passage of forty or fifty years means little to him. The root of this vitality is a combination of humility and self-confidence; it is, perhaps no accident that a word he tends to use is 'symbiosis'.

Kodály is, by turns, elfish and noble. His physique, in spite of the fact that he now needs to take reluctant care over climbing flights of stairs, is splendid; the result of exercise, a good digestion, and a critical appreciation of the art of living. He loves the mountains, retreating to the Mátra from time to time, but also the life of the city. Sensibly, he dresses as the occasion warrants, now, in summer, informal in shirt and shorts, or in cooler weather in track-suit, now, for some official occasion, dark-suited and seigneural. One of his suspicions in that the English, martyrs to formality, have few sensible ideas about dress. About Kodály's daily life there is a charming simplicity. His friends, and they are legion, call, often without announcement; the old lady who was once the figure-skating champion of the world—with a present of cakes according to the recipe of Kodály's mother; the serenely humorous Benedictine—tutoring the master first in Plutarch and then in Sophocles—whose affection for, and gratitude to, Kodály is unbounded; the teacher whose gifts are esteemed, but for whom, after a bereavement, the Kodálys have a special, personal concern. There are others who, not knowing Kodály except from a distance, bring their problems to him, as the one person from whom they may expect to receive guidance and counsel. It may be observed that such comings and goings are watched over with infinite charm and wisdom by Sarolta Kodály, whose competence, zest, and quick humour is both a reflection of and a complement to those qualities in the personality of the master.

It is frequently pointed out that Kodály's position is, in a sense, monarchic, but without crown. While this may well be not wide of the mark, it hides the fact that this kind of status has grown from within, from the private person, and has only developed into a public image because the innate civilised virtues have been carried out of doors without change. It could be that what is meant by a democrat, in its fullest sense, is represented in Kodály. If one were to select the main streams in his conception of democracy they would appear as private charity, and public service, in both of which run the absolute of justice. Kodály speaks of the past, but only as a part of the present. Thus one detects the strong influences of early life. The Christian ideal of charity, the paternal vocation as an official, the intermingled nationalities that formerly comprised a larger Hungary, have been responsible for the outline of Kodály's vision. This has been further sharpened by close experience of social and political change, which he judges neither under prejudice, nor convention, nor theory, but according to simple principles of justice and equity that he would consider to have universal application. There is in all of this a certain *naïveté*—the obverse of great knowledge and wisdom—without which it is possible that no man, certainly none who considers the future, can aspire to greatness.

It is true to say that this *naïveté* also inspires his music; at any rate all that he has written in the last forty years. It is the necessary link between himself, as musician, and the world for which he assumes responsibility. Sophistry in music he abhors, and his views on jazz, for instance, are kinder than on most of the developments within the fields of atonalism, dodecaphony, and serialism. These cults, he says, quite simply, will pass away. At the same time, before the conservative label is casually taken out of its drawer, his interpretation of the function of the musician is this: that 'he should produce something that has not been said'. That, precisely, is what Kodály has done; but with the further intention that what he says shall be lucidly stated and within the limits of accessibility.

For many years Kodály has been the father-protector of Hungarian music. There are few musicians in the country who have not come under his influence, either directly or indirectly. The positive aspect of this is that Hungarian music has established its own independence. The first generation of composers have been zealous in keeping within the boundaries marked by Kodály and Bartók. The second generation, secure in their status as Hungarian composers, are looking on wider horizons, and the next two decades promise much of interest. Music is national, but it is international. On the significance of this Kodály cogitates daily, and his major pronouncements[1] of recent date concentrate thereon. From a backward, largely pastoral country, Hungary had developed into a community with major industrial concerns, with a necessarily greater slant towards urban interests. It is the task of the next musicians to adapt musical education—in the widest sense—to a polytechnical age. In twenty years, says Kodály, the true gipsy tradition will have disappeared, remaining vestigially only in the restaurants of the first-class hotels—as a tourist attraction. Like England, though for different reasons, Hungary has no great instrumental tradition in the past. It was—and the Welsh may take the hint—a land of song. From that song which stemmed from the language Kodály helped to fashion an instrumental idiom and an appreciation of this as a means of communication. In Budapest there are now three major orchestras, all of which give ample opportunity to young composers. That these opportunities exist is in large measure due to Kodály. What use is made of these opportunities is a matter for the younger composers. Kodály is not dogmatic. He hopes that the impulse of native song will continue to serve as a foundation, but is by no means insistent that stylistic adventures should be hindered by unwilling subordination to propositions imposed from without. Self-discipline to Kodály, is the essence of liberty.

Thus he practises a reasonably strict routine, with meticulous attention to his commitments. He is indefatigable in attendance at the Acadamy of Sciences, wherein the preparation of the *Corpus Musicae Popularis Hungaricae* is undertaken. He participates in the oral examination of candidates for doctorates in the Academy of Music. He keeps an open eye for new possibilities in the publication of books or of music. He is available for the discussion of any problems connected with education, and is not inclined to give answers without first testing the reactions of children or students, and teachers: Kodály is a patient listener. He is also a regular concert-goer.

This is the present pattern of a creative life, creative in whole and not only in part. One remarks the methodical lines of the pattern; the patience, the relaxation of mood, the periods of

[1] See p. 199 *et seq.*

quietness. This is the classical aspect of temperament. But there is also a strong strain of restlessness, of impatience, even a sense of ambition as yet unfulfilled. The meeting-point of the two sides is in the humour of conversation, wherein the ripple of quiet wit may suddenly be interrupted by an observation that is ruthlessly critical, even though clothed in language that is measured and urbane. And here we come back to the significance of the word. In language other than his own, Kodály thinks long before selecting the precise term. He will prepare a speech in English, supporting it with phrases from French or German where the lines of communication waver, and each word will be subjected to dictionary scrutiny. The result is often idiomatic, sometimes not. Where it is not, one is aware of the background of universality that once obtained in Latin. If in doubt Kodály seizes a Latin word and turns it into English, sometimes so magnificently that one hesitates to point out that it is not, in fact, English, not even by Johnsonian standards. This reference back to some kind of absolute (the same applies to his insistence on a pure form of Hungarian) is, of course, paralleled in his music. 'What', writes Szabolcsi, 'do Kodály's art and erudition teach? They proclaim the superiority of classical form, acute responsibility for measure, completeness and termination, the flames of imagination and passion and their appeasement in reconciliation with the harmony of life and reality; the obligatory concealment of pain and experiment, the mature 'finality' of expression, but beyond all these, human maturity and dignity, acceptance and execution of historical tasks and individual destiny alike.'[1]

Towards the end of his eighty-first year Kodály, with undiminished zest, went for the first time to Israel, thrilled at the prospect of seeing a newly-emerged nation, to the musical culture of which his own pupils had contributed. His mission was centred on the inaugural address to be delivered to the International Folk Music Council Congress, of which the notes are printed on p. 199. These represent the breadth of Kodály's vision, his aspirations for humanity, his perpetual sense of 'symbiosis'. From Israel he went again to Italy, and, in the hope of visiting Britain yet again,

[1] 'Kodály and Universal Education', in *Zoltano Kodály: Octogenario Sacrum*, Budapest, 1962, p. 9.

then took up the slowly growing score of a new work—a violin concerto for Yehudi Menuhin which might also serve as a birthday piece for the London Symphony Orchestra. . . .

The Kodálys leave their flat. The neighbouring children appear from nowhere to wave to the master. The car stops, at the Opera House, at an hotel, and a small, curious, friendly crowd—enlarged in the season by cosmopolitan elements—greets him. He attends a performance of the *Psalmus*, by the Budapest Municipal Choir and the State Orchestra, in the Károyi kert—the courtyard of a late Baroque town house, now a museum: every seat is booked. The music carries over the city centre, and as it dies away on the air of a summer night the great audience greets the composer with a warmth of affection with which there is nothing comparable. The music, the musician, the life of a nation, and the vital tradition of a people, are united in what Shelley once termed 'the tranquillity of successful patriotism'. As the acclamation ended the thought found words: there is only one man in Hungary who could thus spontaneously be honoured.

Notes for an Address to the International Folk Music Council, July 1963

When I was asked to give an introductory address for the opening of this session, the first question, above all others, that came to my mind was—how to define East and West?

1. A geographical definition is inadequate in relation to music. Tokyo, for instance, has six orchestras, all playing European music, while New York has only one.

2. In respect of moral view-points we could consider as Western all those peoples who accepted the Bible as their moral basis. As the Bible springs from the soil on which we are now standing, we can say we are in the centre of the West. The whole of Western civilisation is founded upon the Bible, but in spite of the many million copies which are read in 300 languages all over the world, and the fact that its principles are—more or less—followed, there are also valuable moral principles in Eastern philosophy, as Albert Schweitzer points out in his book, *Kultur und Ethik*.

3. It is reasonable to ask if we may distinguish East from West according to their several musical systems? But of these there are many more than two, and certain nations use two or more different systems together. Thus in Hungary the pentatonic system, preserved in a wealth of songs of great antiquity, is still alive, and melted down into a symbiosis with other systems—in art—music even with the most modern of techniques.

4. In most phenomena of actual life we notice a mixture of elements derived from different peoples or races. When I saw Epstein's collection of Negro sculptures in London in 1960, I recognised the source of his later works, and they also reminded

me of Picasso. Social dances all over the civilised world are more or less of Negro origin. Jazz elements intrude into even the higher forms of music.

5. At this point we come to folk-song. Our Bulletin is international: the purpose of the I.F.M.C.[1] is to study the folk-music of every people. Folk-lore in the fields of music is gradually changing into enthnomusicology. It deals, almost exclusively, with exotic kinds of music—especially in those countries where the indigenous folk-lore, if existing at all, offers relatively little material for observation.

6. Nowadays, knowledge of foreign poetry is everywhere growing daily. Translations which are made directly from the original by one versed in both languages, and without the necessity of an intermediary, are taking the place of those which only gave an incomplete picture of the original. In this connection I remember two German translations of the same poem by Li-Tai-Po which had diametrically opposite meanings. What we acquire through translations is some idea of the creative imagination of other people.

7. It was a Frenchman, Montaigne, who first emphasised that true poetry remains poetry even if made by Cannibals. It was the beginning of a growing interest for the exotic, which arrived with Goethe in his *West-Östlicher Divan, Chinesische Tageszeiten* and his general idea of a *Weltliteratur*.

8. In music, after more or less casual attempts/Mozart, Weber, Purcell—'Chinese music' (*Fairy Queen*), Marcello—'Jewish music', etc./it was the French who went furthest in the direction of using exotic motives in their music./Saint-Saëns, etc./

The exotic kind of music heard at the Paris Exposition of 1900 fascinated, among others, Debussy, who was also enchanted by Spanish and Russian music. Nevertheless, in spite of alien influences, Debussy, nourished by native music of earlier time such as that of Couperin and Rameau maintained a distinctively French originality./And what about *Turandot, Butterfly*?/

When we in Hungary discovered the oldest layer of our traditional songs/which then we tried to incorporate into higher forms of art/was it not an influence from the East? It was not an influence

[1] International Folk Music Council.

imported from afar but one which had remained alive with the people for 1,500 years. This element went back to the first migration of our ancestors from their original home, and was related to Chinese music. In Hungarian music, then, we find how East and West are living together.

9. As to the situation of music and its public in the far East, we can read interesting reports in the Bulletin of the I.M.C., from the Congress of 1962. Although European music is spreading quickly, at the expense of native music, the chief hindrance to its understanding seems to be the general lack of harmonic and polyphonic feeling, for all Oriental music is strictly monophonic. As European polyphony is hardly 1,000 years old, it does not easily come to terms with the different kinds of native melody. Many Oriental composers, however, are trying to suit their melodies with satisfactory harmonies, and to develop a polyphony agreeable to their own monophonic practice. For instance, the Japanese have produced many interesting examples of such 'symbiosis'. To go further in this direction would greatly facilitate mutual understanding.

Mr. Danielou emphasises that exclusively Occidental 'grand art' is in fact unknown in Europe:

'L'héritage culturel de l'humanité est devenu un héritage commun et la préservation des monuments de l'architecture égyptienne ou des chefs d'œuvre de la music japonaise ou indonésienne nous interessent autant que les Japonais, les Egyptiens ou les Indonésiens. Si cet intéret ne se manifeste pas d'une manière positive sur le plan international il apparait, dans les pays concernes, que ces monuments sont sans importance et il sont alors voués, à plus ou moins bref délai, à la déstruction.'

On the other hand, there is a danger lest people should lose their own individuality. The Hungarian peasant hears on his radio (from 4.35 each morning!) a lot of foreign music, including much that is exotic; he reads in his newspaper of political events, and the troubles of peoples of whom he has never heard before; he learns the names of their leaders and their enemies. In brief, he lives the life of the whole globe. It is, perhaps, a rather dizzy life.

Is it not time to bear in mind Menuhin's warning, sent to the Congress of Rome, which I have already mentioned. I would like to quote it in its entirety, but I must restrict myself to a few sentences:

'Unless the modern man can develop simultaneously a strong and healthy relationship with his own family, his own people, his own background, his own language, music, dance, and cultivate the abstractions and idioms of his own age, he will never be a balanced human being but will remain for ever dazed and confused, a prey to passion and prejudice, in the face of the jungle-onslaught of modern life.

National pride, government schools, national radio and TV must foster to their maximum capacity the arts and crafts, the lore and wisdom of an inherited past. These must constitute the recognisable character of the people.

'For I have no doubt but that beyond this explosive phase of mankind's evolution there lies a more harmonious one when each human voice will have something special and important to say, when each hand will not only wield either sceptre or shovel but will express its owner's personality, his feelings and thoughts.

'For that day and on trust we must preserve and restore every value and every art which brings dignity, nobility, and serenity to the human being.'

Z.K.

Appendix 2

Zoltán Kodály

By M. D. Calvocoressi

STUDYING BARTÓK'S MUSIC, we see that the composer's idio-syncrasies, the freshness of his outlook, the independence of his style, his keen sense of musical humour and musical fitness were developed in close contact with classical tradition on one hand with native traditional music on the other. But the chiefest of those idiosyncrasies, the capacity to disengage and to emphasize the essential characteristics of a motive, to make straight for them and show them under various but never inconsistent aspects, to rely upon the inner logic of musical sense and not upon the mere outer logic of formal working out, can be traced back straight to Liszt. Even if we did not have his own acknowledg-ment of his discovery of the vital principle of Liszt's works, 'beyond externals for which he had little liking', a comparison between what we see in his music and what we see in, say, the 'Faust-Symphonie' would leave no room for doubt.

Many of those very features are to be found in the music of Zoltán Kodály (b. 1882). Like Bartók, Kodály underwent the influence of the German classics—mainly, however, that of Brahms—until the time when he turned to Hungarian folk-music. But at that period he was in a measure influenced by contemporary French music, and specially Debussy's—an influence discernible mainly in a few externals, such as a fondness for certain soft and deep harmonic colour-effects.

The affinities between Kodály and Bartók are most obviously revealed in his two books of Pianoforte Pieces (Op. 2 and 11): his chamber music, on the contrary, would hardly suggest a comparison.

In those pianoforte pieces the first things which strike us are the similarity of the methods with Bartók, and, in nine cases out

of ten, the differences of the results. Take, for instance, the
second number of Op. 2, the second and sixth of Op. 11: they
illustrate the very same principles of treatment as Bartók's
Children's Pieces or *Hungarian Folk-Tunes and Dances*;[1] likewise the
fourth number of Op. 2, with the sudden contrast (p. 12, last
line) of the emphatic comment provided by an episodic motive.
The fifth number of Op. 11 compares closely with Bartók's
Nénies, not only in tone, but in almost every detail of the writing.
Again, in the ninth and tenth numbers of Op. 2 Kodály comes very
close to Bartók.

But more often than not the comparison will be found to rest
on externals and on certain general characteristics. Kodály's
methods are less polyphonic than Bartók's—which is perhaps
one of the reasons why he never experiments in polytonality. He
gives a far greater place to purely harmonic effects, such as, for
instance, the beautiful background in arpeggios of Op. 2, No. 4,
or the chords in the third and seventh numbers of the same opus
(compare the former with Debussy's *Et la Lune descend sur le
Temple qui fut*).

It is, again, by virtue of a skilful, though simple and apparently
crude harmonic device, that the extraordinary effect produced
by the sixth number of Op. 2—a brutal, most telling little piece—
is achieved.

Kodály's humour, in the *Pianoforte Pieces*, is generally as acid as
Bartók's occasionally is, and shows, as a rule, less geniality. The
first number of his Op. 2—a delightful *Valsette*—and the eighth—a
bright little *Scherzando*—may be adduced as exceptions. Equally
rare are expressions of more purely contemplative moods, such
as the third number of Op. 11, the fourth and seventh of Op. 2.

A few general characteristics of his style are equally well
exemplified in all those short pieces and in his chamber music.

One is a direct consequence of his tendency to forego the dis-
cursive forms of amplification and development proper. His music
generally has a distinctly narrative character, even when not
assuming the form of a kind of recitative. I do not mean that
anything in it would justify an attempt to translate its purport into
words—indeed, it would be difficult to imagine any music less

[1] See *Monthly Musical Record*, March 1922, p. 55.

amenable to that favourite sport of certain commentators—but simply that its nature is that of a discourse rather than a meditation: a discourse very definite in tone, broadly and emphatically punctuated, with sharp, sudden swerves and forcible repetitions which seem to aim at driving a point finally home before proceeding to the next.

In the pianoforte pieces all that may be a little bewildering at first. When Theodor Szántó performed the Op. 2 at Paris in 1910, at the Société Musicale Indépendante, the audience evinced bewilderment in unequivocal wise. Those irrepressible members of that audience who attended a later concert at which Kodály's Sonata for 'cello and pianoforte was performed must have been greatly surprised to confront, instead of the further 'eccentricities' which they no doubt expected, a remarkably fine example of music classical in tone and texture, beautiful and original throughout, devoid of abruptness and of any feature affording a pretext for bewilderment.

The first of the two movements of which that Sonata (still unpublished) consists is, in fact, conceived and carried out in a vein of purely emotional reverie; it is instinct with glowing imagination, which in the second section assumes a more whimsical, gayer character. The structure is firm and broad, the tone is sustained throughout.

Equally classical, equally moderate and pregnant are the delightful Serenade for two violins and viola (Op. 12) and the Second String Quartet, Op. 10 (with the first I am unacquainted). The second movement of the Quartet is of surpassing originality, and represents Kodály at his best. In the Serenade the middle movement, meditative in character, is a typical instance of that definiteness of utterance to which I was referring, and also of the whimsical flights in which the composer's imagination indulges so freely. The whole thing consists of a dialogue between the viola and the first violin, one instrument earnest and impassioned in its utterance, the other now interrupting with derisive little interjections or comments, now introducing a fresh topic. Again machinery is one whose workings we were studying in Bartók's Children's Pieces, and which can be traced back straight to Liszt.

Persistent repetition of a pattern, whether rhythm or melodic arabesque, is a feature particularly conspicuous in Kodály's music. Many contemporary composers of all schools resort to the device freely, but none in so noticeable wise, nor with more interesting results. The truth is that musicians of today utilise many elements which preclude conventional forms of working out—for instance, motives whose character does away with all possibility of building up developments upon the contrast between tonic and dominant, of resorting to certain formal types of variation, inversion, and so forth.[1]

Even in certain passages of Bartók's works, we can see that resources such as formal progressions, which under the usual tonal conventions are matters of course, may become obtrusive and out of keeping when those conventions cease to obtain (cases in point occur, I think, in *Duke Blue-beard's Castle*, vocal score, p. 42, line 1, and *The Wooden Prince,* pianoforte score, p. 20, line 4; but I give those instances, and the remark, for what they may be worth). Hence the necessity, certain courses of procedure being eliminated, to resort to new ones.

Whether the device of repetition is a makeshift has often been discussed. It is in any case more straight-forward than the wearisome airs and graces of mere academic working out, and may serve many a better purpose. Sometimes a perfectly satisfactory structure may be evolved out of the repeated volutes of an arabesque, or the repetition may be justified by the purpose of acquiring momentum in view of further progress. Kodály's Sonata for 'cello solo (Op. 8) is a superb instance of broad, firm, and beautiful form in which repetition of patterns occurs freely without ever resulting in monotony. From the architectural point of view, as well as from that of exploiting the instrument's resources to good artistic purpose, it is a wonderful *tour de force*. The Finale, for instance, will test the performer's technique to the utmost, and display it in every possible light, but without ever exceeding the bounds of the possible, and never for mere purposes of effect. As a whole, the Sonata affords as conclusive evidence of skill, imagination, and ingenuity as we may wish to find in the work of any composer.

[1] I remember once giving a specialist in formal extemporisation, by way of experiment, the chief motive of *Islamey* to develop. The result exceeded my expectations.

A Duo for violin and pianoforte and two songs for baritone, with orchestral accompaniment, complete the list of Kodály's works for the time being. Of late years he has not been able to devote much of his time to writing music. Small as it is, his output is varied and attractive enough to justify the wish that we may soon see more from his pen.

The Monthly Musical Record, 1 April, 1922.

[Reprinted by kind permission of the executors of M. D. Calvo-coressi, Esq.]

Bibliography

1. HUNGARIAN:

Emlékkönyv Kodály Zoltán 60. születésnapjára (in Honour of the 60th Birthday of Zoltán Kodály), ed. B. Gunda, Budapest, 1943.

Emlékkönyv Kodály Zoltán 70. születésnapjára (In Honour of the 70th Birthday of Zoltán Kodály), ed. B. Szabolcsi and D. Bartha, Budapest, 1952.

Emlékkönyv Kodály Zoltán 75. születésnapjára (In Honour of the 75th Birthday of Zoltán Kodály), ed. B. Szabolcsi and D. Bartha, Budapest, 1957.

Zoltano Kodály-Octogenario Sacrum[1] (in honour of the 80th birthday of Zoltán Kodály), ed. B. Szabolcsi, Budapest, 1962.

L. Eősze: *Kodály Zoltán élete és munkássága* (Zoltán Kodály: Life and Work), Budapest, 1956, Eng. trans., London, 1962.

A. Molnár: *Kodály Zoltán*, Budapest, 1936.

I. Sonkoly: *Kodály az ember, a művész, a nevelő* (Kodály the Man, the Artist, the Educator), Nyíregyháza, 1948.

A. Szőllősy: *Kodály művészete* (The Art of Kodály), Budapest, 1943.

L. Vargyas: 'Zoltán Kodály' in *Ungarn II*, 12, Budapest, 1942.

Zenei Napok: Kecskemét (in Honour of Kodály's 80th Birthday), 1962.

Magyar Zene—Kodály-Szám, Budapest, 1962.

2. ENGLISH

B. Bartók: 'Kodály's Trio', in *Musical Courier*, New York, 1920.

B. Bartók: 'Gypsy Music or Hungarian Music', in *Musical Quarterly*, New York, 1947.

Ernest Bradbury: 'Kodály and his Symphony', in *Yorkshire Post*, Leeds, 12 February 1963.

János Breuer: *Zoltán Kodály*, Budapest Office of Music Competitions, 1962.

M. D. Calvocoressi: 'Zoltán Kodály', in *Musical Times*, 1913; *Monthly Musical Record*, Vol. LII, 1922, London.

M. D. Calvocoressi: 'Choral Music of Kodály', in *The Listener*, Vol. XV, p. 365, 1936, London.

M. D. Calvocoressi: 'Kodály's Ballet Music', in *The Listener*, Vol. XVIII, p. 449, 1937, London.

A. E. F. Dickinson: 'Kodály's Choral Music', in *Tempo*, No. 15, 1946, London.

[1] With essays in various languages.

A. Földes: 'Kodály', in *Tempo*, No. 46, London, 1958.
István Gábor: 'Musical Education for Children in Budapest', in *New Hungarian Quarterly*, Vol. II, No. 1, p. 200, Budapest, 1961.
Cecil Gray: *A Survey of Contemporary Music*, pp. 249-50, London, 1924.
Julius Káldy: *A History of Hungarian Music*, London, 1903.[1]
Kobbé's Complete Opera Book, rev. and ed. the Earl of Harewood, pp. 1209-14, London, 1945.
Z. Kodály: *Folk Music of Hungary*, London, 1960.
Z. Kodály: 'What is Hungarian in Music?' in *Hungarian Quarterly*, Vol. 5, New York, 1939.
W. H. Mellers: 'Kodály and the Christian Epic', in *Studies in Contemporary Music*, London, 1947; reprinted from *Music and Letters*, 1941.
G. Pannain: 'Zoltán Kodály', in *Modern Composers*, London, 1932.
M. Seiber: 'Kodály: *Missa Brevis*', in *Tempo*, No. 4, London, 1947.
Imre Waldbauer: 'Kodály', in *Cobbett's Cyclopaedic Survey of Chamber Music*, I, pp. 56-64, London, 1929.
J. S. Weissmann: 'The Contemporary Movement in Hungary', in *Music Today*, London, 1949.
J. S. Weissmann: 'Kodály's Later Orchestral Music (I)', in *Tempo*, No. 17, p. 16, London, 1950.
J. S. Weissmann: 'Guide to Contemporary Composers (I and II), in *Tempo*, No. 44, p. 24, 1957, No. 45, p. 26, and No. 46, p. 21, London, 1958.
J. S. Weissmann: 'Kodály's Later Orchestral Music (II)', in *Tempo*, No. 18, p. 17, London, 1950.
J. S. Weissmann: 'Kodály's Symphony: A Morphological Study', in *Tempo*, No. 60, p. 19, London, 1961.
J. S. Weissmann: 'Kodály, Zoltán'; in *Grove's Dictionary*, 5th ed., Vol. IV, p. 785, London, 1954.
The New Hungarian Quarterly:
Vol. III, No. 5, 1962: István Gábor, 'Kodály's Music Pedagogy'.
Vol. III, No. 6, 1962: László Eősze, 'Zoltán Kodály, Octogenarian'.
Vol. III, No. 8, 1962: Zoltán Kodály, 'Confession'.
Zoltán Kodály, 'The task of Musicology in Hungary'.
Mátyás Seiber, 'Kodály the Master'.
Bence Szabolcsi, 'Zoltán Kodály's Youth'.
Pál Járdányi, 'Kodály and the folk-song'.
Dezső Keresztúry, 'Kodály the Writer'.
Tábor Kozma, 'Zoltán Kodály—Achievement and Promise'.
Lajos Vargyas, 'Kodály's Role in Folk-music'.

[1] From *The Millenium of Hungary and its People*, ed. J. de Jekelfalussy (Ministry of Commerce, Budapest), and issued in English by the *Musical Standard*. Káldy was Director of the Royal Hungarian Opera.

Tempo, Winter, 1962-3
    'Kodály at 80.'
    Béla Bartók, 'Zoltán Kodály' (reprinted from *Nyugat*, 1921)
    Edward Greenfield, 'Kodály on Records'.
    Frank Howes, 'Kodály in English'.
    Cynthia Jolly, 'The Art-songs of Kodály'.
    Zoltán Kodály, 'Folk-music and Art-music in Hungary' (Philip
        Maurice Deneke Lecture, Oxford, 3 May 1960).
    András Szőllősy, 'Kodály's Melody'.
    Percy M. Young, 'Kodály as Educationist'.

See also:
Twentieth-century Music, Putnam, New York, 1933.
Complete Book of 20th-Century Music, p. 206, New York, 1959; London,
    1961.
C. A. Macartney: *Hungary—a short History*, Edinburgh, 1962.
Robert Simpson and Oliver Prenn: *Guide to Modern Music on Records*
    (*Nationalist Composers*), p. 130, London, 1958.
Denis Stevens: *A History of Song*, p. 286, London, 1960.
Hungary: Its peoples, places, and politics: The Visit of the Eighty Club in 1906,
    London (T. Fisher Unwin), 1907.

3. GERMAN
H. Lindlar: 'Einige Kodály-Chöre', in *Musik der Zeit*, 9, Bonn, 1954.
Robert Schollum: 'Zoltán Kodály und der Ungarische musikalische
    Volksschule-zug', in *Musik Erziehung*, Vienna, June, 1962.
B. Szabolcsi: 'Die Instrumentalmusik Zoltán Kodálys', in *Musik-
    blätter des Anbruch*, Vienna, 1962.
B. Szabolcsi: 'Die Lieder Zoltán Kodálys', in *Musikblätter des Anbruch*,
    Vienna, 1927.
B. Szabolcsi: 'Die Chöre Zoltán Kodálys', in *Musikblätter des Anbruch*,
    Vienna, 1928.
A. Tóth: *Zoltán Kodály, zu seinem 50. Geburtstag*, Vienna, 1932.
F. Wildgans: 'Zoltán Kodály, ein ungarischer Volksmusiker', *Rondo*,
    No. 1, Vienna, 1953.

4. FRENCH
J. Gergely: 'Zoltan Kodály', in *Fasquelle—Encyclopédie de la Musique*,
    II, Paris, 1959.
E. Haraszti: '*Zoltán Kodály et la musique hongroise*', in *Revue Musicale*,
    Paris, 1947.
S. Kovács: 'La jeune école hongroise', in *Revue Musicale*, Paris, 1911.
A. Tóth: 'Zoltán Kodály', in *Revue Musicale*, Paris, 1929.

5. MISCELLANEOUS

Béla Bartók:—Weg und Werk, ed. B. Szabolcsi, Budapest, 1956.

'*Béla Bartók*'—*International Choral Competition in Debrecen*, August, 1961 (Historical Preface to Programme).

Corpus Musicae Popularis Hungaricae, Vols. I-VI, Béla Bartók, Zoltán Kodály, and others.

J. Gergely: *Zoltán Kodály, Musico Hungaro e Mestro Universal*, Publicacoes Europa-America, 1954.

Z. Kodály, (ed.): *Studia Musicologica*, Vol. I, Budapest, 1961.

Zoltáno Kodály Octogenario sacrum (Studies in English, French German, Russian and Spanish), ed. B. Szabolcsi, Budapest, 1962.

Lajos Lesznai: *Béla Bartók*, Leipzig, 1962.

Albert Siklós: *Hangszereléstan (Orchestration)*, Budapest 1909.

B. Szabolcsi: *Geschichte der ungarischen Musik*, Budapest 1964.

D. Tóth: *Un musicista ungherese: Zoltán Kodály*, Budapest 1938.

Péter Várnai: *Music Belongs to Everybody*, Budapest 1963.

6. FILMS

The Children are singing
Music } Hungarofilm

Index of Works and Recordings

THIS INDEX IS not comprehensive, insofar as Kodály's output of small choral pieces is very considerable, and of these a large part is available only with Hungarian text. At the same time every care has been taken to ensure that all choral works which are issued with English words (as well as those with Hungarian words that are of general importance) are included, while it is hoped that the rest of the composer's published works are indicated.

Certain works were published by houses other than those who now control them. For the sake of convenience the present imprint is given, while the dates are those of first publication rather than of composition. The latter will generally be found in the text of the book.

The numbers at right refer to pages where works are discussed.

B.H. = Boosey & Hawkes
E.M. = Editio Musica (Budapest)
M.K. = Magyar Kórus
O.U.P. = Oxford University Press
R. = Rózsavölgyi
U.E. = Universal Edition

In Section VIII recordings under the labels H.L.P., H.L.P.X., and L.P.K., are from the Hungarian Longplay Catalogue (Kultúra, Budapest). Recordings of vocal works are in Hungarian, except where the original text was in another language.

In respect of literary works (IX) English titles are given, but the text is Hungarian unless otherwise stated.

1. For Solo Voice

(a) WITH PIANOFORTE ACCOMPANIMENT

16 Songs (Op. 1)	1921	E.M., 42-6, 191
2 Songs (Op. 5)[1]	1916	B.H., 39, 66, 72
7 Songs (Op. 6)[2]	1923	B.H., 66, 67
5 Songs (Op. 9)[2]	1924	B.H., 39, 66, 67
3 Songs (Op. 14)[2]	1929	B.H., 66, 68
4 Songs[1]	1925	B.H., 107,n.1

[1] With English text.   [2] With German text.

2. Choral Works

(*a*) FOR HIGH VOICES, (FEMALE OR CHILDREN'S CHOIR)
WITH ENGLISH TEXT

[1] Also available for mixed voices.
[2] Contributed to Classical Songs for Children,, ed. Countess of Harewood and R. Duncan.

(b) FOR MALE VOICES—WITH ENGLISH TEXT

2 *Drinking Songs*—(1) *Bordal*, (2) *Mulató Gajd*	1913-17	U.E.
The Bachelor—*Kit Kéne Élvenni*	1935	U.E.
The Ruins—*Huszt*	1936	U.E.
The Peacocks—*Felszállott a Páva*	1951	U.E., 96
Songs from Karád—*Karádi Nóták*	1951	B.H.

(c) FOR MIXED VOICES, *A CAPPELLA*, WITH ENGLISH TEXT

Evening—*Este*	1904	U.E., 51
A Birthday Greeting—*Nagyszalontai Köszöntő*	1931	U.E.
Mátra Pictures—*Mátrai Képek*	1931	U.E., 95, 97-9, 107, 109, 180
The Aged—*Öregek*	1933	U.E.
Jesus and the Traders—*Jézus és a Kufárok*	1934	U.E., 95, 97, 99-101, 130, 141
Too Late—*Akik Mindig Elkésnek*	1934	U.E.
Transylvanian Lament—*Székely Keserves*	1934	U.E., 95
Ode to Franz Liszt—*Liszt Ferenchez*	1936	U.E., 95, 96
Hymn to King Stephen—*Ének Szent István Királyhoz*	1938	B.H., 124
Norwegian Girls—*Norvég Lányok*	1940	B.H.
Battle Song—*Csatadal*	1943	B.H., 125
Psalm CXXI—*121-ik Zsoltár*	1943	B.H., 125
Cohors Generosa—(*Latin text*)	1944	B.H.
Cease your bitter weeping[1]	1951	B.H., 146n.1
Hymn of Zrinyi—*Zrinyi Szózata*	1955	B.H., 138-40, 173
I will look for Death	1959	B.H.
Media vita in morte sumus—(*Latin text*)	1962	B.H.
Communion Anthem—*Első áldozás*	1963	B.H.
Veni, veni Emmanuel—(*Latin and English text*)	1963	B.H.
An Ode for Music (Collins and Shakespeare (?))—For Cork Choral Festival, 1963	1963	B.H.
A Song of Faith—*A Magyarokhoz*	1964	B.H., 95, 175
An Ode (O'Shaughnessy), for the Quatercentenary of Merton College, Oxford	1964	ms.

[1] Also available for high voices, arr. M. Seiber.

(d) FOR MIXED VOICES, WITH ORCHESTRA; AND VARIOUS VOCAL GROUPS WITH INSTRUMENTS

Psalmus Hungaricus[1]	1923	U.E., 27, 74-81, 82, 84, 85, 109, 138, 168, 171, 176, 177, 180, 191, 198
Budavári Te Deum—(Latin Text)[1]	1936	U.E., 27, 78n.1, 96, 101-3, 117, 123, 150, 175, 193
Missa Brevis—(Latin text)	1944	B.H., 27, 122, 127-30, 143, 155, 171, 175
Kálló Folk Dances (or *Kálló Double Dance*)[2] *Kállai Kettős*	1952	B.H., 136-7, 185
Shepherds' Christmas Dance—Karácsonyi Pásztortánc (female voices and wind inst.)	1936	U.E.
Soldier's Song—Katonadal (male voices, trumpet, and drum)	1951	B.H., 137
5 Tantum Ergo (female voices; nos. 1, 4, 5 with org. acc.) (Latin text)	1928	U.E.
Pange lingua (mixed voices, org.) (Latin text)	1931	U.E., 127
Psalm CXIV (mixed voices, org.)	1958	B.H., 137

(e) CHORAL WORKS NOT YET AVAILABLE WITH ENGLISH TEXT[2]

FOR HIGH VOICES

4 Italian Madrigals (Italian text) *Négy Olasz Madrigál*	1949	E.M., 109

FOR MIXED VOICES

Evening Song—Esti Dal	1938	E.M.
The Forgotten Song of Bálint Balassi— Balassi Bálint Elfelejtett Éneke	1942	M.K.
Dirge—Sirató Ének	1947	M.K.
Wish for Peace—1801—Békességóhajtás	1953	E.M., 137
Sík Sándor's Te Deum—Sík Sándor Te Deuma	1962	E.M.

FOR MALE VOICES

The Son of an enslaved Country—Rab Hazának Fia *Still by a Miracle our Country stands— Isten Csodája*	1947	M.K.

[1] Miniature score.   [2] See also List of Recordings, p. 220.

3. Dramatic Works

4. Editorial Work

5. Chamber Music

[1] Miniature scores available.   [2] See also Orchestral Works.

ARRANGEMENTS

3 Chorale Preludes, J. S. Bach, trs. for 'cello and pfte.	1924	U.E.
Fantasia Cromatica, J. S. Bach, trs. for vla. solo (ed. W. Primrose)		B.H.
Prelude and Fugue in E flat minor, Book I, J. S. Bach, for 'cello. and pfte.		B.H.[1]
Prelude and Fugue in B.Mi. Book I, J. S. Bach, for str. qu.		B.H.[1]
'Lute' Prelude in C Minor (Schm. 999) J. S. Bach, for vl. and pfte.		B.H.[1]

6. Orchestral Works

Háry János: Suite[2]	1927	U.E., 42, 85, 86, 87, 88, 116, 143, 154, 173, 191
Theatre Overture	1927	U.E.
Summer Evening[3]	1906–30	U.E., 39-40, 109-10, 153, 156, 171, 172
Dances from Marosszék (also arranged as ballet)[3]	1930	U.E., 110, 111, 136, 143
Dances from Galánta (also arranged as ballet)[3]	1933	U.E., 8, 25, 110-11, 123, 136, 161, 162, 176, 191, 193
Ballet Music	1936	U.E., 150
Variations on a Hungarian Folk-song(The Peacock)[3]	1939	B.H., 111-18, 120, 150, 154, 161, 162, 176, 191, 193
Concerto for Orchestra[1]	1939	B.H., 118-20, 154, 156, 161, 172
Minuetto Serio (from *Czinka Panna*)	1953	E.M.
Symphony[3]	1961	B.H., 112, 128, 149, 150-151, 152-64, 170, 173, 175

[1] Forthcoming.   [2] Available in miniature score.
[3] Miniature scores available.

7. Educational

The Choral Method[1] (ed. Percy M. Young)	B.H., 123, 149
50 Songs for Little Children	1964, 145
333 Sight-reading Exercises	1963, 126, 145
Bicinia Hungarica (4 books of two-part songs)	1962, 1, 25-6, 126, 137, 155
33 Two-part Exercises	1964
44 Two-part Exercises	1964
55 Two-part Exercises	1964
Tricinia: 29 Three-part Exercises	1964, 135
15 Two-part Exercises	1961, 126
Let us Sing Correctly	1961, 126
Epigrams	1963
Sol-Mi (8 books), with Jenő Ádám	1945 M.K.
Song-book for Primary Schools, with Jenő Ádám	1948 Hung. Min. of Ed.

8. Recordings

FOR SOLO VOICE AND PFTE.

Hungarian Folk-songs	HLP 3513 LPK 10008 LPK 10012 DGG/DGM 19117 DGG/LPEM 19171
A közelítő tél (The Approaching Winter) *Kádár Kata (Mother Listen)*	} HLP 146
Árva vagyok; Megizenem az édesanyámnak; *Árva madár; Ne búsuljon*—from the Folk-song cycle, *Magyar Népzene*	} EP 1690

FOR HIGH VOICES

Ave Maria *Egyetem Begyetem (Rhymed Song for Children)* *Három gömöri népdal (Three Folk Songs from Gömör)* *Táncnóta, (Dancing Song)* *Villő (The Straw Guy)* *Esti Dal (Evening Song)*	} Delyse/ECB 3148

[1] Originally designed for use in Hungarian schools this series has been edited for English-speaking pupils in collaboration with Kodály.

Jesus and the Traders	Cantate 640217
Psalmus Hungaricus & Te Deum[1]	HLPX 1011/Artia ALP 152
Te Deum	Westminster XWN, 18455
Missa Brevis[1]	HLPX 1016/HMV-ALP 1687

DRAMATIC WORKS

Háry János	HLPX 1023-5
Háry János (excerpts)	LPK 1515
The Spinning Room	HLPX 1009-10

CHAMBER MUSIC

Adagio (for vla. and pfte.)	HLPX 1026
String Quartet, No. 1.	HLPX 147
Dances from Marosszék	
Méditation sur un motif de Claude Debussy	
Children's Dances	for pfte. HLP 1553
Valsette	
Sonata for 'Cello and Pfte.	
Sonata for Unaccompanied 'Cello	Supraphon SUA 10383
String Quartet, No. 2.	
Serenade for 2 Vl. and Vla.	HLP 1501
7 Pieces for Pfte.	HLPX 1038
Csendes mise orgonára (Mass for Organ)	LPX 107

ORCHESTRAL WORKS

Háry János: Suite	HLP 1539/Mercury MMA 11270/Capitol P 8508
Dances from Galánta, and Marosszék	HLP 1500/Mercury MMA 11077
"Peacock" Variations	HLP 132 and LPX 1101
Concerto for Orchestra[1]	DGG LPM 18687
Summer Evening[1]	and LPX 1072

9. Principal Critical and Musicological Works

'Collection from Mátyusföld', *Ethnographia*, 1905, p. 300.
'The Verse Construction of the Hungarian Folk-song', *Nyelvtudományi Közlemények*, Vol. XXXVI, 1906, pp. 95-136.
'Ballads', *Ethnographia*, 1907, pp. 38, 108, 153, 230.

[1] Conducted by Kodály.

[1] Almost identical with *Folk Music and Art Music in Hungary*, the Philip Maurice Deneke Lecture, delivered at Oxford, 3 May 1960: see *Tempo*, Winter, 1962-3, pp. 28-36.

'The Future of Folk-song Research', *Akadémiai Értesitő*, 1952, p. 491.
'Hungarian Dances of 1729', *Papers of Hungarian Academy of Sciences*, 1952, p. 17.
János Arany's Folk-song Collection, Budapest, 1952.
'János Arany's Collection of Melodies', *Papers of Hungarian Academy of Sciences*, 1935, p. 215.
What is a Good Musician?, Editio Musica, 1954.
'Remarks about the Lecture of Bence Szabolcsi on Popular and Individual Art Compositions in Music', *Papers of Hungarian Academy of Sciences*, 1953, p. 293.
'From Szentirmay to Bartók,' *Papers of Hungarian Academy of Sciences*, 1955, p. 223.
'On Béla Bartók' (address of 26 September 1956), *Papers of Hungarian Academy of Sciences*, 1957, p. 11.
'The Tasks of Musicology in Hungary'[1] (in English), *Studia Musicologica* (ed. Kodály) Vol. I, 1961, pp. 5-8.
'Confession'[2] (in English), *The New Hungarian Quarterly*, Vol. III, No. 8, 1962, pp. 3-9.

[1] Also reprinted in *The New Hungarian Quarterly*, Vol. III, No. 8, 1962, pp. 10-13.
[2] English version of an address delivered on December 23, 1932, and published in *Nyugat*, 1933.

General Index

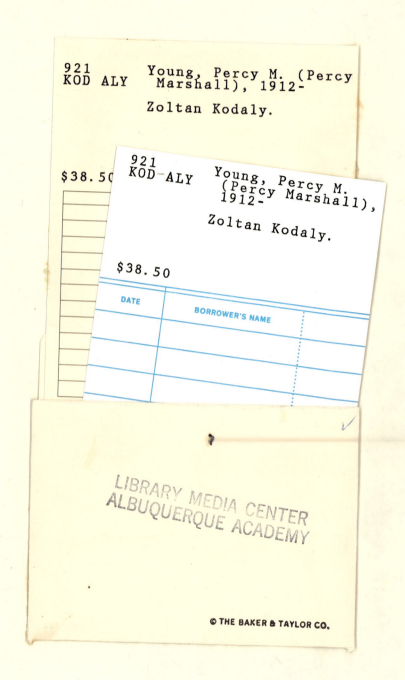